Heterogeneous Computing with OpenCL

Revised OpenCL 1.2 Edition

Heterogeneous Computing with OpenCL

Revised OpenCL 1.2 Edition

Benedict R. Gaster

Lee Howes

David R. Kaeli

Perhaad Mistry

Dana Schaa

ELSEVIER

AMSTERDAM • BOSTON • HEIDELBERG • LONDON
NEW YORK • OXFORD • PARIS • SAN DIEGO
SAN FRANCISCO • SINGAPORE • SYDNEY • TOKYO

Morgan Kaufmann is an imprint of Elsevier

Acquiring Editor: Todd Green
Project Manager: Paul Prasad Chandramohan
Designer: Alan Studholme

Morgan Kaufmann is an imprint of Elsevier
225 Wyman Street, Waltham, MA 02451, USA

Notices

Knowledge and best practice in this field are constantly changing. As new research and experience broaden our understanding, changes in research methods or professional practices may become necessary. Practitioners and researchers must always rely on their own experience and knowledge in evaluating and using any information or methods described herein. In using such information or methods they should be mindful of their own safety and the safety of others, including parties for whom they have a professional responsibility.

To the fullest extent of the law, neither the Publisher nor the authors, contributors, or editors, assume any liability for any injury and/or damage to persons or property as a matter of product liability, negligence or otherwise, or from any use or operation of any methods, products, instructions, or ideas contained in the material herein.

Library of Congress Cataloging-in-Publication Data
Application submitted

British Library Cataloguing-in-Publication Data
A catalogue record for this book is available from the British Library.

ISBN: 978-0-12-405894-1

For information on all MK publications
visit our website at www.mkp.com

Printed in the United States of America
12 13 14 15   10 9 8 7 6 5 4 3 2 1

Contents

Foreword to the Revised OpenCL 1.2 Edition

I need your help. I need you to read this book and start using OpenCL. Let me explain.

The fundamental building blocks of computing have changed over the past 10 years. We have moved from the single-core processors many of us started with long ago to shared memory multicore processors, to highly scalable "many core" processors, and finally to heterogeneous platforms (e.g., a combination of a CPU and a GPU). If you have picked up this book and are thinking of reading it, you are most likely well aware of this fact. I assume you are also aware that software needs to change to keep up with the evolution of hardware.

And this is where I need your help. I've been working in parallel computing since 1985 and have used just about every class of parallel computer. I've used more parallel programming environments than I could name and have helped create more than a few. So I know how this game works. Hardware changes and programmers like us are forced to respond. Our old code breaks and we have to reengineer our software. It's painful, but it's a fact of life.

Money makes the world go around so hardware vendors fight for competitive advantage. This drives innovation and, over the long run, is a good thing. To build attention for "their" platforms, however, these vendors "help" the poor programmers by creating new programming models tied to their hardware. And this breeds confusion. Well-meaning but misguided people use, or are forced to use, these new programming models and the software landscape fragments. With different programming models for each platform, the joy of creating new software is replaced with tedious hours reworking our software for each and every new platform that comes along.

At certain points in the history of parallel computing, as the software landscape continues to fragment, a subset of people come together and fight back. This requires a rare combination of a powerful customer that controls a lot of money, a collection of vendors eager to please that customer, and big ideas to solve the programming challenges presented by a new class of hardware. This rare set of circumstances can take years to emerge, so when it happens, you need to jump on the opportunity. It happened for clusters and massively parallel supercomputers with MPI (1994). It happened for shared memory computers with OpenMP (1997). And more recently, this magical combination of factors has come together for heterogeneous computing to give us OpenCL.

I can't stress how important this development is. If OpenCL fails to dominate the heterogeneous computing niche, it could be many years before the right set of circumstances come together again. If we let this opportunity slip away and we fall back on our old, proprietary programming model ways, we could be sentencing our software developers to years of drudgery.

So I need your help. I need you to join the OpenCL revolution. I need you to insist on portable software frameworks for heterogeneous platforms. When possible, avoid programming models tied to a single hardware vendor's products. Open standards help everyone. They enable more than a product line. They enable an industry, and if you are in the software business, that is a very good thing.

OpenCL, however, is an unusually complex parallel programming standard. It has to be. I am aware of no other parallel programming model that addresses such a wide array of systems: GPUs, CPUs, FPGAs, embedded processors, and combinations of these systems. OpenCL is also complicated by the goals of its creators. You see, in creating OpenCL, we decided the best way to impact the industry would be to create a programming model for the performance-oriented programmer wanting full access to the details of the system. Our reasoning was that, over time, high-level models would be created to map onto OpenCL. By creating a common low-level target for these higher level models, we'd enable a rich marketplace of ideas and programmers would win. OpenCL, therefore, doesn't give you many abstractions to make your programming job easier. You have to do all that work yourself.

OpenCL can be challenging, which is where this book comes in. You can learn OpenCL by downloading the specification and writing code. That is a difficult way to go. It is much better to have trailblazers who have gone before you establish the context and then walk you through the key features of the standard. Programmers learn by example, and this book uses that fact by providing a progression of examples from trivial (vector addition) to complex (image analysis). This book will help you establish a firm foundation that you can build on as you master this exciting new programming model.

Read this book. Write OpenCL code. Join the revolution. Help us make the world safe for heterogeneous computing. Please . . . I need your help. We all do.

Tim Mattson
Principal Engineer
Intel Corp.

Foreword to the First Edition

For more than two decades, the computer industry has been inspired and motivated by the observation made by Gordon Moore (A.K.A "Moore's law") that the density of transistors on die was doubling every 18 months. This observation created the anticipation that the performance a certain application achieves on one generation of processors will be doubled within two years when the next generation of processors will be announced. Constant improvement in manufacturing and processor technologies was the main drive of this trend since it allowed any new processor generation to shrink all the transistor's dimensions within the "golden factor", 0.3 (ideal shrink) and to reduce the power supply accordingly. Thus, any new processor generation could double the density of transistors, to gain 50% speed improvement (frequency) while consuming the same power and keeping the same power density. When better performance was required, computer architects were focused on using the extra transistors for pushing the frequency beyond what the shrink provided, and for adding new architectural features that mainly aim at gaining performance improvement for existing and new applications.

During the mid 2000s, the transistor size became so small that the "physics of small devices" started to govern the characterization of the entire chip. Thus frequency improvement and density increase could not be achieved anymore without a significant increase of power consumption and of power density. A recent report by the International Technology Roadmap for Semiconductors (ITRS) supports this observation and indicates that this trend will continue for the foreseeable future and it will most likely become the most significant factor affecting technology scaling and the future of computer based system.

To cope with the expectation of doubling the performance every known period of time (not 2 years anymore), two major changes happened (1) instead of increasing the frequency, modern processors increase the number of cores on each die. This trend forces the software to be changed as well. Since we cannot expect the hardware to achieve significantly better performance for a given application anymore, we need to develop new implementations for the same application that will take advantage of the multicore architecture, and (2) thermal and power become first class citizens with any design of future architecture. These trends encourage the community to start looking at heterogeneous solutions: systems which are assembled from different subsystems, each of them optimized to achieve different optimization points or to address different workloads. For example, many systems combine "traditional" CPU architecture with special purpose FPGAs or Graphics Processors (GPUs). Such an integration can be done at different levels; e.g., at the system level, at the board level and recently at the core level.

Developing software for homogeneous parallel and distributed systems is considered to be a non-trivial task, even though such development uses well-known paradigms and well established programming languages, developing methods, algorithms, debugging tools, etc. Developing software to support general-purpose heterogeneous systems is relatively new and so less mature and much more difficult. As heterogeneous systems are becoming unavoidable, many of the major software and hardware manufacturers start creating software environments to support them. AMD proposed the use of the Brook language developed in Stanford University, to handle streaming computations, later extending the SW environment to include the Close to Metal (CTM)and the Compute Abstraction Layer (CAL) for accessing their low level streaming hardware primitives in order to take advantage of their highly threaded parallel architecture. NVIDIA took a similar approach, co-designing their recent generations of GPUs and the CUDA programming environment to take advantage of the highly threaded GPU environment. Intel proposed to extend the use of multi-core programming to program their Larrabee architecture. IBM proposed the use of message-passing-based software in order to take advantage of its hetero-geneous, non-coherent cell architecture and FPGA based solutions integrate libraries written in VHDL with C or C++ based programs to achieve the best of two envi-ronments. Each of these programming environments offers scope for benefiting do-main-specific applications, but they all failed to address the requirement for general purpose software that can serve different hardware architectures in the way that, for example, Java code can run on very different ISA architectures.

The Open Computing Language (OpenCL) was designed to meet this important need. It was defined and managed by the nonprofit technology consortium Khronos The language and its development environment "borrows" many of its basic con-cepts from very successful, hardware specific environments such as CUDA, CAL, CTM, and blends them to create a hardware independent software development en-vironment. It supports different levels of parallelism and efficiently maps to homo-geneous or heterogeneous, single- or multiple-device systems consisting of CPUs, GPUs, FPGA and potentially other future devices. In order to support future devices, OpenCL defines a set of mechanisms that if met, the device could be seamlessly in-cluded as part of the OpenCL environment. OpenCL also defines a run-time support that allows to manage the resources, combine different types of hardware under the same execution environment and hopefully in the future it will allow to dynamically balance computations, power and other resources such as memory hierarchy, in a more general manner.

This book is a text book that aims to teach students how to program heteroge-neous environments. The book starts with a very important discussion on how to pro-gram parallel systems and defines the concepts the students need to understand before starting to program any heterogeneous system. It also provides a taxonomy that can be used for understanding the different models used for parallel and distrib-uted systems. Chapters 2 – 4 build the students' step by step understanding of the basic structures of OpenCL (Chapter 2) including the host and the device architecture (Chapter 3). Chapter 4 provides an example that puts together these concepts using a not trivial example.

Chapters 5 and 6 extend the concepts we learned so far with a better understand-ing of the notions of concurrency and run-time execution in OpenCL (Chapter 5) and the dissection between the CPU and the GPU (Chapter 6). After building the basics, the book dedicates 4 Chapters (7-10) to more sophisticated examples. These sections are vital for students to understand that OpenCL can be used for a wide range of applications which are beyond any domain specific mode of operation. The book also demonstrates how the same program can be run on different platforms, such as Nvidia or AMD. The book ends with three chapters which are dedicated to advanced topics.

No doubt that this is a very important book that provides students and researchers with a better understanding of the world of heterogeneous computers in general and the solutions provided by OpenCL in particular. The book is well written, fits students' different experience levels and so, can be used either as a text book in a course on OpenCL, or different parts of the book can be used to extend other courses; e.g., the first two chapters are well fitted for a course on parallel programming and some of the examples can be used as a part of advanced courses.

Dr. Avi Mendelson

Microsoft R&D Israel
Adjunct Professor, Technion

Preface

OUR HETEROGENEOUS WORLD

Our world is heterogeneous in nature. This kind of diversity provides a richness and detail that is difficult to describe. At the same time, it provides a level of complexity and interaction in which a wide range of different entities are optimized for specific tasks and environments.

In computing, heterogeneous computer systems also add richness by allowing the programmer to select the best architecture to execute the task at hand or to choose the right task to make optimal use of a given architecture. These two views of the flexibility of a heterogeneous system both become apparent when solving a computational problem involves a variety of different tasks. Recently, there has been an upsurge in the computer design community experimenting with building heterogeneous systems. We are seeing new systems on the market that combine a number of different classes of architectures. What has slowed this progression has been a lack of standardized programming environment that can manage the diverse set of resources in a common framework.

OPENCL

OpenCL has been developed specifically to ease the programming burden when writing applications for heterogeneous systems. OpenCL also addresses the current trend to increase the number of cores on a given architecture. The OpenCL framework supports execution on multi-core central processing units, digital signal processors, field programmable gate arrays, graphics processing units, and heterogeneous accelerated processing units. The architectures already supported cover a wide range of approaches to extracting parallelism and efficiency from memory systems and instruction streams. Such diversity in architectures allows the designer to provide an optimized solution to his or her problem—a solution that, if designed within the OpenCL specification, can scale with the growth and breadth of available architectures. OpenCL's standard abstractions and interfaces allow the programmer to seamlessly "stitch" together an application within which execution can occur on a rich set of heterogeneous devices from one or many manufacturers.

THIS TEXT

Until now, there has not been a single definitive text that can help programmers and software engineers leverage the power and flexibility of the OpenCL programming standard. This is our attempt to address this void. With this goal in mind, we have not attempted to create a syntax guide—there are numerous good sources in which programmers can find a complete and up-to-date description of OpenCL syntax.

Instead, this text is an attempt to show a developer or student how to leverage the OpenCL framework to build interesting and useful applications. We provide a number of examples of real applications to demonstrate the power of this programming standard.

Our hope is that the reader will embrace this new programming framework and explore the full benefits of heterogeneous computing that it provides. We welcome comments on how to improve upon this text, and we hope that this text will help you build your next heterogeneous application.

Acknowledgments

We thank Manju Hegde for proposing the book project, Jay Owen for connecting the participants on this project with each other and finally Todd Green from Morgan Kaufmann for his project management, input and deadline pressure.

On the technical side, we thank Jay Cornwall for his thorough work editing an early version of this text, and we thank Takahiro Harada, Justin Hensley, Budirijanto Purnomo, Frank Swehosky and Dongping Zhang for their significant contributions to individual chapters, particularly the sequence of case studies that could not have been produced without their help.

About the Authors

Benedict R. Gaster is a software architect working on programming models for next-generation heterogeneous processors, particularly examining high-level abstractions for parallel programming on the emerging class of processors that contain both CPUs and accelerators such as GPUs. He has contributed extensively to the OpenCL's design and has represented AMD at the Khronos Group open standard consortium. He has a Ph.D. in computer science for his work on type systems for extensible records and variants.

Lee Howes has spent the past 3 1/2 years working at AMD on a range of topics related to GPU computing and graphics programming. Lee currently focuses on programming models for the future of heterogeneous computing. His interests lie in declaratively representing mappings of iteration domains to data, methods for making low-level hardware features usable in high level input languages and in communicating complicated architectural concepts and optimizations succinctly to a developer audience. Lee has a Ph.D. in computer science from Imperial College London for work in the mapping of iteration spaces to memory regions.

David Kaeli received a B.S. and Ph.D. in electrical engineering from Rutgers University and an M.S. in computer engineering from Syracuse University. He is Associate Dean of Undergraduate Programs in the College of Engineering and a Full Professor on the ECE faculty at Northeastern University, where he directs the Northeastern University Computer Architecture Research Laboratory (NUCAR). Prior to joining Northeastern in 1993, he spent 12 years at IBM, the last 7 at T. J. Watson Research Center, Yorktown Heights, NY. He has co-authored more than 200 critically reviewed publications. His research spans a range of areas, including microarchitecture to back-end compilers and software engineering. He leads a number of research projects in the area of GPU computing. He currently serves as the Chair of the IEEE Technical Committee on Computer Architecture. He is an IEEE Fellow and a member of the ACM.

Perhaad Mistry is a Ph.D. candidate at Northeastern University. He received a B.S. in electronics engineering from the University of Mumbai and an M.S. in computer engineering from Northeastern University. He is currently a member of the Northeastern University Computer Architecture Research Laboratory (NUCAR) and is advised by Dr. David Kaeli. He works on a variety of parallel computing projects. He has designed scalable data structures for the physics simulations for GPGPU platforms and has also implemented medical reconstruction algorithms for heterogeneous devices. His current research focuses on the design of profiling tools for heterogeneous computing. He is studying the potential of using standards such as OpenCL for building tools that simplify parallel programming and performance analysis across the variety of heterogeneous devices available today.

Dana Schaa received a B.S. in computer engineering from California Polytechnic State University, San Luis Obispo, and an M.S. in electrical and computer engineering from Northeastern University, where he is also currently a Ph.D. candidate. His research interests include parallel programming models and abstractions, particularly for GPU architectures. He has developed GPU-based implementations of several medical imaging research projects ranging from real-time visualization to image reconstruction in distributed, heterogeneous environments. He married his wonderful wife, Jenny, in 2010, and they live together in Boston with their charming cats.

Introduction to Parallel Programming

INTRODUCTION

Today's computing environments are becoming more multifaceted, exploiting the capabilities of a range of multi-core microprocessors, central processing units (CPUs), digital signal processors, reconfigurable hardware (FPGAs), and graphics processing units (GPUs). Presented with so much heterogeneity, the process of developing efficient software for such a wide array of architectures poses a number of challenges to the programming community.

Applications possess a number of workload behaviors, ranging from control intensive (e.g., searching, sorting, and parsing) to data intensive (e.g., image processing, simulation and modeling, and data mining). Applications can also be characterized as compute intensive (e.g., iterative methods, numerical methods, and financial modeling), where the overall throughput of the application is heavily dependent on the computational efficiency of the underlying hardware. Each of these workload classes typically executes most efficiently on a specific style of hardware architecture. No single architecture is best for running all classes of workloads, and most applications possess a mix of the workload characteristics. For instance, control-intensive applications tend to run faster on superscalar CPUs, where significant die real estate has been devoted to branch prediction mechanisms, whereas data-intensive applications tend to run fast on vector architectures, where the same operation is applied to multiple data items concurrently.

OPENCL

The Open Computing Language (OpenCL) is a heterogeneous programming framework that is managed by the nonprofit technology consortium Khronos Group. OpenCL is a framework for developing applications that execute across a range of device types made by different vendors. It supports a wide range of levels of parallelism and efficiently maps to homogeneous or heterogeneous, single- or multiple-device systems consisting of CPUs, GPUs, and other types of devices limited only by the imagination of vendors. The OpenCL definition offers both a device-side language and a host management layer for the devices in a system.

The device-side language is designed to efficiently map to a wide range of memory systems. The host language aims to support efficient plumbing of complicated concurrent programs with low overhead. Together, these provide the developer with a path to efficiently move from algorithm design to implementation.

OpenCL provides parallel computing using task-based and data-based parallelism. It currently supports CPUs that include x86, ARM, and PowerPC, and it has been adopted into graphics card drivers by AMD, Apple, Intel, and NVIDIA. Support for OpenCL is rapidly expanding as a wide range of platform vendors have adopted OpenCL and support or plan to support it for their hardware platforms. These vendors fall within a wide range of market segments, from the embedded vendors (ARM and Imagination Technologies) to the HPC vendors (AMD, Intel, NVIDIA, and IBM). The architectures supported include multi-core CPUs, throughput and vector processors such as GPUs, and fine-grained parallel devices such as FPGAs.

Most important, OpenCL's cross-platform, industrywide support makes it an excellent programming model for developers to learn and use, with the confidence that it will continue to be widely available for years to come with ever-increasing scope and applicability.

THE GOALS OF THIS BOOK

The first edition of this book was the first of its kind to present OpenCL programming in a fashion appropriate for the classroom. In this second edition we update the content for the latest version of the OpenCL standard. The book is organized to address the need for teaching parallel programming on current system architectures using OpenCL as the target language, and it includes examples for CPUs, GPUs, and their integration in the accelerated processing unit (APU). Another major goal of this text is to provide a guide to programmers to develop well-designed programs in OpenCL targeting parallel systems. The book leads the programmer through the various abstractions and features provided by the OpenCL programming environment. The examples offer the reader a simple introduction and more complicated optimizations, and they suggest further development and goals at which to aim. It also discusses tools for improving the development process in terms of profiling and debugging such that the reader need not feel lost in the development process.

The book is accompanied by a set of instructor slides and programming examples, which support the use of this text by an OpenCL instructor. Please visit http://heterogeneouscomputingwithopencl.org/ for additional information.

THINKING PARALLEL

Most applications are first programmed to run on a single processor. In the field of high-performance computing, classical approaches have been used to accelerate computation when provided with multiple computing resources. Standard approaches include "divide-and-conquer" and "scatter–gather" problem decomposition methods, providing the programmer with a set of strategies to effectively exploit the parallel resources available in high-performance systems. Divide-and-conquer methods iteratively break a problem into subproblems until the subproblems fit well on the computational resources provided. Scatter–gather methods send a subset of the input data set to each parallel resource and then collect the results of the computation and combine them into a result data set. As before, the partitioning takes account of the size of the subsets based on the capabilities of the parallel resources. Figure 1.1 shows how popular applications such as sorting and a vector–scalar multiply can be effectively mapped to parallel resources to accelerate processing.

The programming task becomes increasingly challenging when faced with the growing parallelism and heterogeneity present in contemporary parallel processors. Given the power and thermal limits of complementary metal-oxide semiconductor (CMOS) technology, microprocessor vendors find it difficult to scale the frequency of these devices to derive more performance and have instead decided to place multiple processors, sometimes specialized, on a single chip. In doing so, the problem of extracting parallelism from an application is left to the programmer, who must decompose the underlying algorithms in the applications and map them efficiently to a diverse variety of target hardware platforms.

In the past 5 years, parallel computing devices have been increasing in number and processing capabilities. GPUs have also appeared on the computing scene and are

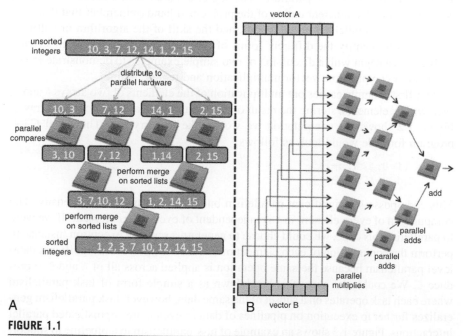

A

FIGURE 1.1

(A) Simple sorting and (B) dot product examples.

providing new levels of processing capability at very low cost. Driven by the demand for real-time three-dimensional graphics rendering, a highly data-parallel problem, GPUs have evolved rapidly as very powerful, fully programmable, task and data-parallel architectures. Hardware manufacturers are now combining CPU cores and GPU cores on a single die, ushering in a new generation of heterogeneous computing. Compute-intensive and data-intensive portions of a given application, called kernels, may be offloaded to the GPU, providing significant performance per watt and raw performance gains, while the host CPU continues to execute nonkernel tasks.

Many systems and phenomena in both the natural world and the man-made world present us with different classes of parallelism and concurrency:

- Molecular dynamics
- Weather and ocean patterns
- Multimedia systems
- Tectonic plate drift
- Cell growth
- Automobile assembly lines
- Sound and light wave propagation

Parallel computing, as defined by Almasi and Gottlieb (1989), is "a form of computation in which many calculations are carried out simultaneously, operating on the principle that large problems can often be divided into smaller ones, which are then solved concurrently (i.e., in parallel)." The degree of parallelism that can be achieved is dependent on the inherent nature of the problem at hand (remember that there exists significant parallelism in the world), and the skill of the algorithm or software designer is to identify the different forms of parallelism present in the underlying problem. We begin with a discussion of two simple examples to demonstrate inherent parallel computation: vector multiplication and text searching.

Our first example carries out multiplication of the elements of two arrays A and B, each with N elements, storing the result of each multiply in a corresponding array C. Figure 1.2 shows the computation we would like to carry out. The serial C++ program for code would look as follows:

```
for (i=0; i<N; i++)
    C[i] = A[i] * B[i];
```

This code possesses significant parallelism but very little arithmetic intensity. The computation of every element in C is independent of every other element. If we were to parallelize this code, we could choose to generate a separate execution instance to perform the computation of each element of C. This code possesses significant data-level parallelism because the same operation is applied across all of A and B to produce C. We could also view this breakdown as a simple form of task parallelism where each task operates on a subset of the same data; however, task parallelism generalizes further to execution on pipelines of data or even more sophisticated parallel interactions. Figure 1.3 shows an example of task parallelism in a pipeline to support filtering of images in frequency space using an FFT.

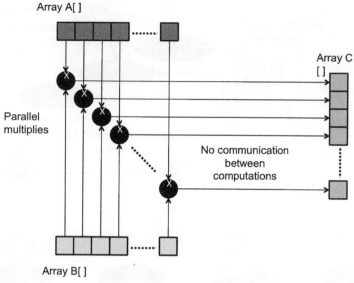

Array A[ ]

Parallel
multiplies

Array C
[ ]

No communication
between
computations

Array B[ ]

FIGURE 1.2

Multiplying two arrays: This example provides for parallel computation without any need for communication.

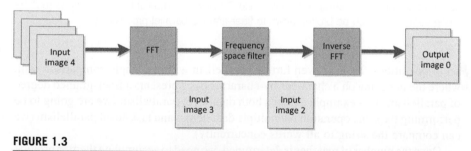

Input image 4

FFT

Frequency space filter

Inverse FFT

Output image 0

Input image 3

Input image 2

FIGURE 1.3

Filtering a series of images using an FFT shows clear task parallelism as a series of tasks operate together in a pipeline to compute the overall result.

Let us consider a second example. The computation we are trying to carry out is to find the number of occurrences of a string of characters in a body of text (Figure 1.4). Assume that the body of text has already been parsed into a set of N words. We could choose to divide the task of comparing the string against the N potential matches into N comparisons (i.e., tasks), where each string of characters is matched against the text string. This approach, although rather naïve in terms of search efficiency, is highly parallel. The process of the text string being compared against the set of potential words presents N parallel tasks, each carrying out the same

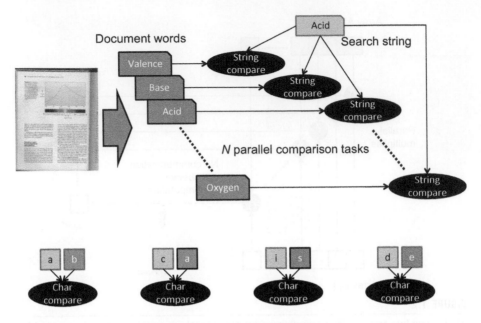

Finer-grained character-by-character parallelism

FIGURE 1.4

An example of both task-level and data-level parallelism. We can have parallel tasks that count the occurrence of string in a body of text. The lower portion of the figure shows that the string comparison can be broken down to finer-grained parallel processing.

set of operations. There is even further parallelism within a single comparison task, where the matching on a character-by-character basis presents a finer-grained degree of parallelism. This example exhibits both data-level parallelism (we are going to be performing the same operation on multiple data items) and task-level parallelism (we can compare the string to all words concurrently).

Once the number of matches is determined, we need to accumulate them to provide the total number of occurrences. Again, this summing can exploit parallelism. In this step, we introduce the concept of "reduction," where we can utilize the availability of parallel resources to combine partials sums in a very efficient manner. Figure 1.5 shows the reduction tree, which illustrates this summation process in log N steps.

CONCURRENCY AND PARALLEL PROGRAMMING MODELS

Here, we discuss concurrency and parallel processing models so that when attempting to map an application developed in OpenCL to a parallel platform, we can select the right model to pursue. Although all of the following models can be supported in OpenCL, the underlying hardware may restrict which model will be practical to use.

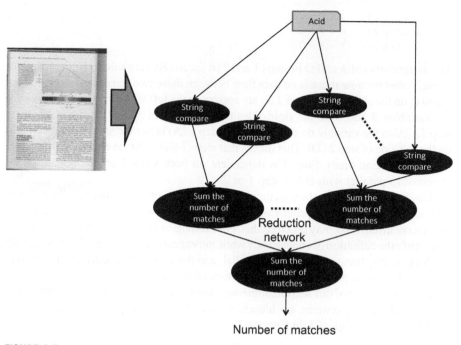

Reduction
network

Number of matches

FIGURE 1.5

After all string comparisons are completed, we can sum up the number of matches in a combining network.

Concurrency is concerned with two or more activities happening at the same time. We find concurrency in the real world all the time—for example, carrying a child in one arm while crossing a road or, more generally, thinking about something while doing something else with one's hands.

When talking about concurrency in terms of computer programming, we mean a single system performing multiple tasks independently. Although it is possible that concurrent tasks may be executed at the same time (i.e., in parallel), this is not a requirement. For example, consider a simple drawing application, which is either receiving input from the user via the mouse and keyboard or updating the display with the current image. Conceptually, receiving and processing input are different operations (i.e., tasks) from updating the display. These tasks can be expressed in terms of concurrency, but they do not need to be performed in parallel. In fact, in the case in which they are executing on a single core of a CPU, they cannot be performed in parallel. In this case, the application or the operating system should switch between the tasks, allowing both some time to run on the core.

Parallelism is concerned with running two or more activities in parallel with the explicit goal of increasing overall performance. For example, consider the following assignments:

```
step 1)    A = B + C
step 2)    D = E + G
step 3)    R = A + D
```

The assignments of A and D in steps 1 and 2 (respectively) are said to be independent of each other because there is no data flow between these two steps (i.e., the variables E and G on the right side of step 2 do not appear on the left side step 1, and vice versa, the variables B and C on the right sides of step 1 do not appear on the left side of step 2.). Also the variable on the left side of step 1 (A) is not the same as the variable on the left side of step 2 (D). This means that steps 1 and 2 can be executed in parallel (i.e., at the same time). Step 3 is dependent on both steps 1 and 2, so cannot be executed in parallel with either step 1 or 2.

Parallel programs must be concurrent, but concurrent programs need not be parallel. Although many concurrent programs can be executed in parallel, interdependencies between concurrent tasks may preclude this. For example, an interleaved execution would still satisfy the definition of concurrency while not executing in parallel. As a result, only a subset of concurrent programs are parallel, and the set of all concurrent programs is itself a subset of all programs. Figure 1.6 shows this relationship.

In the remainder of this section, some well-known approaches to programming concurrent and parallel systems are introduced with the aim of providing a foundation before introducing OpenCL in Chapter 2.

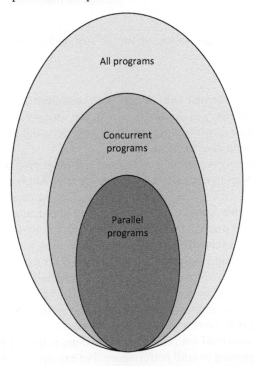

FIGURE 1.6

Parallel and concurrent programs are subsets of programs.

Threads and Shared Memory

A running program may consist of multiple subprograms that maintain their own independent control flow and that are allowed to run concurrently. These subprograms are defined as *threads*. Communication between threads is via updates and access to memory appearing in the same address space. Each thread has its own pool of local memory—that is, variables—but all threads see the same set of global variables. A simple analogy that can be used to describe the use of threads is the concept of a main program that includes a number of subroutines. The main program is scheduled to run by the operating system and performs necessary loading and acquisition of system and user resources to run. Execution of the main program begins by performing some serial work and then continues by creating a number of tasks that can be scheduled and run by the operating system concurrently using threads.

Each thread benefits from a global view of memory because it shares the same memory address space of the main program. Threads communicate with each other through global memory. This can require synchronization constructs to ensure that more than one thread is not updating the same global address.

A memory consistency model is defined to manage load and store ordering. All processors see the same address space and have direct access to these addresses with the help of other processors. Mechanisms such as locks/semaphores are commonly used to control access to shared memory that is accessed by multiple tasks. A key feature of the shared memory model is the fact that the programmer is not responsible for managing data movement, although depending on the consistency model implemented in the hardware or runtime system, some level of memory consistency may have to be enforced manually. This relaxes the requirement to specify explicitly the communication of data between tasks, and as a result, parallel code development can often be simplified.

There is a significant cost to supporting a fully consistent shared memory model in hardware. For multiprocessor systems, the hardware structures required to support this model become a limiting factor. Shared buses become bottlenecks in the design. The extra hardware required typically grows exponentially in terms of its complexity as we attempt to add additional processors. This has slowed the introduction of multi-core and multiprocessor systems at the low end, and it has limited the number of cores working together in a consistent shared memory system to relatively low numbers because shared buses and coherence protocol overheads become bottlenecks. More relaxed shared memory systems scale further, although in all cases scaling shared memory systems comes at the cost of complicated and expensive interconnects.

Most multi-core CPU platforms support shared memory in one form or another. OpenCL supports execution on shared memory devices.

Message-Passing Communication

The message-passing communication model enables explicit intercommunication of a set of concurrent tasks that may use memory during computation. Multiple tasks can reside on the same physical device and/or across an arbitrary number of devices.

Tasks exchange data through communications by sending and receiving explicit messages. Data transfer usually requires cooperative operations to be performed by each process. For example, a send operation must have a matching receive operation.

From a programming perspective, message-passing implementations commonly comprise a library of hardware-independent routines for sending and receiving messages. The programmer is responsible for explicitly managing communication between tasks. Historically, a variety of message-passing libraries have been available since the 1980s. MPI is currently the most popular message-passing middleware. These implementations differ substantially from each other, making it difficult for programmers to develop portable applications.

Different Grains of Parallelism

In parallel computing, granularity is a measure of the ratio of computation to communication. Periods of computation are typically separated from periods of communication by synchronization events. The grain of parallelism is constrained by the inherent characteristics of the algorithms constituting the application. It is important that the parallel programmer selects the right granularity in order to reap the full benefits of the underlying platform because choosing the right grain size can help to expose additional degrees of parallelism. Sometimes this selection is referred to as "chunking," determining the amount of data to assign to each task. Selecting the right chunk size can help provide for further acceleration on parallel hardware. Next, we consider some of the trade-offs associated with identifying the right grain size.

- Fine-grained parallelism
  - Low arithmetic intensity.
  - May not have enough work to hide long-duration asynchronous communication.
  - Facilitates load balancing by providing a larger number of more manageable (i.e., smaller) work units.
  - If the granularity is too fine, it is possible that the overhead required for communication and synchronization between tasks can actually produce a slower parallel implementation than the original serial execution.
- Coarse-grained parallelism
  - High arithmetic intensity.
  - Complete applications can serve as the grain of parallelism.
  - More difficult to load balance efficiently.

Given these trade-offs, which granularity will lead to the best implementation? The most efficient granularity is dependent on the algorithm and the hardware environment in which it is run. In most cases, if the overhead associated with communication and synchronization is high relative to the time of the computation task at hand, it will generally be advantageous to work at a coarser granularity. Fine-grained parallelism can help reduce overheads due to load imbalance or memory delays (this is particularly true on a GPU, which depends on near-zero-overhead fine-grained thread switching to hide memory latencies). Fine-grained parallelism can even occur at an instruction level (this approach is used in very long instruction word (VLIW) and superscalar architectures).

Data Sharing and Synchronization

Consider the case in which two applications run that do not share any data. As long as the runtime system or operating system has access to adequate execution resources, they can be run concurrently and even in parallel. If halfway through the execution of one application it generated a result that was subsequently required by the second application, then we would have to introduce some form of synchronization into the system, and parallel execution—at least across the synchronization point—becomes impossible.

When writing concurrent software, data sharing and synchronization play a critical role. Examples of data sharing in concurrent programs include

- the input of a task is dependent on the result of another task—for example, in a producer/consumer or pipeline execution model; and
- when intermediate results are combined together (e.g., as part of a reduction, as in our word search example shown in Figure 1.4).

Ideally, we would only attempt to parallelize portions of an application that are void of data dependencies, but this is not always possible. Explicit synchronization primitives such as barriers or locks may be used to support synchronization when necessary. Although we only raise this issue here, later chapters revisit this question when support for communication between host and device programs or when synchronization between tasks is required.

STRUCTURE

The remainder of the book is organized as follows:

Chapter 1 (this chapter) introduces many concepts related to the development of parallel algorithms and software. The chapter covers concurrency, threads, and different grains of parallelism: many of the fundamentals of parallel software development.

Chapter 2 presents an introduction to OpenCL, including key concepts such as kernels, platforms, and devices, the four different abstraction models, and developing your first OpenCL kernel. Understanding these different models is critical to fully appreciate the richness of OpenCL's programming model.

Chapter 3 presents some of the architectures OpenCL does or might target, including x86 CPUs, GPUs, and APUs. The text includes discussion of different styles of architectures including SIMD and VLIW. This chapter also covers the concepts of multi-core and throughput-oriented systems, as well as the new advances in heterogeneous architectures.

Chapter 4 introduces basic matrix multiplication, image rotation and convolution implementations to help the reader learn OpenCL by example.

Chapter 5 discusses concurrency and execution in the OpenCL programming model. In this chapter we discuss kernels, work items and the OpenCL execution and memory hierarchies. We also show how queuing and synchronization work in OpenCL such that the reader gains an understanding of how to write OpenCL programs that interact with memory correctly.

Chapter 6 shows how OpenCL maps to an example architecture. For this study we choose a system comprising an AMD Bulldozer CPU and an AMD Radeon HD7970 GPU. This chapter allows us to show how the mappings of the OpenCL programming model for largely serial architectures such as CPUs and vector/throughput architectures such as GPUs differ, giving some idea how to optimize for specific architectural styles.

Chapter 7 discusses data management on heterogeneous systems, with particular focus on developing guidelines on how to optimize data transfers on different platforms using OpenCL. The chapter concludes with a case study where the performance of a reduction kernel is considered when different data management strategies are used.

Chapter 8 presents a case study that accelerates a convolution algorithm. Issues related to memory space utilization and efficiency are considered as well as work item scheduling, wavefront occupancy, and overall efficiency. These techniques are the foundations necessary for developing high performance code using OpenCL.

Chapter 9 presents another case study, looking at how to optimize the performance of a Histogramming application. In particular, it highlights how careful design of work-group size and memory access patterns can make a vast difference to performance in memory bound applications such as Histogram.

Chapter 10 discusses how to leverage a heterogeneous CPU-GPU environment. The target application is a mixed particle simulation (as illustrated on the cover) where work is distributed across both the CPU and GPU depending on the grain size of particles in the system.

Chapter 11 shows how to use OpenCL extensions using the device fission and double precision extensions as examples.

Chapter 12 shows that non C and C++ application developers can access the benefits of OpenCL via a selection of API wrapper frameworks and Embedded Domain Specific Languages. This main component of the chapter is an in depth look at accessing OpenCL from the functional programming language Haskell.

Chapter 13 introduces the reader to debugging and analyzing OpenCL programs. The right debugging tool can save a developer 100s of wasted programs, allowing her instead to learn the specific computer language and solve the problem at hand.

Chapter 14 looks at the profiling techniques briefly mentioned in chapter 13 in more depth, applying them to a real application. A medical image analysis pipeline is ported from a traditional CPU multithreaded execution and optimized for execution using OpenCL on a GPU. In this chapter we see both static analysis and profiling and the tradeoffs involved in optimizing a real application for data-parallel execution.

Reference

Almasi, G. S., & Gottlieb, A. (1989). *Highly Parallel Computing*. Redwood City, CA: Benjamin Cummings.

Further Reading and Relevant Websites

Chapman, B., Jost, G., van der Pas, R., & Kuck, D. J. (2007). *Using OpenMP: Portable Shared Memory Parallel Programming*. Cambridge, MA: MIT Press.

Duffy, J. (2008). *Concurrent Programming on Windows*. Upper Saddle River, NJ: Addison-Wesley.

Gropp, W., Lusk, E., & Skjellum, A. (1994). *Using MPI: Portable Parallel Programming with the Message-Passing Interface*. MIT Press Scientific and Engineering Computation Series. Cambridge, MA: MIT Press.

Herlihy, M., & Shavit, N. (2008). *The Art of Multiprocessor Programming*. Burlington, MA: Morgan Kaufmann.

Khronos Group. *OpenCL*. www.khronos.org/opencl.

Mattson, T. G., Sanders, B. A., & Massingill, B. L. (2004). *Patterns for Parallel Programming*. Upper Saddle River, NJ: Addison-Wesley.

NVIDA. *CUDA Zone*. http://www.nvidia.com/object/cuda_home_new.html.

AMD. OpenCL Zone. http://developer.amd.com/openclzone.

Introduction to OpenCL

2

INTRODUCTION

This chapter introduces OpenCL, the programming fabric that will allow us to weave our application to execute concurrently. Programmers familiar with C and C++ should have little trouble understanding the OpenCL syntax. We begin by reviewing the OpenCL standard.

The OpenCL Standard

Open programming standards designers are tasked with a very challenging objective: arrive at a common set of programming standards that are acceptable to a range of competing needs and requirements. The Khronos consortium that manages the OpenCL standard has done a good job addressing these requirements. The consortium has developed an applications programming interface (API) that is general enough to run on significantly different architectures while being adaptable enough that each hardware platform can still obtain high performance. Using the core language and correctly following the specification, any program designed for one vendor can execute on another's hardware. The model set forth by OpenCL creates portable, vendor- and device-independent programs that are capable of being accelerated on many different hardware platforms.

The OpenCL API is a C with a C++ Wrapper API that is defined in terms of the C API. There are third-party bindings for many languages, including Java, Python, and .NET. The code that executes on an OpenCL device, which in general is not the same device as the host CPU, is written in the OpenCL C language. OpenCL C is a restricted version of the C99 language with extensions appropriate for executing data-parallel code on a variety of heterogeneous devices.

The OpenCL Specification

The OpenCL specification is defined in four parts, called models, that can be summarized as follows:

1. Platform model: Specifies that there is one processor coordinating execution (the *host*) and one or more processors capable of executing OpenCL C code (the *devices*). It defines an abstract hardware model that is used by programmers when writing OpenCL C functions (called *kernels*) that execute on the devices.
2. Execution model: Defines how the OpenCL environment is configured on the host and how kernels are executed on the device. This includes setting up an OpenCL context on the host, providing mechanisms for host–device interaction, and defining a concurrency model used for kernel execution on devices.
3. Memory model: Defines the abstract memory hierarchy that kernels use, regardless of the actual underlying memory architecture. The memory model closely resembles current GPU memory hierarchies, although this has not limited adoptability by other accelerators.
4. Programming model: Defines how the concurrency model is mapped to physical hardware.

In a typical scenario, we might observe an OpenCL implementation executing on a host x86 CPU, which is using a GPU device as an accelerator. The platform model defines this relationship between the host and device. The host sets up a kernel for the GPU to run and instantiates it with some specified degree of parallelism. This is the execution model. The data within the kernel is allocated by the programmer to specific parts of an abstract memory hierarchy. The runtime and driver will map these abstract memory spaces to the physical hierarchy. Finally, hardware thread contexts that execute the kernel must be created and mapped to actual GPU hardware units. This is done using the programming model. Throughout this chapter, these ideas are discussed in further detail.

This chapter begins by introducing how OpenCL kernels are written and the parallel execution model that they use. The OpenCL host API is then described and demonstrated using a running example–vector addition. The full listing of the vector addition example is given at the end of the chapter.

Kernels and the OpenCL Execution Model

Kernels are the parts of an OpenCL program that actually execute on a device. The OpenCL API enables an application to create a context for management of the execution of OpenCL commands, including those describing the movement of data between host and OpenCL memory structures and the execution of kernel code that processes this data to perform some meaningful task.

Like many CPU concurrency models, an OpenCL kernel is syntactically similar to a standard C function; the key differences are a set of additional keywords and the execution model that OpenCL kernels implement. When developing concurrent programs for a CPU using OS threading APIs or OpenMP, for example, the programmer considers the physical resources available (e.g., CPU cores) and the overhead of creating and switching between threads when their number substantially exceeds the resource availability. With OpenCL, the goal is often to represent parallelism programmatically at the finest granularity possible. The generalization of the OpenCL interface and the low-level kernel language allows efficient mapping to a wide range of hardware. The following discussion presents three versions of a function that performs an element-wise vector addition: a serial C implementation, a threaded C implementation, and an OpenCL implementation.

The code for a serial C implementation of the vector addition executes a loop with as many iterations as there are elements to compute. Each loop iteration adds the corresponding locations in the input arrays together and stores the result into the output array:

```
// Perform an element-wise addition of A and B and store in C.
// There are N elements per array.
void vecadd(int *C, int* A, int *B, int N) {
    for(int i = 0; i < N; i++) {
        C[i] = A[i] + B[i];
    }
}
```

For a simple multi-core device, we could either use a low-level coarse-grained threading API, such as Win32 or POSIX threads, or use a data-parallel model such as OpenMP. Writing a coarse-grained multithreaded version of the same function would require dividing the work (i.e., loop iterations) between the threads. Because there may be a large number of loop iterations and the work per iteration is small, we would need to chunk the loop iterations into a larger granularity (a technique called *strip mining*, (Cooper and Torczon, 2011)). The code for the multithreaded version may look as follows:

```
// Perform and element-wise addition of A and B and store in C.
// There are N elements per array and NP CPU cores.
void vecadd(int *C, int* A, int *B, int N, int NP, int tid) {
    int ept = N/NP; // elements per thread
    for(int i = tid*ept; i < (tid+1)*ept; i++) {
        C[i] = A[i] + B[i];
    }
}
```

OpenCL is closer to OpenMP than the threading APIs of Win32 and POSIX, supporting data-parallel execution but retaining a low level of control. The unit of concurrent execution in OpenCL C is a *work-item*. As with the two previous examples, each work-item executes the kernel function body. Instead of manually strip mining the loop, we will often map a single iteration of the loop to a work-item. We tell the OpenCL runtime to generate as many work-items as elements in the input and output arrays and allow the runtime to map those work-items to the underlying hardware, and hence CPU or GPU cores, in whatever way it deems appropriate. Conceptually, this is very similar to the parallelism inherent in a functional "map" operation (c.f., mapReduce) or a data-parallel for loop in a model such as OpenMP. When an OpenCL device begins executing a kernel, it provides intrinsic functions that allow a work-item to identify itself. In the following code, the call to get_global_id(0) allows the programmer to make use of the position of the current work-item in the simple case to regain the loop counter:

```
// Perform an element-wise addition of A and B and store in C
// N work-items will be created to execute this kernel.
__kernel
void vecadd(__global int *C, __global int* A, __global int *B) {
    int tid = get_global_id(0); // OpenCL intrinsic function
    C[tid] = A[tid] + B[tid];
}
```

Given that OpenCL describes execution in fine-grained work-items and can dispatch vast numbers of work-items on architectures with hardware support for fine-grained threading, it is easy to have concerns about scalability. The hierarchical concurrency model implemented by OpenCL ensures that scalable execution can be achieved even while supporting a large number of work-items. When a kernel is executed, the programmer specifies the number of work-items that should be created as an n-*dimensional range* (NDRange). An NDRange is a one-, two-, or three-dimensional index space of work-items that will often map to the dimensions of either the input or the output data. The dimensions of the NDRange are specified as an *N*-element array of type size_t, where *N* represents the number of dimensions used to describe the work-items being created.

In the vector addition example, our data will be one-dimensional and, assuming that there are 1024 elements, the size can be specified as a one-, two-, or three-dimensional vector. The host code to specify an ND Range for 1024 elements is as follows:

```
size_t indexSpaceSize[3] = {1024, 1, 1};
```

Achieving scalability comes from dividing the work-items of an NDRange into smaller, equally sized workgroups (Figure 2.1). An index space with *N* dimensions requires workgroups to be specified using the same *N* dimensions; thus, a three-dimensional index space requires three-dimensional workgroups.

Work items within a workgroup have a special relationship with one another: They can perform barrier operations to synchronize and they have access to a shared memory address space. Because workgroup sizes are fixed, this communication does not have a need to scale and hence does not affect scalability of a large concurrent dispatch.

For the vector addition example, the workgroup size might be specified as

```
size_t workGroupSize[3] = {64, 1, 1};
```

If the total number of work-items per array is 1024, this results in creating 16 workgroups (1024 work-items/(64 work-items per workgroup) = 16 workgroups). Note

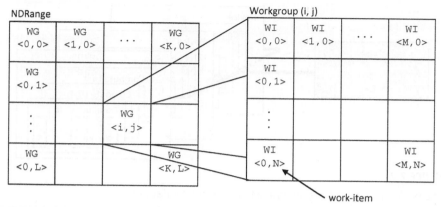

FIGURE 2.1

Work-items are created as an NDRange and grouped in workgroups.

that OpenCL requires that the index space sizes are evenly divisible by the work-group sizes in each dimension. For hardware efficiency, the workgroup size is usually fixed to a favorable size, and we round up the index space size in each dimension to satisfy this divisibility requirement. In the kernel code, we can specify that extra work-items in each dimension simply return immediately without outputting any data.

For programs such as vector addition in which work-items behave independently (even within a workgroup), OpenCL allows the local workgroup size to be ignored by the programmer and generated automatically by the implementation; in this case, the developer will pass NULL instead.

PLATFORM AND DEVICES

The OpenCL platform model defines the roles of the host and devices and provides an abstract hardware model for devices.

Host–Device Interaction

In the platform model, there is a single host that coordinates execution on one or more devices. Platforms can be thought of as vendor-specific implementations of the OpenCL API. The devices that a platform can target are thus limited to those with which a vendor knows how to interact. For example, if Company A's platform is chosen, it cannot communicate with Company B's GPU.

The platform model also presents an abstract device architecture that programmers target when writing OpenCL C code. Vendors map this abstract architecture to the physical hardware. With scalability in mind, the platform model defines a

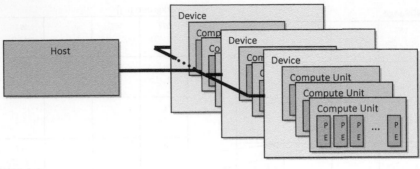

FIGURE 2.2

The platform model defines an abstract architecture for devices.

device as an array of *compute units*, with each compute unit functionally independent from the rest. Compute units are further divided into *processing elements*. Figure 2.2 illustrates this hierarchical model.

The platform device model closely corresponds to the hardware model of some GPUs. For example, the AMD Radeon 7970 graphics card (device) comprises 32 vector processors (compute units). Each compute unit has 4 16-lane SIMD engines for a total of 64 lane (processing elements). Each SIMD lane on the 7970 executes a scalar instruction. This allows the device to execute a total of 2048 instructions at a time on the processing elements.

The API function `clGetPlatformIDs()` is used to discover the set of available platforms for a given system:

```
cl_int
clGetPlatformIDs(cl_uint num_entries,
                 cl_platform_id *platforms,
                 cl_uint *num_platforms)
```

`clGetPlatformIDs()` will often be called twice by an application. The first call passes an `unsigned int` pointer as the `num_platforms` argument and `NULL` is passed as the `platforms` argument. The pointer is populated with the available number of platforms. The programmer can then allocate space to hold the platform information. For the second call, a `cl_platform_id` pointer is passed to the implementation with enough space allocated for `num_entries` platforms. After platforms have been discovered, the `clGetPlatformInfo()` call can be used to determine which implementation (vendor) the platform was defined by. The full source code listing at the end of the chapter demonstrates this process.

The `clGetDeviceIDs()` call works very similar to `clGetPlatformIDs()`. It takes the additional arguments of a platform and a device type but otherwise the same three-step process occurs. The `device_type` argument can be used to limit the devices to GPUs only (`CL_DEVICE_TYPE_GPU`), CPUs only (`CL_DEVICE_TYPE_CPU`), all devices (`CL_DEVICE_TYPE_ALL`), as well as other options. As with platforms, `clGetDeviceInfo()` is called to retrieve information such as name, type, and vendor from each device. Discovering devices is illustrated in the full source code listing at the end of the chapter:

```
cl_int
clGetDeviceIDs(cl_platform_id platform,
               cl_device_type device_type,
               cl_uint num_entries,
               cl_device_id *devices,
               cl_uint *num_devices)
```

The `CLInfo` program in the AMD APP SDK uses the `clGetPlatformInfo()` and `clGetDeviceInfo()` commands to print detailed information about the OpenCL supported platforms and devices in a system. Hardware details such as memory sizes and bus widths are available using these commands. A snippet of the output from the `CLInfo` program is shown here:

```
$ ./CLInfo
Number of platforms:              1

Platform Profile:                 FULL_PROFILE
Platform Version:                 OpenCL 1.2 AMD-APP (938.1)
Platform Name:                    AMD Accelerated Parallel Processing
Platform Vendor:                  Advanced Micro Devices, Inc.

Number of devices:                2

Device Type:                      CL_DEVICE_TYPE_GPU
Board name:                       AMD Radeon HD 7900 Series
Device Topology:                  PCI[ B#1, D#0, F#0 ]
Max compute units:                32
Max work items dimensions:        3
Max work group size:              512
Preferred vector width char:      16
Local memory type:                Scratchpad
Local memory size:                32768
Name:                             Tahiti
Vendor:                           Advanced Micro Devices, Inc.
Device OpenCL C version:          OpenCL C 1.2
Driver version:                   CAL 1.4.1741 (VM)
Device Type:                      CL_DEVICE_TYPE_CPU
Device ID:                        4098
Max compute units:                2
Max work group size:              1024
Name:                             Intel(R) Core(TM)2 CPU 6300 @ 1.86 GHz
Vendor:                           GenuineIntel
Device OpenCL C version:          OpenCL C 1.2
```

THE EXECUTION ENVIRONMENT

Before a host can request that a kernel be executed on a device, a context must be configured on the host that enables it to pass commands and data to the device.

Contexts

In OpenCL, a *context* is an abstract container that exists on the host. A context coordinates the mechanisms for host–device interaction, manages the memory objects that are available to the devices, and keeps track of the programs and kernels that are created for each device.

The API function to create a context is `clCreateContext()`. The `properties` argument is used to restrict the scope of the context. It may provide a specific platform, enable graphics interoperability, or enable other parameters in the future. Limiting the context to a given platform allows the programmer to provide contexts for multiple platforms and fully utilize a system comprising resources from a mixture of vendors. Next, the number and IDs of the devices that the programmer wants to associate with the context must be supplied. OpenCL allows user callbacks to be provided when creating a context that can be used to report additional error information that might be generated throughout its lifetime. The full source code listing at the end of the chapter demonstrates the creation of a context:

```
cl_context
clCreateContext (const cl_context_properties *properties,
                 cl_uint num_devices,
                 const cl_device_id *devices,
                 void (CL_CALLBACK *pfn_notify)(
                                  const char *errinfo,
                                  const void *private_info,
                                  size_t cb,
                                  void *user_data),
                 void *user_data,
                 cl_int *errcode_ret)
```

The OpenCL specification also provides an API call that alleviates the need to build a list of devices. `clCreateContextFromType()` allows a programmer to create a context that automatically includes all devices of the specified type (e.g., CPUs, GPUs, and all devices). After creating a context, the function `clGetContextInfo()` can be used to query information such as the number of devices present and the device structures.

In OpenCL, the process of discovering platforms and devices and setting up a context is tedious. However, after the code to perform these steps is written once, it can be reused for almost any project.

Command Queues

Communication with a device occurs by submitting commands to a *command queue*. The command queue is the mechanism that the host uses to request action by the device.

Once the host decides which devices to work with and a context is created, one command queue needs to be created per device (i.e., each command queue is associated with only one device). Whenever the host needs an action to be performed by a device, it will submit commands to the proper command queue. The API `clCreateCommandQueue()` is used to create a command queue and associate it with a device:

```
cl_command_queue
clCreateCommandQueue(
     cl_context context,
     cl_device_id device,
     cl_command_queue_properties properties,
     cl_int* errcode_ret)
```

The properties parameter of `clCreateCommandQueue()` is a bit field that is used to enable profiling of commands (`CL_QUEUE_PROFILING_ENABLE`) and/or to allow out-of-order execution of commands (`CL_QUEUE_OUT_OF_ ORDER_EXEC_MODE_ ENABLE`). Profiling is discussed in Chapter 12. With an in-order command queue (the default), commands are pulled from the queue in the order they were received. Out-of-order queues allow the OpenCL implementation to search for commands that can possibly be rearranged to execute more efficiently. If out-of-order queues are used, it is up to the user to specify dependencies that enforce a correct execution order. The full source code listing at the end of the chapter creates a command queue.

Any API that specifies host–device interaction will always begin with *clEnqueue* and require a command queue as a parameter. For example, the `clEnqueueReadBuffer()` command requests that the device send data to the host, and `clEnqueueNDRangeKernel()` requests that a kernel is executed on the device. These calls are discussed later in this chapter.

Events

Any operation that enqueues a command into a command queue—that is, any API call that begins with *clEnqueue*—produces an *event*. Events have two main roles in OpenCL:

1. Representing dependencies
2. Providing a mechanism for profiling

In addition to producing event objects, API calls that begin with *clEnqueue* also take a "wait list" of events as a parameter. By generating an event for one API call and passing it as an argument to a successive call, OpenCL allows us to represent dependencies. A kernel enqueued using a *clEnqueue* call will not begin executing until all events in its wait list have been satisfied. Chapter 5 provides examples of representing dependencies using events.

OpenCL events can also be used to profile, using associated timers, commands enqueued. Chapter 13 describes how to use OpenCL events for profiling.

Memory Objects

OpenCL applications often work with large arrays or multidimensional matrices. This data needs to be physically present on a device before execution can begin. In order for data to be transferred to a device, it must first be encapsulated as a *memory object*. OpenCL defines two types of memory objects: *buffers* and *images*. Buffers are equivalent to arrays in C, created using malloc(), where data elements are stored contiguously in memory. Images, on the other hand, are designed as opaque objects, allowing for data padding and other optimizations that may improve performance on devices.

Whenever a memory object is created, it is valid only within a single context. Movement to and from specific devices is managed by the OpenCL runtime as necessary to satisfy data dependencies.

Buffers

Conceptually, it may help to visualize a memory object as a pointer that is valid on a device. This is similar to a call to malloc, in C, or a C++'s new operator. The API function clCreateBuffer() allocates the buffer and returns a memory object:

```
cl_mem clCreateBuffer(
    cl_context context,
    cl_mem_flags flags,
    size_t size,
    void *host_ptr,
    cl_int *errcode_ret)
```

Creating a buffer requires supplying the size of the buffer and a context in which the buffer will be allocated; it is visible for all devices associated with the context. Optionally, the caller can supply flags that specify that the data is read-only, write-only, or read-write. Other flags also exist that specify additional options for creating and initializing a buffer. One simple option is to supply a host pointer with data used to initialize the buffer. The full source code listing at the end of the chapter demonstrates the creation of two input buffers and one output buffer.

Data contained in host memory is transferred to and from an OpenCL buffer using the commands clEnqueueWriteBuffer() and clEnqueueReadBuffer(), respectively. If a kernel that is dependent on such a buffer is executed on a discrete accelerator device such as a GPU, the buffer may be transferred to the device. The buffer is linked to a context, not a device, so it is the runtime that determines the precise time the data is moved.

The API calls for reading and writing to buffers are very similar. The signature for clEnqueueWriteBuffer() is

```
cl_int
clEnqueueWriteBuffer (
    cl_command_queue command_queue,
    cl_mem buffer,
```

```
cl_bool blocking_write,
size_t offset,
size_t cb,
const void *ptr,
cl_uint num_events_in_wait_list,
const cl_event *event_wait_list,
cl_event *event)
```

Similar to other enqueue operations, reading or writing a buffer requires a command queue to manage the execution schedule. In addition, the enqueue function requires the buffer, the number of bytes to transfer, and an offset within the buffer. The `blocking_write` option should be set to `CL_TRUE` if the transfer into an OpenCL buffer should complete before the function returns—that is, it will block until the operation has completed. Setting `blocking_write` to `CL_FALSE` allows `clEnqueueWriteBuffer()` to return before the write operation has completed. The full source code listing at the end of the chapter enqueues commands to write input data to buffers on a device, and read the output data back to the host.

Images

Images are OpenCL memory objects that abstract the storage of physical data to allow for device-specific optimizations. They are not required to be supported by all OpenCL devices and an application is required to check, using `clGetDeviceInfo()`, if they are supported or not, otherwise behavior is undefined. Unlike buffers, images cannot be directly referenced as if they were arrays. Further, adjacent data elements are not guaranteed to be stored contiguously in memory. The purpose of using images is to allow the hardware to take advantage of spatial locality and to utilize the hardware acceleration available on many devices. The architectural design and tradeoffs for images are discussed in detail in Chapter 5.

In versions 1.0 and 1.1 of the OpenCL standard, only 2D and 3D images were supported using the commands `clCreateImage2D()` and `clCreateImage3D()`, respectively. In version 1.2 of the standard, a more general interface was introduced using `clCreateImage()`, which also supports 1D images.

Unlike buffers that do not have a data type or dimensions, an image is created using descriptors that provide specific details to the hardware about the data. The elements of an image are represented by a format descriptor (`cl_image_format`). The format descriptor specifies how the image elements are stored in memory based the on the concept of channels. The *channel order* specifies the number of elements that make up an image element (up to 4 elements, based on the traditional use of RGBA pixels), and the *channel type* specifies the size of each element. These elements can be sized anywhere from 1 to 4 bytes and in various different formats. e.g. integer or floating point. Other metadata is provided by an image descriptor (`cl_image_desc`), which includes the type of the image and the dimensions.

```
cl_mem
clCreateImage(
    cl_context context,
    cl_mem_flags flags,
    const cl_image_format *image_format,
    const cl_image_desc *image_desc,
    void *host_ptr,
    cl_int *errcode_ret)
```

There are also additional parameters compared to buffers when reading or writing an image. Read or write operations take a 3-element origin (similar to the buffer offset) that defines the location within the image that the transfer will begin, and another 3-element region parameter that defines the extent of the data that will be transferred.

Within a kernel, images are accessed with built-in functions specific to the data type. For example, the function `read_imagef()` is used for reading floats and `read_imageui()` for unsigned integers. When data is read from an image, a sampler object is required. Samplers specify how out-of-bounds image accesses are handled, whether interpolation should be used, and if coordinates are normalized. Writing to a location in an image requires manual conversion to the proper storage data format (i.e., storing in the proper channel and with the proper size). Chapter 4 provides an example of an OpenCL program that uses images.

Flush and Finish

The flush and finish commands are two different types of barrier operations for a command queue. The `clFinish()` function blocks until all of the commands in a command queue have completed; its functionality is synonymous with a synchronization barrier. The `clFlush()` function blocks until all of the commands in a command queue have been removed from the queue. This means that the commands will definitely be in-flight but will not necessarily have completed.

```
cl_int clFlush(cl_command_queue command_queue);
cl_int clFinish(cl_command_queue command_queue);
```

Creating an OpenCL Program Object

OpenCL C code (written to run on an OpenCL device) is called a *program*. A program is a collection of functions called kernels, where kernels are units of execution that can be scheduled to run on a device.

OpenCL programs are compiled at runtime through a series of API calls. This runtime compilation gives the system an opportunity to optimize for a specific device. There is no need for an OpenCL application to have been prebuilt against the AMD, NVIDIA, or Intel runtimes, for example, if it is to run on devices produced by all of these vendors. OpenCL software links only to a common runtime layer (called the ICD); all platform-specific SDK activity is delegated to a vendor runtime through a dynamic library interface.

The process of creating a kernel is as follows:

1. The OpenCL C source code is stored in a character string. If the source code is stored in a file on a disk, it must be read into memory and stored as a character array.
2. The source code is turned into a program object, `cl_program`, by calling `clCreateProgramWithSource()`.
3. The program object is then compiled, for one or more OpenCL devices, with `clBuildProgram()`. If there are compile errors, they will be reported here.

The precise binary representation used is vendor specific. In the AMD runtime, there are two main classes of devices: x86 CPUs and GPUs. For x86 CPUs, `clBuildProgram()` generates x86 instructions that can be directly executed on the device. For the GPUs, it will create AMD's GPU intermediate language (IL), a high-level intermediate language that represents a single work-item but that will be just-in-time compiled for a specific GPU's architecture later, generating what is often known as ISA (i.e., code for a specific instruction set architecture). NVIDIA uses a similar approach, calling its intermediate representation PTX. The advantage of using such an IL is to allow the GPU ISA to change from one device or generation to another in what is still a very rapidly developing architectural space.

One additional feature of the build process is the ability to generate both the final binary format and various intermediate representations and serialize them (e.g., write them out to disk). As with most objects, OpenCL provides a function to return information about program objects, `clGetProgramInfo()`. One of the flags to this function is `CL_PROGRAM_BINARIES`, which returns a vendor-specific set of binary objects generated by `clBuildProgram()`.

In addition to `clCreateProgramWithSource()`, OpenCL provides `clCreateProgramWithBinary()`, which takes a list of binaries that matches its device list. The binaries are previously created using `clGetProgramInfo()`.

The OpenCL Kernel

The final stage to obtain a `cl_kernel` object that can be used to execute kernels on a device is to extract the kernel from the `cl_program`. Extracting a kernel from a program is similar to obtaining an exported function from a dynamic library. The name of the kernel that the program exports is used to request it from the compiled program object. The name of the kernel is passed to `clCreateKernel()`, along with the program object, and the kernel object will be returned if the program object was valid and the particular kernel is found.

A few more steps are required before the kernel can actually be executed. Unlike calling functions in regular C programs, we cannot simply call a kernel by providing a list of arguments.

Executing a kernel requires dispatching it through an enqueue function. Due both to the syntax of the C language and to the fact that kernel arguments are persistent (and hence we need not repeatedly set them to construct the argument list for such a dispatch), we must specify each kernel argument individually using the function `clSetKernelArg()`. This function takes a kernel object, an index specifying the argument number, the size of the argument, and a pointer to the argument. When a kernel is executed, this information is used to transfer arguments to the device. The type information in the kernel parameter list is then used by the runtime to unbox (similar to casting) the data to its appropriate type. The process of setting kernel arguments is illustrated in the full source code listing at the end of the chapter.

After any required memory objects are transferred to the device and the kernel arguments are set, the kernel is ready to be executed. Requesting that a device begin executing a kernel is done with a call to `clEnqueueNDRangeKernel()`:

```
cl_int
clEnqueueNDRangeKernel(
    cl_command_queue command_queue,
    cl_kernel kernel,
    cl_uint work_dim,
    const size_t *global_work_offset,
    const size_t *global_work_size,
    const size_t *local_work_size,
    cl_uint num_events_in_wait_list,
    const cl_event *event_wait_list,
    cl_event *event)
```

Look at the signature for the function. A command queue must be specified so the target device is known. Similarly, the kernel object identifies the code to be executed. Four fields are related to work-item creation. The `work_dim` parameter specifies the number of dimensions (one, two, or three) in which work-items will be created. The `global_work_size` parameter specifies the number of work-items in each dimension of the NDRange, and `local_work_size` specifies the number of work-items in each dimension of the workgroups. The parameter `global_work_offset` can be used to provide global IDs to the work-items that do not start at 0. As with all *clEnqueue* commands, an `event_wait_list` is provided, and for non-NULL values the runtime will guarantee that all corresponding events will have completed before the kernel begins execution. The `clEnqueueNDRangeKernel()` call is asynchronous: it will return immediately after the command is enqueued in the command queue and likely before the kernel has even started execution. Either `clWaitForEvents()` or `clFinish()` can be used to block execution on the host until the kernel completes. The code to configure the work-items for the vector addition kernel and enqueue it for execution is shown in the full source code listing at the end of the chapter.

At this point, we have presented all of the required host API commands needed to enable the reader to run a complete OpenCL program.

MEMORY MODEL

In general, memory subsystems vary greatly between computing platforms. For example, all modern CPUs support automatic caching, although many GPUs do not. To support code portability, OpenCL's approach is to define an abstract memory model that programmers can target when writing code and vendors can map to their actual memory hardware. The memory spaces defined by OpenCL are discussed here and shown in Figure 2.3.

These memory spaces are relevant within OpenCL programs. The keywords associated with each space can be used to specify where a variable should be created or where the data that it points to resides.

Global memory is visible to all compute units on the device (similar to the main memory on a CPU-based host system). Whenever data is transferred from the host to the device, the data will reside in global memory. Any data that is to be transferred back from the device to the host must also reside in global memory. The keyword __global is added to a pointer declaration to specify that data referenced by the pointer resides in global memory. For example, in the OpenCL C code at the end of the chapter __global float* A, the data pointed to by A resides in global memory (although we will see that A actually resides in private memory).

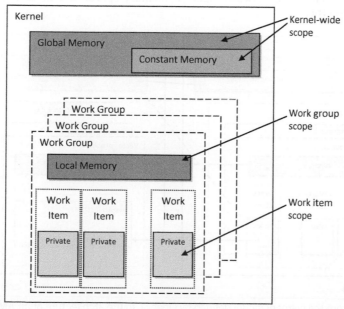

FIGURE 2.3

The abstract memory model defined by OpenCL.

Constant memory is not specifically designed for every type of read-only data but, rather, for data where each element is accessed simultaneously by all work-items. Variables whose values never change (e.g., a data variable holding the value of π) also fall into this category. Constant memory is modeled as a part of global memory, so memory objects that are transferred to global memory can be specified as constant. Data is mapped to constant memory by using the __constant keyword.

Local memory is a scratchpad memory whose address space is unique to each compute device. It is common for it to be implemented as on-chip memory, but there is no requirement that this be the case. Local memory is modeled as being shared by a workgroup. As such, accesses may have much shorter latency and much higher bandwidth than global memory. Calling clSetKernelArg() with a size, but no argument, allows local memory to be allocated at runtime, where a kernel parameter is defined as a __local pointer (e.g., __local float* sharedData). Alternatively, arrays can be statically declared in local memory by appending the keyword __local (e.g., __local float[64] sharedData), although this requires specifying the array size at compile time.

Private memory is memory that is unique to an individual work-item. Local variables and nonpointer kernel arguments are private by default. In practice, these variables are usually mapped to registers, although private arrays and any spilled registers are usually mapped to an off-chip (i.e., long-latency) memory.

The memory spaces of OpenCL closely model those of modern GPUs. Figure 2.4 details the relationship between OpenCL memory spaces and those found on an AMD 7970 GPU.

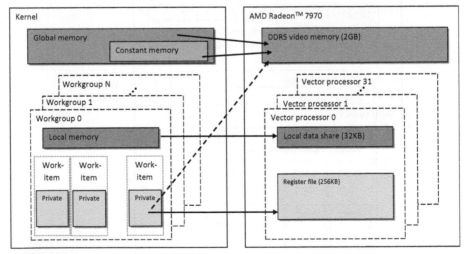

FIGURE 2.4

Mapping from the memory model defined by OpenCL to the architecture of an AMD Radeon 7970 GPU. Simple private memory will be stored in registers; complex addressing or excessive use will be stored in DRAM.

WRITING KERNELS

As previously described, OpenCL C kernels are similar to C functions and can be thought of as instances of a parallel map operation. The function body, like the mapped function, will be executed once for every work-item created. We utilize the code for the OpenCL kernel `cache` to illustrate how this mapping is accomplished.

Kernels begin with the keyword `__kernel` and must have a return type of `void`. The argument list is as for a C function with the additional requirement that the address space of any pointer must be specified. Buffers can be declared in global memory (`__global`) or constant memory (`__constant`). Images are assigned to global memory. Access qualifiers (`__read_only`, `__write_only`, and `__read_write`) can also be optionally specified because they may allow for compiler and hardware optimizations.

The `__local` qualifier is used to declare memory that is shared between all work-items in a workgroup. This concept is often one of the most confusing for new OpenCL programmers. When a local pointer is declared as a kernel parameter, such as `__local float *sharedData`, it is a pointer to an array shared by the entire workgroup. In other words, only one array will be created per workgroup, and all work-items in the workgroup can access it.

An alternative approach for declaring local memory allocations is to declare a variable at a kernel-scope level:

```
__kernel void aKernel(...){
   // Shared by all work-items in the group
   __local float sharedData[32];
   ...
}
```

This appears to have kernel lexical scope, but the same named entity is shared by all work-items in an entire workgroup, just as is the `__local` parameter, and the approaches are equivalent. Although it is important to note that a `__local` parameter can be set to a different size for each dispatch, a `__local` declaration within a kernel is fixed at compilation time.

When programming for OpenCL devices, particularly GPUs, performance may increase by using local memory to cache data that will be used multiple times by a work-item or by multiple work-items in the same workgroup (i.e., data with temporal locality). When developing a kernel, we can achieve this with an explicit assignment from a global memory pointer to a local memory pointer, as shown in the following example code:

```
__kernel void cache(
   __global float* data,
   __local float* sharedData) {
   int globalId = get_global_id(0);
```

```
int localId = get_local_id(0);
// Cache data to local memory
sharedData[localId] = data[globalId];
...
}
```

Once a work-item completes its execution, none of its state information or local memory storage is persistent. Any results that need to be kept must be transferred to global memory.

FULL SOURCE CODE EXAMPLE FOR VECTOR ADDITION

The following example listing is the complete host code for implementing the vector addition example discussed in this chapter.

```
// This program implements a vector addition using OpenCL

// System includes
#include <stdio.h>
#include <stdlib.h>

// OpenCL includes
#include <CL/cl.h>

// OpenCL kernel to perform an element-wise addition
const char* programSource =
"__kernel                                              \n"
"void vecadd(__global int *A,                          \n"
"            __global int *B,                          \n"
"            __global int *C)                          \n"
"{                                                     \n"
"                                                      \n"
"   // Get the work-item's unique ID                   \n"
"   int idx = get_global_id(0);                        \n"
"                                                      \n"
"   // Add the corresponding locations of              \n"
"   // 'A' and 'B', and store the result in 'C'.       \n"
"   C[idx] = A[idx] + B[idx];                          \n"
"}                                                     \n"
;
int main() {
    // This code executes on the OpenCL host

    // Host data
    int *A = NULL; // Input array
    int *B = NULL; // Input array
    int *C = NULL; // Output array

    // Elements in each array
    const int elements = 2048;
```

```
// Compute the size of the data
size_t datasize=sizeof(int)*elements;

// Allocate space for input/output data
A=(int*)malloc(datasize);
B=(int*)malloc(datasize);
C=(int*)malloc(datasize);

// Initialize the input data
int i;
for(i=0; i<elements; i++) {
    A[i]=i;
    B[i]=i;
}

// Use this to check the output of each API call
cl_int status;

// Retrieve the number of platforms
cl_uint numPlatforms=0;
status=clGetPlatformIDs(0, NULL, &numPlatforms);

// Allocate enough space for each platform
cl_platform_id *platforms=NULL;
platforms=(cl_platform_id*)malloc(
    numPlatforms*sizeof(cl_platform_id));

// Fill in the platforms
status=clGetPlatformIDs(numPlatforms, platforms, NULL);

// Retrieve the number of devices
cl_uint numDevices=0;
status=clGetDeviceIDs(platforms[0], CL_DEVICE_TYPE_ALL, 0,
    NULL, &numDevices);

// Allocate enough space for each device
cl_device_id *devices;
devices=(cl_device_id*)malloc(
    numDevices*sizeof(cl_device_id));

// Fill in the devices
status=clGetDeviceIDs(platforms[0], CL_DEVICE_TYPE_ALL,
    numDevices, devices, NULL);

// Create a context and associate it with the devices
cl_context context;
context=clCreateContext(NULL, numDevices, devices, NULL,
    NULL, &status);

// Create a command queue and associate it with the device
cl_command_queue cmdQueue;
cmdQueue=clCreateCommandQueue(context, devices[0], 0,
    &status);
```

```
// Create a buffer object that will contain the data
// from the host array A
cl_mem bufA;
bufA=clCreateBuffer(context, CL_MEM_READ_ONLY, datasize,
    NULL, &status);

// Create a buffer object that will contain the data
// from the host array B
cl_mem bufB;
bufB=clCreateBuffer(context, CL_MEM_READ_ONLY, datasize,
    NULL, &status);

// Create a buffer object that will hold the output data
cl_mem bufC;
bufC=clCreateBuffer(context, CL_MEM_WRITE_ONLY, datasize,
    NULL, &status);

// Write input array A to the device buffer bufferA
status=clEnqueueWriteBuffer(cmdQueue, bufA, CL_FALSE,
    0, datasize, A, 0, NULL, NULL);

// Write input array B to the device buffer bufferB
status=clEnqueueWriteBuffer(cmdQueue, bufB, CL_FALSE,
    0, datasize, B, 0, NULL, NULL);

// Create a program with source code
cl_program program=clCreateProgramWithSource(context, 1,
    (const char**)&programSource, NULL, &status);

// Build (compile) the program for the device
status=clBuildProgram(program, numDevices, devices,
    NULL, NULL, NULL);

// Create the vector addition kernel
cl_kernel kernel;
kernel=clCreateKernel(program, "vecadd", &status);

// Associate the input and output buffers with the kernel
status=clSetKernelArg(kernel, 0, sizeof(cl_mem), &bufA);
status=clSetKernelArg(kernel, 1, sizeof(cl_mem), &bufB);
status=clSetKernelArg(kernel, 2, sizeof(cl_mem), &bufC);

// Define an index space (global work size) of work
// items for execution. A workgroup size (local work size)
// is not required, but can be used.
size_t globalWorkSize[1];

// There are 'elements' work-items
globalWorkSize[0]=elements;

// Execute the kernel for execution
status=clEnqueueNDRangeKernel(cmdQueue, kernel, 1, NULL,
    globalWorkSize, NULL, 0, NULL, NULL);
```

```
    // Read the device output buffer to the host output array
    clEnqueueReadBuffer(cmdQueue, bufC, CL_TRUE, 0,
        datasize, C, 0, NULL, NULL);

    // Verify the output
    int result=1;
    for(i=0; i<elements; i++) {
        if(C[i] !=i+i) {
            result=0;
            break;
        }
    }
    if(result) {
        printf("Output is correct\n");
    } else {
        printf("Output is incorrect\n");
    }

    // Free OpenCL resources
    clReleaseKernel(kernel);
    clReleaseProgram(program);
    clReleaseCommandQueue(cmdQueue);
    clReleaseMemObject(bufA);
    clReleaseMemObject(bufB);
    clReleaseMemObject(bufC);
    clReleaseContext(context);

    // Free host resources
    free(A);
    free(B);
    free(C);
    free(platforms);
    free(devices);

    return 0;
}
```

VECTOR ADDITION WITH C++ WRAPPER

The Khronos Group has defined a C++ wrapper API to go along with the OpenCL standard. The C++ API corresponds closely to the C API (e.g. cl::Memory maps to cl_mem), but offers the benefits of the higher-level language such as classes and exception handling. The following source code listing provides a vector addition example that corresponds to the prior C version.

```
#define __NO_STD_VECTOR // Use cl::vector instead of STL version
#define __CL_ENABLE_EXCEPTIONS
```

```cpp
#include<CL/cl.hpp>

#include<iostream>
#include<fstream>
#include<string>

int main() {
   const int N_ELEMENTS=1024;
   int *A=new int[N_ELEMENTS];
   int *B=new int[N_ELEMENTS];
   int *C=new int[N_ELEMENTS];

   for(int i=0; i<N_ELEMENTS; i++) {
     A[i]=i;
     B[i]=i;
   }
try {
   // Query for platforms
   cl::vector<cl::Platform>platforms;
   cl::Platform::get(&platforms);

   // Get a list of devices on this platform
   cl::vector<cl::Device>devices;
   platforms[0].getDevices(CL_DEVICE_TYPE_GPU, &devices);

   // Create a context for the devices
   cl::Context context(devices);

   // Create a command queue for the first device
   cl::CommandQueue queue =
     cl::CommandQueue(context, devices[0]);

   // Create the memory buffers
   cl::Buffer bufferA=cl::Buffer(context,
     CL_MEM_READ_ONLY, N_ELEMENTS * sizeof(int));
   cl::Buffer bufferB=cl::Buffer(context,
     CL_MEM_READ_ONLY, N_ELEMENTS * sizeof(int));
   cl::Buffer bufferC=cl::Buffer(context,
     CL_MEM_WRITE_ONLY, N_ELEMENTS * sizeof(int));

   // Copy the input data to the input buffers using the
   // command queue for the first device
   queue.enqueueWriteBuffer(bufferA, CL_TRUE, 0,
     N_ELEMENTS * sizeof(int), A);
   queue.enqueueWriteBuffer(bufferB, CL_TRUE, 0,
     N_ELEMENTS * sizeof(int), B);

   // Read the program source
   std::ifstream sourceFile("vector_add_kernel.cl");
   std::string sourceCode(
      std::istreambuf_iterator<char>(sourceFile),
```

```cpp
    (std::istreambuf_iterator<char>()));
  cl::Program::Sources source(1,
    std::make_pair(sourceCode.c_str(),
    sourceCode.length()+1));

  // Make program from the source code
  cl::Program program=cl::Program(context, source);

  // Build the program for the devices
  program.build(devices);

  // Make kernel
  cl::Kernel vecadd_kernel(program, "vecadd");

  // Set the kernel arguments
  vecadd_kernel.setArg(0, bufferA);
  vecadd_kernel.setArg(1, bufferB);
  vecadd_kernel.setArg(2, bufferC);

  // Execute the kernel
  cl::NDRange global(N_ELEMENTS);
  cl::NDRange local(256);
  queue.enqueueNDRangeKernel(vecadd_kernel,
    cl::NullRange, global, local);

  // Copy the output data back to the host
  queue.enqueueReadBuffer(bufferC, CL_TRUE, 0,
    N_ELEMENTS * sizeof(int), C);

  // Verify the result
  bool result=true;
  for (int i=0; i<N_ELEMENTS; i++) {
    if (C[i]!=A[i]+B[i]) {
      result=false;
      break;
    }
  }
  if (result)
    std::cout<< "Success!"<< std::endl;
  else
    std::cout<< "Failed!"<< std::endl;
  }
catch(cl::Error error)
{
  std::cout<< error.what()<< "("<<
      error.err()<< ")"<< std::endl;
}
  return 0;
}
```

SUMMARY

In this chapter, we provided an introduction to the basics of using the OpenCL standard when developing parallel programs. We described the four different abstraction models defined in the standard and presented examples of OpenCL implementations to place some of the abstraction in context.

In Chapter 3, we discuss OpenCL device architectures, including a range of instruction set styles, threading issues, and memory topics.

Reference

Cooper, K., & Torczon, L. (2011). *Engineering a Compiler*. Burlington, MA: Morgan Kaufmann.

OpenCL Device Architectures

INTRODUCTION

OpenCL has been developed by a wide range of industry groups to satisfy the need to standardize on programming models that can achieve good or high performance across the range of devices available on the market. Each of these companies has specific goals in mind for OpenCL and targets for what features OpenCL should have to be able to run correctly on a specific architecture. To this end, OpenCL has a range of features that attempt to allow detection of unique hardware capabilities. For example, OpenCL has a relaxed consistency block-based parallelism model intended to run relatively efficiently on serial, symmetric multiprocessing (SMP), multithreaded, and single instruction multiple data (SIMD) or vector devices. In this chapter, we discuss some of these devices and the overall design space in which they sit.

Although OpenCL is designed to be a platform-independent application programming interface (API), at the algorithm level and consequently at the level of kernel implementation, true platform independence in terms of performance is still a goal (versus a reality). As developers, we need to understand the potential advantages of different hardware features, the key runtime characteristics of these devices, and where these devices fit into the different classes of computer architectures. Once the reader is equipped with this deeper understanding of the targeted hardware, he or she can make informed choices when designing parallel algorithms and software. The reader should also better appreciate the philosophy behind OpenCL's design in terms of programming, memory, and runtime models.

HARDWARE TRADE-OFFS

Given the history of OpenCL and its early use for graphics APIs and pixel shaders, it is easy to understand how OpenCL has developed as a leading language targeted for GPU programming. As a result, OpenCL has become a popular programming API for the high-performance computing market. However, as the number of platforms supporting OpenCL grows (particularly in the embedded systems space), the overall impact of OpenCL should increase substantially.

What is not necessarily clear from this discussion is what a GPU really is and how it differs from these "other devices." When we develop general-purpose code for a GPU is the device still a graphics processor, or some more generic entity. If it is a graphics processor is that due to the device carrying some amount of graphics-specific logic, or is it the architectural style overall?

More questions arise when we try to think about this question in any detail. How many cores does a GPU have? To answer that question, we have to decide on a definition of "core." What is a "many-core" device, and is it significantly different from a "multi-core" device? In general, different architectures choose different approaches to increase performance for a given power/transistor budget. Rather than simply being a raw compute power/electrical power/area trade-off, hardware developers have always also had to consider programming effort. The trade-off between these factors has created a wide divergence in designs.

Multi-core CPUs allow us to maintain clock frequencies and complexity that are comparable to single core CPUs, while adding more cores as transistor sizes reduce. With careful design, power consumption can be kept within reasonable limits. SIMD and very long instruction word (VLIW) architectures attempt to further increase the amount of useful work being performed by improving the ratio of arithmetic operations to control logic. In such cases, it can be difficult to generate workloads to keep the arithmetic logic units (ALUs) satisfied. Multithreading approaches this from a different angle. Rather than increasing the ratio of useful to computation to control logic, it increases the amount of useful work available to occupy computation logic during periods in which indirectly useful work is occupying noncompute logic such as memory pipelines. Thereby multithreading increases the utilization of the device we already have. Threading can be seen from the software side, in which case it can apply to multi-core chips as much as to single core designs, but it can also be viewed in terms of single cores managing multiple software threads. Caches and memory system trade-offs allow different architectures to target different data access patterns while trading off transistors for different uses.

In all these cases, we can apply the trade-offs to an individual core or a set of cores, depending on our definition of core. However, we do not need to apply the same trade-off across an entire device. Heterogeneity can enable hardware optimizations for multiple types of algorithms running simultaneously, offering better performance on both and hence overall. The traditional, and at the present time common, example of this at the system level is the GPU + CPU combination we see in modern PCs (along with other lower performance processors scattered throughout the system). The latest generations of high-performance processors combine these two aspects into a single device, something that AMD calls the accelerated processing unit (APU).

In reality, we see combinations of these factors in different designs with different target markets, application, and price points. In this section, we examine some of these architectural features and discuss to what degree different common architectures apply them.

Performance Increase by Frequency, and Its Limitations

The easiest way, as a developer, to think about code we are writing is to create software that executes linearly: Perform one task, complete that task, perform another task. It is considerably more difficult for a developer to write parallel code, this is true even for limited SIMD or vector parallelism as is common in graphics. Multi-component pixels make this relatively simple as the logical entity maps well to the programming concept. In other applications, where the logical concepts do not map as effectively to programming vectors, extracting SIMD operations can be substantially more difficult. For this reason, architectures have historically aimed to increase the performance of a single, narrow, thread of execution before moving to parallelism, with extreme, multi-threaded parallelism relegated to high-performance specialist machines in particular markets.

Shrinking of CMOS circuitry has allowed distances between transistors to scale fairly consistently for an extended period of time. The shrinking of distances and reduction in size of the capacitors allowed hardware architects to clock circuits at a higher rate. In turn, this led to Gordon Moore's famous self-fulfilling prophecy about transistor density and its misinterpretations into the realm of execution frequency and overall performance. Certainly, increasing frequency allowed the performance of nonparallel code to increase consistently during that time, such that it became an expectation for software developers until the early 21st century.

During the past decade, it has become obvious that continued scaling of clock frequencies of CPUs is not practical, largely due to power and heat dissipation constraints. The reason for this is that power consumption is dependent on frequency in a nonlinear manner. CMOS dynamic power consumption is approximated by the combination of dynamic and static power:

$$P = ACV^2F + VI_{leak}$$

where

A is the activity factor, or fraction of the number of transistors in the circuit that are switching;

C is the capacitance of the circuit;

V is the voltage applied across the circuit;

F is the switching frequency; and

I_{leak} is an estimate of the current due to leakage of transistors.

It appears from this equation that power is linear with frequency. In reality, to increase the frequency, one has to increase the rate of flow of charge into and out of the capacitors in the circuit. This requires a comparable increase in voltage, which both scales the dynamic term and also increases the latter, static, term in the equation. For a long time, voltages could reduce with each process generation such that frequency scaling would not increase the power consumption uncontrollably. However, as process technology has reached the small sizes we see today, we can no longer scale the voltage down without increasing the error rate of transistor switching and hence frequency scaling requires voltage increases. The increase in power consumption and heat dissipation from any increase in frequency is then substantial.

As a second problem, increasing clock frequency on-chip requires either increasing off-chip memory bandwidth to provide data fast enough to not stall the linear workload running through the processor or increasing the amount of caching in the system.

If we are unable to continue increasing the frequency with the goal of obtaining higher performance, we require other solutions. The heart of any of these solutions is to increase the number of operations performed on a given clock cycle.

Superscalar Execution

Superscalar and, by extension, out-of-order execution is one solution that has been included on CPUs for a long time; it has been included on x86 designs since the beginning of the Pentium era. In these designs, the CPU maintains dependence information between instructions in the instruction stream and schedules work onto unused functional units when possible. An example of this is shown in Figure 3.1.

The major beneficiary of out-of-order logic is the software developer. By extracting parallelism from the programmer's code automatically within the hardware, serial code performs faster without any extra developer effort. Indeed, superscalar designs predate frequency scaling limitations by a decade or more, even in popular mass-produced devices, as a way to increase overall performance superlinearly. However, it is not without its disadvantages.

Out-of-order scheduling logic requires a substantial investment in transistors and hence CPU die area to maintain queues of in-flight instructions and maintain information on inter-instruction dependencies to deal with dynamic schedules throughout the device. In addition, speculative instruction execution quickly becomes necessary to expand the window of out-of-order instructions to execute in parallel. Such speculative execution results in throwaway work and hence wasted energy. As a result, out-of-order execution in a CPU has shown diminishing returns; the industry has taken other approaches to increasing performance as transistor size has decreased, even on the high-performance devices in which superscalar logic was formerly feasible. On embedded and special-purpose devices, extraction of parallelism from serial code has never been as much of a goal, and such designs have historically been less common in these areas.

Good examples of superscalar processors are numerous, from Seymour Cray's CDC 6600 to numerous RISC designs in the 1990s. Currently, high-end CPUs are mostly superscalar. Many GPUs also show superscalar capabilities.

VLIW

VLIW is a heavily compiler-dependent method for increasing instruction-level parallelism in a processor. Rather than depending entirely on complex out-of-order control logic that maintains dependences in hardware, as we saw when discussing superscalar execution, VLIW moves this dependence analysis work into the compiler. Instead of providing a scalar instruction stream, each issued instruction in a

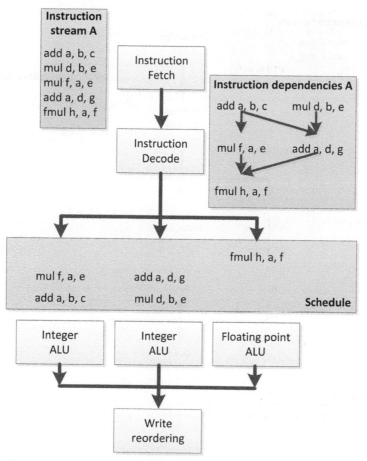

FIGURE 3.1

Out-of-order execution of an instruction stream of simple assembly-like instructions. Note that in this syntax, the destination register is listed first. Add a, b, c is a = b + c.

VLIW processor is a long instruction word comprising multiple instructions intended to be issued in parallel. This instruction will be mapped directly to the execution pipelines of the processor.

An example of VLIW execution is shown in Figure 3.2. This is the same set of instructions as we saw in Figure 3.1, but rather than being fetched serially, they are fetched in three horizontally arranged packets of up to three instructions. We now see that the dependence structure of this instruction stream is linear, and the hardware will treat it that way rather than extracting and tracking a more complicated dependence graph. The VLIW instruction packets are decoded, and each individual part of the instruction stream maps to a given computation unit in the processor for execution. In some VLIW designs, as in this example, the computation units are

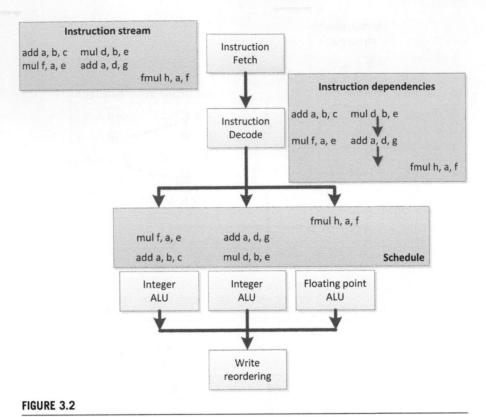

FIGURE 3.2

VLIW execution based on the out-of-order diagram in Figure 3.1.

heterogeneous and hence some instructions will only ever be scheduled into a given lane of the VLIW packet stream. Other architectures present more homogeneous hardware such that any instruction can be issued in any location and only dependence information limits the possibilities.

In the example in Figure 3.2, we see that the instruction schedule has gaps: The first two VLIW packets are missing a third entry, and the third is missing its first and second entries. Obviously, the example is very simple, with few instructions to pack, but it is a common problem with VLIW architectures that efficiency can be lost due to the compiler's inability to fully fill packets. This can be due to limitations in the compiler or simply due to an inherent lack of parallelism in the instruction stream. In the latter case, the situation will be no worse than for out-of-order execution but more efficient as the scheduling hardware is reduced in complexity. The former case would end up as a trade-off between efficiency losses from unfilled execution slots and gains from reduced hardware control overhead. In addition, there is an extra cost in compiler development to take into account when performing a cost/benefit analysis for VLIW execution over hardware schedule superscalar execution.

VLIW designs commonly appear in DSP chips. High-end consumer devices currently include the Intel Itanium line of CPUs (known as Explicitly Parallel Instruction Computing) and AMD's R600 GPUs.

SIMD and Vector Processing

SIMD and its generalization in vector parallelism aim for improved efficiency from a slightly different angle compared with the other previously discussed concepts. Whereas VLIW and hardware-managed superscalar both address extracting independent instruction parallelism from unrelated instructions in an instruction stream, SIMD and vector parallelism directly allow the hardware instructions to target data parallel execution.

A single SIMD instruction encapsulates a request that the same operation be performed on multiple data elements in parallel. Contrast this with the scalar operation performed by each instruction in the other approaches to parallelism. Vector computation generalizes this approach and usually works over long sequences of data elements, often pipelining computations over the data rather than executing on all elements simultaneously, and more generally supports gathered read and scattered write operations to and from memory.

If we again look at a variation on the running example as seen in Figure 3.3, we can see that the instruction stream is now issued linearly rather than out of order.

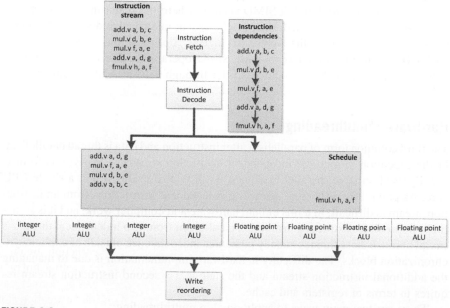

FIGURE 3.3

SIMD execution where a single instruction is scheduled in order but executes over multiple ALUs at the same time.

However, each of these instructions now executes over a vector of four ALUs at the same time. The integer instructions issue one by one through the four-way integer vector ALU on the left, and the floating point instructions issue similarly through the four-way floating point ALU on the right. Note that although in this example we are issuing the instructions linearly, there is no reason to assume that we cannot perform these operations within a superscalar or VLIW pipeline, and we will see architectures that do just that in later discussion.

The advantage of SIMD execution is that relative to ALU work, the amount of scheduling and instruction decode logic can both be decreased. We are now performing four operations with a single instruction and a single point in the dependence schedule.

Of course, as with the previous proposals, there are trade-offs. A significant amount of code is not data parallel, and hence it is not possible to find vector instructions to issue. In other cases, it is simply too difficult for the compiler to extract data parallelism from code. For example, vectorization of loops is an ongoing challenge, with little success in anything but the simplest cases. In these cases, we end up with unutilized ALUs and thus transistor wastage.

Vector processors originate in the supercomputer market, but SIMD designs are common in many market segments. CPUs often include SIMD pipelines with explicit SIMD instructions in a scalar instruction stream, including the various forms of Streaming SIMD Extension (SSE) and AVX on x86 chips, the AltiVec extensions for PowerPC, and ARM's NEON extensions. GPU architectures historically included explicit SIMD operations to support pixel vectors, and many modern GPUs also execute over wide implicit SIMD vectors, where the scalar instruction stream describes a single lane. Indeed, such machines can be considered vector machines because in many cases the vector is logical. For example, AMD's Radeon HD7970 architecture executes 64-wide SIMD operations. These wide vector instructions are pipelined over multiple cycles through a 16-lane SIMD unit.

Hardware Multithreading

The third common form of parallelism after instruction and data is thread parallelism, or the execution of multiple independent instruction streams. Clearly, this form is heavily used on large, parallel machines, but it is also useful within a single CPU core. As previously discussed, extracting independent instructions from an instruction stream is difficult, in terms of both hardware and compiler work, and it is sometimes impossible. Extracting instruction parallelism from two independent threads is trivial because those threads already guarantee independence outside of explicit synchronization blocks. The difficulty in hardware implementation is due to managing the additional instruction stream and the state that a second instruction stream requires in terms of registers and cache.

There are two main ways to apply on-chip multithreading:

Simultaneous multithreading
Temporal multithreading

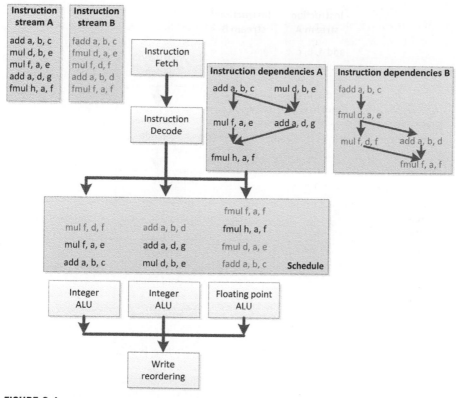

FIGURE 3.4

The out-of-order schedule seen in Figure 3.1 combined with a second thread and executed simultaneously.

Simultaneous multithreading (SMT) is visualized in Figure 3.4. In this approach, instructions from multiple threads are interleaved on the execution resources by an extension to the superscalar scheduling logic that tracks both instruction dependencies and source threads. The goal is for the execution resources to be more effectively utilized, and in the figure that is the case. A higher proportion of execution slots are occupied with useful work. The cost of this approach is that state storage must be increased and the instruction dependence and scheduling logic becomes more complicated as it manages two distinct sets of dependencies, resources, and execution queues.

Figure 3.5 shows the simpler time-sliced version of chip multithreading. In this case, each thread is executed in consecutive execution slots in round-robin fashion. For the purposes of simplification, the diagram shows a single shared ALU.

The following are advantages of this approach:

- The logic to handle the scheduling is simple.
- Pipeline latency can be covered by scheduling more threads, reducing the amount of forwarding logic.

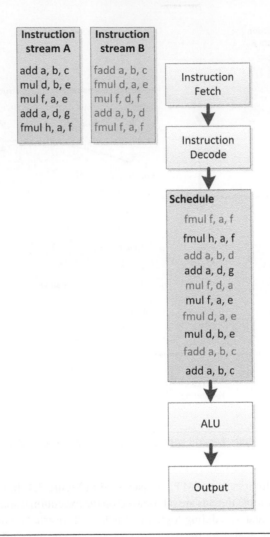

FIGURE 3.5

Two threads scheduled in time slice fashion.

- Stalls of a single thread due to a cache miss, waiting for a branch to be computed, or similar events can be covered by changing the order of thread execution and running more threads than necessary to cover pipeline latency.

This last case is the most useful in scaling to complicated problems. Many architectures are able to run more threads than necessary. When a thread reaches some sort of stall, it can be removed from the ready queue such that only threads in the ready queue are scheduled for execution. Once the stall ends, the thread can be placed back in the ready queue. In this manner, although a single thread might execute more slowly than on an out-of-order machine, the total throughput of the machine is kept

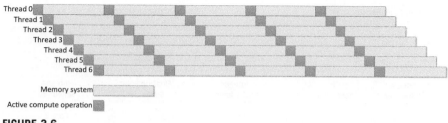

FIGURE 3.6

Taking temporal multithreading to an extreme as throughput computing: A large number of threads interleave execution to keep the device busy, whereas each individual thread takes longer to execute than the theoretical minimum.

high and utilization of compute resources can be maintained without overcomplicating the control logic. Taken to an extreme, this sort of heavy multithreading can be viewed as throughput computing: maximizing throughput at the possible expense of latency. The principle is shown in Figure 3.6.

Both forms of chip multithreading are common. The MTA design from Tera is a classic time-sliced multithreading supercomputer. The MTA design suffered from manufacturing difficulties; however, Cray's subsequent implementation, the MTA-2 design, utilized 128 register sets per CPU using fast thread switching between threads within this state and skipping stalled threads. The XMT design extends this further to fit multithreaded processors in standard AMD Opteron-based Cray systems. Sun's Niagara series of chips implements a multi-core multithreaded design (8 per core) to achieve low power and high throughput on data-center workloads. Intel's Pentium 4 and then later Nehalem and successor designs implement a form of SMT known as "hyperthreading." Modern GPU designs runs numerous threads in a temporal fashion on each core, where the number is generally resource limited: On the current generation of AMD GPUs, this is usually 8–10 threads per core to cover latency and stalls.

Multi-Core Architectures

Conceptually at least, the obvious approach to increasing the amount of work performed per clock cycle is to simply clone a single CPU core multiple times on the chip. In the simplest case, each of these cores executes largely independently, sharing data through the memory system, usually through a cache coherency protocol. This design is a scaled down version of traditional multisocket server SMP systems that have been used to increase performance for decades, in some cases to extreme degrees.

However, multi-core systems come in different guises, and it can be very difficult to define a core. For example, a mainstream CPU, at the high end, generally includes a wide range of functional blocks such that it is independent of other cores on the chip, barring interfacing logic, memory controllers, and so on, that would be unlikely to count as cores. However the line can be blurred. For example, AMD's "Bulldozer" (high-power core) design shown alongside the simpler "Bobcat" (low-power core)

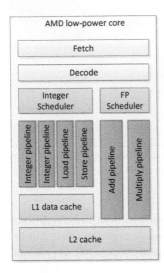 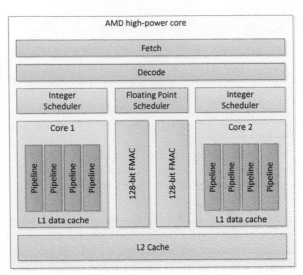

FIGURE 3.7

The AMD Bobcat and Bulldozer high-level designs (not shown to any shared scale). Bobcat (left) follows a traditional approach mapping functional units to cores, in a low-power design. Bulldozer (right) combines two cores within a module, offering sharing of some functional units. The two shades in the Bulldozer diagram show the difference between functional blocks that are shared between cores and those that are not.

design in Figure 3.7 shares functional units between pairs of cores in a replicable unit termed a module. A single thread will run on each core in a traditional fashion while the hardware interleaves floating point instructions onto the shared floating point pipelines. The aim of such a design is to raise efficiency by improving occupancy of functional units.

In a similar manner, GPU designs show a different definition of core. Modern GPUs have tens of cores—at the current high end there are between 16 and 32, with levels of complexity that depend on the specific architecture. Many GPU designs, such as the Graphics Core Next-based (AMD, 2012) designs from AMD and the Fermi and Kepler derivatives from NVIDIA follow a relatively CPU-like design. However, some designs diverge substantially, for example if we look at the AMD Radeon HD 6970 high-level diagram shown in Figure 3.8, we see a similar approach to Bulldozer taken to an extreme. Although the device has 24 SIMD cores, by looking at the execution units in the fairest way to compare with traditional CPUs, those SIMD cores only execute ALU operations—both floating point and integer. Instruction scheduling, decode, and dispatch are executed by the wave scheduler units. The wave schedulers are so named because the unit of scheduling is a wide SIMD thread context known as a wavefront. Indeed, on the 6970, there are two of these to prevent overly high complexity, whereas lower capability parts in the series use only one and scale the number of SIMD cores.

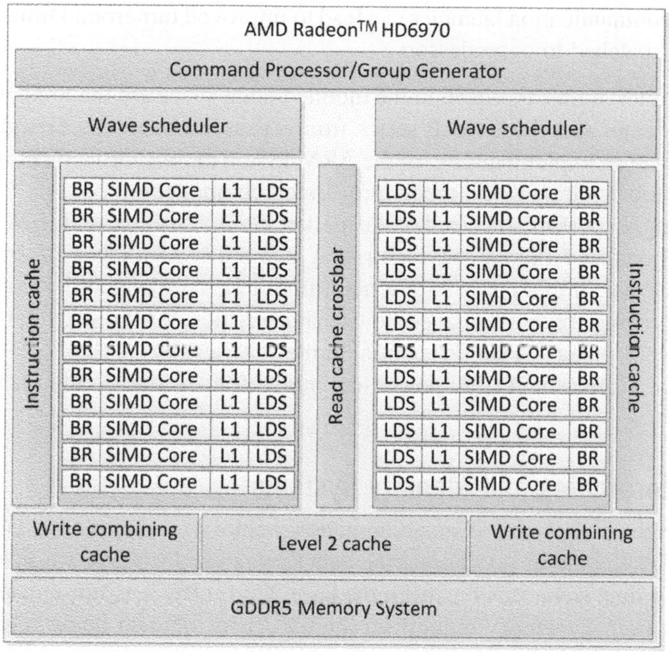

FIGURE 3.8

The AMD Radeon™ HD6970 GPU architecture. The device is divided into two halves where instruction control: scheduling and dispatch is performed by the level wave scheduler for each half. The 24 16-lane SIMD cores execute four-way VLIW instructions on each SIMD lane and contain private level 1 caches and local data shares (LDS).

Integration: Systems-on-Chip and the APU

In the embedded space, a more heterogeneous approach to multi-core design is common. To achieve low power, embedded developers have constructed complicated systems-on-chip (SoCs) combining varied components into a compact and cost-effective design. Combining specialized components in this way allows devices to be optimized for a particular use case and power envelope, which is particularly important in markets such as the design of mobile phones.

Benefits from SoCs are the following:

- Combining multiple elements into a single device allows for a single manufacturing process and a single product to deal with, allowing for lower manufacturing costs.
- The smaller number of packages takes up less space in a final device, allowing for lower device cost and smaller form factor, which are vital in markets such as mobile telephony.
- Smaller distances mean less power used during communication and easier sharing of data through a single memory system.

- Lower communication latencies can lead to improved turnaround times for workloads dispatched to coprocessors.

Good examples of this approach in the mobile phone space are the Snapdragon SoC from Qualcomm and the OMAP series from Texas Instruments. Designs such as these combine an implementation of the ARM ISA, a mobile GPU, memory controllers, and various wireless and media processing components.

At the higher performance end of the market, Sony, Toshiba, and IBM developed the Cell Broadband engine processor that combines a number of small, high-performance but simple cores with a main traditional full-capability core with the aim of improving the performance/Watt characteristics. AMD and Intel have both developed combined CPU/GPU SoCs termed APUs by AMD, enabling high-performance graphics and CPU power in a more efficient single chip package.

Cache Hierarchies and Memory Systems

Whereas in the early years of supercomputers memory bandwidth and latency were such that CPUs could always access the data they needed when it was needed, it has been a long time since this has been the case. Currently, it is not unusual that the latency between a memory request on the CPU and the data being returned from memory is hundreds or even thousands of CPU cycles. On a single threaded CPU, out-of-order logic would be impossibly complicated to cover that much latency.

Fortunately, most applications do not make entirely independent memory accesses. In general, memory access patterns express some degree of locality, which will be either of the following:

- Spatial: Two or more memory accesses read or write addresses that are near each other, by some measure, in memory.
- Temporal: Two or more memory accesses read or write the same address (i.e., the same read is performed at different times).

These two forms of locality lead to the conclusion that if we can store a value read from memory and its neighbors, later reads will be able to reuse that data. As a result, CPU designers have added complicated layers of intermediate memory caches to support this optimization.

Caches come in varied designs, but they can be divided into two general categories that are applied dependent on the workload. CPU caches tend to be designed to minimize latency. To achieve this, caches are large with complicated hierarchies to move as much of the data as close to the CPU core as possible. Out-of-order logic can only cover a limited amount of latency, so the fewer cycles to access data, the better. In addition, keeping data close to the execution units minimizes power consumption: Long-distance data movement is a significant component of CPU power usage.

Throughput processors are more latency tolerant, using threading to cover the cycles between request and data return. In these designs, the goal of caching is less to minimize latency, so the large multilevel hierarchy is less common, and more to reduce traffic across the limited memory buses. Smaller caches that allow neighboring accesses to be caught but are concerned less with very long periods of reuse are often seen in these situations, acting more as spatial filters. Wide SIMD units and programming models aim for efficient coalesced memory access to increase the size of memory transactions issues. The result is that dedicating logic to arithmetic units becomes a better use of transistors. In addition, higher latency, higher bandwidth memory interconnects allow this design to work more efficiently, although system-level issues such as pin availability and necessity to allow swapping of memory chips are equally important in this decision. One extension of this bias toward spatial locality that we often see in GPU design is to lay memory out such that two-dimensional accesses are efficiently cached.

Some designs including GPUs and the cell processor include software-managed scratchpad memory spaces as well as or in place of cache hierarchies. These buffers enable higher performance at a given power and area budget, but they require more complicated programming.

The reality of any given design is that it balances caching levels and features based on the expected workloads for the processor. Unfortunately, there is no right answer for all processor design/workload combinations.

THE ARCHITECTURAL DESIGN SPACE

In the real world, we do not see many architectures that fit cleanly into just one of the previously mentioned categories. The reality is that computer architecture is a huge design space with enormous variation in all directions. Common current architectures sit in that design space at various points.

This is most important in helping us realize that some of the publicly held viewpoints of today's architectures can be overly simplistic. For example, in the domain of GPUs, we often encounter statements such as the following:

- CPUs are serial, GPUs are parallel.
- CPUs have a small number of cores, GPUs have hundreds.
- GPUs run thousands of threads, CPUs run one (or two).

The reality of any design is far more complicated than that, with wide variation in internal buffers, number of pipelines, type of pipelines, and so on. The theme of this chapter is to show that the difference between GPUs and CPUs, or indeed most modern architectures, is not fundamental. The majority of the visible architectural differences we commonly see today are simply points on a sliding scale, a set of parameterization knobs applied to basic designs. These are the differences the average programmer needs to understand: Only the expert need be concerned with ratios between buffer sizes and arranging instructions for hardware co-issue.

In this section, we discuss several real architectures and where they fit in the design space trading off some of the features we discussed previously. It is hoped that this will help to give a more nuanced feel for architectural trade-offs and help develop views on what algorithms may or may not work well on real architectures. Figure 3.9 gives a graphical hint toward some of the architectural trade-offs while ignoring caching to keep the diagram somewhat simple. In the design, we limit ourselves to extreme simplifications. The goal is to show that the wide SIMD and state storage design of GPUs is a long way along a spectrum from simple CPUs in terms of use of area, and that maximum performance and ease of achieving good performance depend on these design choices.

CPU Designs

The devices that most people are used to developing on can be loosely described as "CPUs." Even within this space, there is considerable variation in how different forms of parallelism are utilized.

Low-Power CPUs

At the very lowest end of the power spectrum, CPU cores are very simple, in-order cores. At this level, power consumption is the most important factor in design, with performance a secondary consideration. Such designs often do not support floating point operations and have no need for parallelism.

Currently, the most widespread low-power CPU ISA is the ARM ISA developed in IP form by ARM Holdings. The ARM architecture originated in the Acorn RISC machine concept from Acorn Computers as a desktop architecture, but recently the simplicity of the architecture has made it dominant in the mobile and embedded markets, with a foray into Acorn's own desktop projects from 1996 to 1998 as the DEC-manufactured StrongARM. ARM designs come in a wide variety of forms because the ISA IP is licensed to manufacturers who are at liberty to design their own cores. Usually, ARM cores are combined within SoCs with other units such as cellular modems, embedded graphics processors, video accelerators, and similar devices.

Most variants on the ARM ISA have been in-order cores with three to seven pipeline stages. The Cortex-A8, -A9, and -A15 cores, based on the ARMv7 ISA, are superscalar and multi-core with up to four symmetric cores. The ARMv7-based cores may also support the Neon SIMD instructions, giving 64- and 128-bit SIMD operations in each core.

The AMD Bobcat CPU core that was shown in Figure 3.7 is the low-power core in AMD's current CPU lineup designed for a power range of 1–10 W. To achieve the low-power figures, Bobcat cores are clocked more slowly than the high-end parts as well as being carefully designed to reduce overhead—at the cost of lower peak performance. Bobcat is a 64-bit design, supports two-way out-of-order issue, and also has a 64-bit SIMD unit that can multicycle SSE operations.

Intel's Atom design takes a slightly different approach to performance compared with AMD's Bobcat. Atom does not support out-of-order execution, and as a result, single threaded performance suffers. However, Atom does support a form

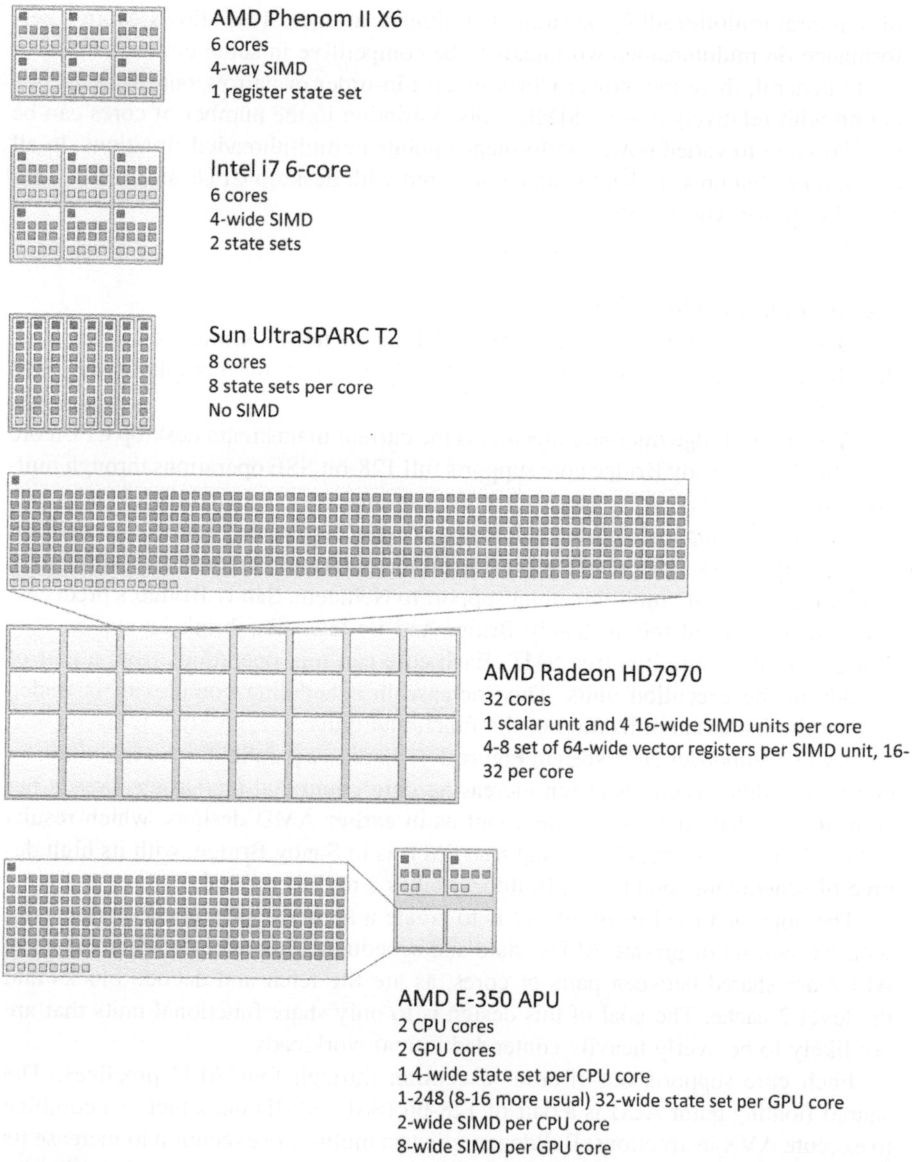

AMD Phenom II X6
6 cores
4-way SIMD
1 register state set

Intel i7 6-core
6 cores
4-wide SIMD
2 state sets

Sun UltraSPARC T2
8 cores
8 state sets per core
No SIMD

AMD Radeon HD7970
32 cores
1 scalar unit and 4 16-wide SIMD units per core
4-8 set of 64-wide vector registers per SIMD unit, 16-32 per core

AMD E-350 APU
2 CPU cores
2 GPU cores
1 4-wide state set per CPU core
1-248 (8-16 more usual) 32-wide state set per GPU core
2-wide SIMD per CPU core
8-wide SIMD per GPU core

FIGURE 3.9

A selection of the architectures discussed in this section giving a graphical hint toward their trade-offs in use of silicon area. Note, in particular, the preference for state storage in the GPU designs compared with the CPU designs. Note that the definition of "ALU" in this diagram is somewhat flexible. We are counting both integer ALUs and floating point ALUs but not necessarily counting separate multiplication and addition ALUs as distinct even when they can dual issue. The important factor is the rough ratio to state, not the precise numbers for a given device.

of temporal multithreading executing two threads at once. This allows Atom's performance on multithreaded workloads to be competitive in some circumstances.

In general, these low-power CPUs support in-order or narrow out-of-order execution with relatively narrow SIMD units. Variation in the number of cores can be used to scale to varied power/performance points in multithreaded situations. In all cases, these features are kept simple compared with desktop CPUs as a method for reducing power consumption.

Mainstream Desktop CPUs

Mainstream desktop CPUs from AMD and Intel do not look much different from the Bobcat design. In each case, they slightly increase the complexity of each element.

The Sandy Bridge microarchitecture is the current mainstream desktop CPU core from Intel. The Sandy Bridge core supports full 128-bit SSE operations through multiple pipelines and issues up to six operations of mixed types in parallel. In addition, Sandy Bridge supports 256-bit Advanced Vector Extensions (AVX) operations, allowing up to 16 single precision floating point operations per cycle. As with Atom, Intel added hardware multithreading support to Nehalem, Sandy Bridge's predecessor, and maintained this in Sandy Bridge and its later die shrink known as "Ivy Bridge". In this case, it is true SMT: Each core can mix operations from a pair of threads in the execution units. This increase in scheduling complexity is traded against the increased utilization of the functional units.

AMD's Bulldozer core, seen in Figure 3.7, increases parallel thread execution by taking a middle ground between increasing core count and increasing threads per core. Rather than increasing core count as in earlier AMD designs, which results in large per-core overhead, or using true SMT as in Sandy Bridge, with its high degree of scheduling complexity, Bulldozer takes a middle ground.

The approach used in Bulldozer is to create a second independent integer core with its own set of private ALUs, state and scheduler. However, the floating point ALUs are shared between pairs of cores, as are the fetch and decode blocks and the level 2 cache. The goal of this design is to only share functional units that are not likely to be overly heavily contended in real workloads.

Each core supports out-of-order execution through four ALU pipelines. The shared floating point ALU is a pair of 128-bit (SSE) SIMD units that can combine to execute AVX instructions. Bulldozer relies on multi-core execution to increase its thread count. However, each core is a relatively small area, so a higher core density should be possible compared with earlier designs that reproduced all floating point and scheduling resources on a per-core basis.

With mainstream CPUs, then, we see wide multi-issue out-of-order hardware, high clock speeds, and large caches—all features intended to maintain high single threaded performance with reasonably high power draw. In-core multithreading is kept minimal or nonexistent, and SIMD units are set at a width that does not waste too much area when not in use.

Intel Itanium 2

Intel's Itanium architecture and its more successful successor, the Itanium 2, represent an interesting attempt to make a mainstream server processor based on VLIW techniques. The Itanium architecture includes a large number of registers (128 integers and 128 floating points). It uses a VLIW approach known as EPIC, in which instructions are stored in 128-bit three-instruction bundles. The CPU fetches two bundles per cycle from L1 cache and hence executes six instructions per clock cycle. There are two 64-bit SIMD units on each core, and the processor is designed to be efficiently combined into multi-core and multi-socket servers.

The goal of EPIC is to move the problem of exploiting parallelism from runtime to compile time. It does this by feeding back information from execution traces into the compiler. It is the task of the compiler to package instructions into the VLIW/EPIC packets, and as a result, performance on the architecture is highly dependent on compiler capability. To assist with this numerous masking, dependence flags between bundles, pre-fetch instructions, speculative loads, and rotating register files are built into the architecture. To improve the throughput of the processor, Itanium 2 implementations support two-way temporal multithreading, switching threads on certain events such as memory accesses that are likely to have long latency.

Niagara

The Niagara design (Figure 3.10), originally from Sun and under continuing development at Oracle, takes a throughput computing multithreaded approach to server workloads. Workloads on many servers, particularly transactional and web workloads, are often heavily multithreaded, with a large number of lightweight integer threads using the memory system. The Niagara, or UltraSPARC Tx and later SPARC Tx CPUs are designed to efficiently execute a large number of threads to maximize overall work throughput with minimal power consumption. Each of the cores is designed to be simple and efficient, with no complex out-of-order execution logic. Each core is designed to interleave operations from eight threads through two execution units. Figure 3.9 shows how much state is present compared with decode logic or ALUs, showing a clear preference for latency hiding and simplicity of logic compared with the mainstream x86 designs.

To support these threads, the design requires multiple sets of registers but as a trade-off requires less speculative register storage than a superscalar design. In addition, coprocessors allow acceleration of cryptographic operations, and an on-chip Ethernet controller improves network throughput. The UltraSPARC T2 (Grohoski, 2006) has 8 cores with eight threads each. The SPARC T3 expands this to 16 cores, with eight threads each.

The latest generation, the SPARC T4, backs off slightly from the earlier multithreading design. Oracle claims that per-thread performance is increased by 5x over the SPARC T3. Each CPU core supports out of order execution and can switch to a single thread mode where a single thread can use all of the resources that previously had to be dedicated to multiple threads. In this sense the SPARC T4 is closer to other modern SMT designs such as those from Intel.

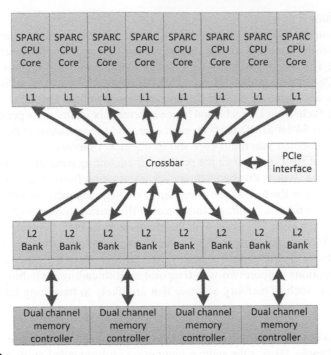

FIGURE 3.10

Diagrammatic representation of the Niagara 2 CPU from Sun/Oracle. The design intends to make a high level of threading efficient: Note its relative similarity to the GPU design seen in Figure 3.8. Given enough threads, we can cover all memory access time with useful compute without extracting ILP through complicated hardware techniques.

GPU Architectures

Like CPUs, GPU architectures come in a wide variety of options. Here, we briefly discuss several before going into more depth about OpenCL programming for the AMD architecture. GPUs tend to be heavily multithreaded with sophisticated hardware task management because the graphics workloads they are designed to process consist of complex vertex, geometry, and pixel processing task graphs. These tasks and the pixels they process are highly parallel, which gives a substantial amount of independent work to process for devices with multiple cores and highly latency-tolerant multithreading. It is important to understand that barring sophisticated mechanisms to manage task queues, or to hide SIMD execution behind hardware management systems, GPUs are simply multithreaded processors with their parameterization aimed at processing large numbers of pixels very efficiently.

Handheld GPUs

Handheld GPUs have only recently started to gain general-purpose capabilities, with ARM and Imagination Technologies, in particular, now offering fully OpenCL-compliant IP. At this scale, GPUs consist of a small number of cores, typically one to four, where each executes a large number of individual threads on a small pixel-size SIMD unit not entirely dissimilar to an SSE vector pipeline. For example, ARM's Mali-T604 architecture uses three types of computation pipeline in each of up to four cores. Intercore task management supports managing workloads across the cores: Much GPU threading in general is hardware controlled rather than exposed to the operating system. An embedded design such as the Mali-T604 can share the same global memory as embedded CPUs, reducing the need to copy data across memory spaces; in the ARM design, this data is fully cached.

At the High End: AMD Radeon HD7970 and NVIDIA GTX580

High-end desktop GPUs and their derivatives for the HPC and workstation segments aim more for performance than maximal power efficiency. To achieve high memory bandwidth, a large number of pins are dedicated to memory traffic, and high bandwidth-per-pin (possibly lower latency) memory protocols may be used such as GDDR5. These devices use a mixture of features to improve compute throughput, including wide SIMD arrays to maximize arithmetic throughput for a given number of issued instructions. The AMD Radeon HD7970 architecture seen in Figure 3.11 has 16 SIMD lanes in hardware and uses vector pipelining to execute a 64-element vector over four cycles. The NVIDIA GTX580 architecture (Figure 3.12) also uses a 16-wide SIMD unit and executes a 32-element vector over two cycles. Both devices are multithreaded, supporting numerous wide SIMD threads on each core. On the AMD architecture, for example, each core possesses one scalar core and four SIMD units associated with a banked register file: each of those four SIMD units can have up to 10 vector threads (wavefronts) in flight, one of which can be chosen on each issue cycle for that SIMD unit. That gives a total of up to 40 per core and hence 1280 active vector threads across the entire device (or 81920 individual work items). The NVIDIA design offers similarly high numbers: however in both cases the actual concurrency is limited by the amount of state each thread uses and the realistic number is likely to be much lower.

In both the AMD and NVIDIA architectures the intermediate language that programs the device is a lane-wise SIMD model such that the instruction stream represents a single lane of the SIMD unit, an approach that NVIDIA calls "Single Instruction Multiple Thread" (SIMT) and has also be called "SPMD-on-SIMD". The ISA that this compiles down to may or may not be lane-wise, and in the AMD case it is an explicit scalar + vector ISA where program counters are managed explicitly on a per-wavefront basis and divergent branches are managed using explicit mask registers. We will discuss this in more detail in Chapter 6.

Instruction level parallelism is achieved in varying ways. The HD7970 design issues multiple instructions per cycle, each from a different active program counter, where one vector instruction will be issued on each cycle to a different vector unit. The GTX580 can co-issue two threads at once over two execution pipelines. Older AMD designs such as the HD6970 used VLIW instruction issue. In fact the HD6970 and HD7970 are very similar in their execution unit design, the difference lies largely in the instruction issue such that one issues in a compiler-structured fashion from one thread and the other issues at runtime from four threads. All of these designs are

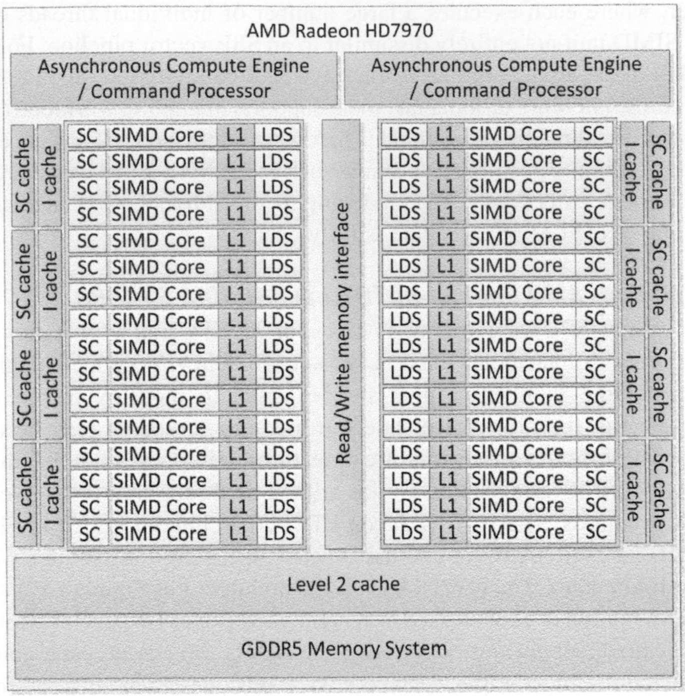

FIGURE 3.11

The AMD HD7970 architecture. The device has 32 cores in 8 clusters. Each core consists of a scalar execution unit, that handles branches and basic integer operations, and four SIMD ALUs. Each of the four SIMD units may have an instruction issued per cycle and the schedule selects a single instruction from one of the active hardware threads, or "wavefronts" to issue to the SIMD unit, as well as a scalar operation and a memory operation.

superscalar in that execution resources can issue memory access, arithmetic and other operations from threads running on the same core, but not necessarily the same thread and in this sense they are throughput architectures optimizing for the throughput of a set of threads over the latency of one.

Like the mobile GPUs on the market, the high-end AMD and NVIDIA models comprise multiple cores. Defining a core as the closest reasonable mapping to the equivalent in a CPU, the HD7970 has 32 cores (each with 4 vector units) and the NVIDIA design has 16 (with two vector units and clocked at double rate). Each core has a scratchpad memory buffer known as *local memory* in OpenCL which is allocated on a per-workgroup basis.

In Figure 3.9 we see a rough comparison of state usage in different styles of device. It should be clear that the high-end GPU design is heavily weighted towards thread state: allowing fast switching between multiple program instances and high throughput.

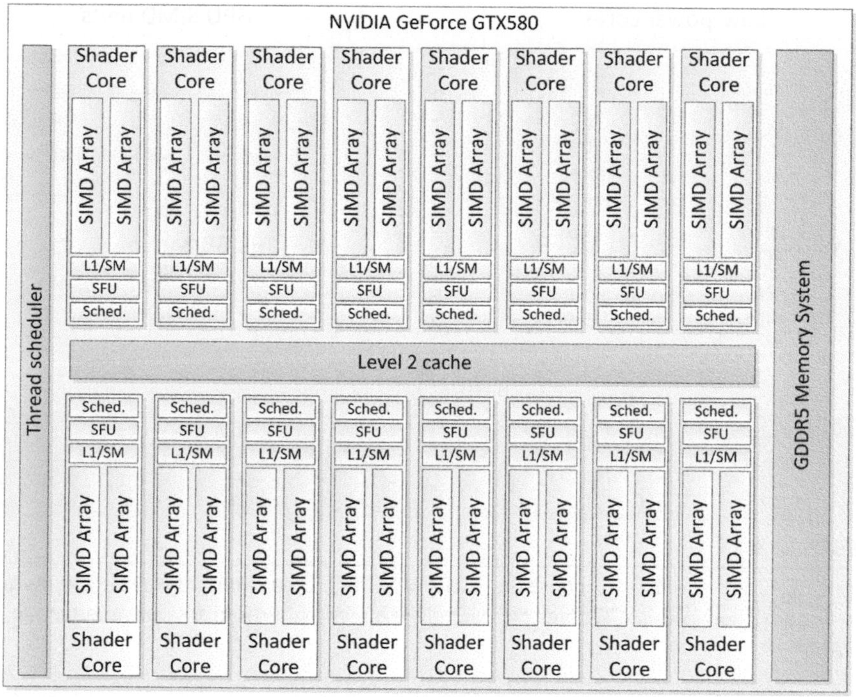

FIGURE 3.12

The NVIDIA GTX580 architecture. This device has 16 cores, with two SIMD arrays of 16 lanes in each core. Each core includes a shared memory/level one cache and a separate array of special function units to perform more complicated operations. The fine-grained scheduler chooses hardware threads, or "warps," to map to each SIMD array as they are available to execute.

APU and APU-Like Designs

SoCs have been common in embedded markets for a long time. Currently, there is a move toward SoCs being used for much higher performance systems and applications. Such fused processors, most obviously combining CPU and GPU designs, in addition to the less strongly marketed video decoders random number generators and encryption circuits, begin to encroach on the netbook, notebook, and low-end desktop spaces. It is easy to imagine such designs moving into high-end desktops. In this space we might see the power saving capabilities of integration combined with the substantial compute capability of a discrete GPU that need only be enabled when higher performance is needed, thus offering power savings overall.

Currently, the major architectures in this market are AMD's Bobcat-based, Phenom II-based and Bulldozer-based Fusion products (Advanced Micro Devices, 2011) and Intel's Sandy Bridge and Ivy Bridge ranges.

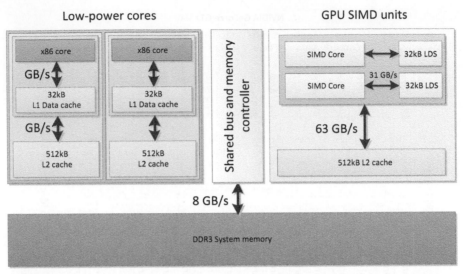

FIGURE 3.13

The E350 "Zacate" AMD APU consists of two 8-wide SIMD cores with five-way VLIW units and two "Bobcat" low-power x86 cores connected via a shared bus and a single interface to DRAM.

The AMD designs targeted at low-end netbook and subnotebook machines with a 9–18 W power budget are known as Ontario or Zacate and are based on the low-power Bobcat CPU core combined with a low-end GPU. These components are produced together on a single silicon die on a 40-nm process. The highest spec model in the range is shown in Figure 3.13. In this case, the GPU is an eight-wide SIMD unit based on the five-way VLIW of the 5xxx GPU generation from which the architecture is derived. The two Bobcat cores have two-way SIMD units, each allowing SSE instructions to be issued from each core over two cycles. AMD's higher performance APU, Trinity, is based on a derivative of the Bulldozer core and a significantly higher performance GPU.

Intel's Ivy bridge APU design (Figure 3.14) is based on four cores of the Sandy Bridge microarchitecture core discussed previously. The GPU is part of the ongoing development of Intel's in-house embedded GPU design. This latest revision of Intel's GPU core has full OpenCL and DirectX 11 capabilities.

The APU architectures offer scope for sharing data structures between GPU and CPU cores such that the major communication bottleneck of many GPU compute workloads is alleviated. This means that latency can be improved for workloads dispatched to the GPU and more tightly integrated algorithms between GPU and CPU cores can be created that are currently not practical due to performance constraints arising from the latency of the PCI express bus. This improvement comes at the cost of CPU-style memory bandwidth shared between both devices, losing the very high-bandwidth exotic memory interfaces of discrete GPUs. It is likely that this trade-off

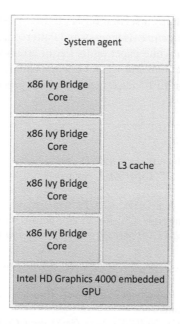

FIGURE 3.14

The Intel Ivy Bridge with Intel HD4000 graphics present. Although not termed an "APU" by Intel, the concept is the same as the devices under that category from AMD. Intel combines four Ivy Bridge x86 cores, the 22nm die shrink of the Sandy Bridge microarchitecture, with an improved version of its embedded graphics processor.

is advantageous in the wide range of algorithms that are inefficient when implemented purely on the GPU. This advantage may come either because the GPU's throughput-based design being suboptimal for serial code, and the APU design may reduce turnaround time of mixing CPU and GPU code, or because the algorithms are communication-bottlenecked.

SUMMARY

In this chapter, we discussed the types of architecture that OpenCL might run on and the trade-offs in the architectural design space that these architectures embody. After examining OpenCL more closely, in Chapter 6 we discuss how the OpenCL model maps to a specific architecture in the form of a combination of AMD FX8150 CPU and HD7970 GPU.

The content of this chapter will benefit from further reading; however, for many of the specific devices, concise references can be difficult to find. The fourth edition of *Computer Organization and Design* (Patterson and Hennessy, 2008) discusses many architectural issues in-depth, including the AMD Opteron, Intel Nehalem (predecessor to Sandy Bridge, sharing many features), UltraSPARC T2, and various other designs. It also contains a section on NVIDIA's GPU architecture. The fifth edition of *Computer Architecture* (Hennessy and Patterson, 2011) extends these concepts. NVIDIA released a white paper on its Fermi architecture in 2009 (NVIDIA, 2009). Chapter 2 of the Itanium 2 processor manual (Intel, 2002) gives a reasonably high-level overview of the EPIC implementation and processor pipeline.

References

Advanced Micro Devices, Incorporated. (2011). *AMD Fusion Family of APUs: Enabling a Superior, Immersive PC Experience.* Sunnyvale, CA: Advanced Micro Devices, Incorporated.

Advanced Micro Devices, Incorporated. (2012). *White paper: AMD Graphics Core Next (GCN) Architecture.* Sunnyvale, CA: Advanced Micro Devices, Incorporated.

Grohoski, G. (2006). *Niagara-2: A Highly Threaded Server-on-a-Chip.* 18th Hot Chips Symposium, August.

Hennessy, J. L., & Patterson, D. A. (2011). *Computer Architecture: A Quantitative Approach* (5th ed.). Burlington, MA: Morgan Kaufmann.

Intel Corporation. (2002). *Intel Itanium 2 Processor: Hardware Developer's Manual.* Santa Clara, CA: Intel Corporation.

NVIDIA Corporation. (2009). *NVIDIA's Next Generation CUDA Compute Architecture: Fermi.* Santa Clara, CA: NVIDIA Corporation.

Patterson, D. A., & Hennessy, J. L. (2008). *Computer Organization and Design* (4th ed.). Burlington, MA: Morgan Kaufmann.

Basic OpenCL Examples

4

INTRODUCTION

In Chapter 2, we discussed the OpenCL specification and how it can be used to implement programs for heterogeneous platforms. Chapter 3 covered the architecture of some possible OpenCL targets. In this chapter, we discuss a few more complex examples, which build on the simple examples such as vector addition discussed in Chapter 2. We cover the implementation of both the host and the device code in a methodical manner.

The aim of this chapter is to give the reader more intuition of how OpenCL can be used to write data-parallel programs. The implementations in this chapter are complete OpenCL examples. However, they have not been tuned to take advantage of any particular device architecture. The aim is to provide the user with implementation guidelines for OpenCL applications and to discuss implementations that can serve as a baseline for the architecture-specific optimization of applications in later chapters.

EXAMPLE APPLICATIONS

In this section, we discuss the implementation of some example OpenCL applications. The examples covered here include image rotation, matrix multiplication, and image convolution.

Simple Matrix Multiplication Example

A simple serial C implementation of matrix multiplication is shown here (remember that OpenCL host programs can be written in either C or using the OpenCL C++ Wrapper API). The code iterates over three nested `for` loops, multiplying Matrix A by Matrix B and storing the result in Matrix C. The two outer loops are used to iterate over each element of the output matrix. The innermost loop will iterate over the individual elements of the input matrices to calculate the result of each output location.

```
// Iterate over the rows of Matrix A
for(int i = 0; i < heightA; i++) {
  // Iterate over the columns of Matrix B
  for(int j = 0; j < widthB; j++) {
    C[i][j] = 0;
    // Multiply and accumulate the values in the current row
    // of A and column of B
    for(int k = 0; k < widthA; k++) {
      C[i][j] += A[i][k] * B[k][j];
    }
  }
}
```

It is straightforward to map the serial implementation to OpenCL, as the two outer *for-loops* work independently of each other. This means that a separate work-item can be created for each output element of the matrix. The two outer for-loops are mapped to the two-dimensional range of work-items for the kernel.

The independence of output values inherent in matrix multiplication is shown in Figure 4.1. Each work-item reads in its own row of Matrix A and its column of Matrix B. The data being read is multiplied and written at the appropriate location of the output Matrix C.

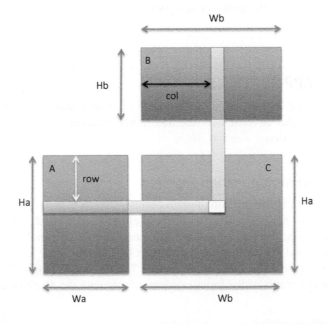

FIGURE 4.1

Each output value in a matrix multiplication is generated independently of all others.

```
// widthA = heightB for valid matrix multiplication
__kernel void simpleMultiply(
    __global float* outputC,
    int widthA,
    int heightA,
    int widthB,
    int heightB,
    __global float* inputA,
    __global float* inputB) {

    //Get global position in Y direction
    int row = get_global_id(1);
    //Get global position in X direction
    int col = get_global_id(0);

    float sum = 0.0f;

    //Calculate result of one element of Matrix C
    for (int i = 0; i < widthA; i++) {
        sum += inputA[row*widthA+i] * inputB[i*widthB+col];
    }

    outputC[row*widthB+col] = sum;
}
```

Now that we have understood the implementation of the data-parallel kernel, we need to write the OpenCL API calls that move the data to the device. The implementation steps for the rest of the matrix multiplication application are summarized in Figure 4.2. We need to create a context for the device we wish to use. Using the context, we create the command queue, which is used to send commands to the device. Once the command queue is created, we can send the input data to the device, run the parallel kernel, and read the resultant output data back from the device.

Step 1: Set Up Environment

In this step, we declare a context, choose a device type, and create the context and a command queue. Throughout this example, the ciErrNum variable should always be checked to see if an error code is returned by the implementation.

```
cl_int ciErrNum;

// Use the first platform
cl_platform_id platform;
ciErrNum = clGetPlatformIDs(1, &platform, NULL);

// Use the first device
cl_device_id device;
ciErrNum = clGetDeviceIDs(
    platform,
    CL_DEVICE_TYPE_ALL,
    1,
    &device,
    NULL);
```

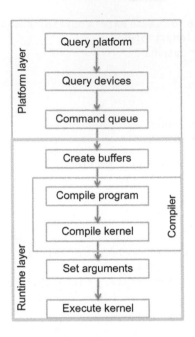

FIGURE 4.2

Programming steps to writing a complete OpenCL application.

```
cl_context_properties cps[3] = {
    CL_CONTEXT_PLATFORM, (cl_context_properties)platform, 0};

// Create the context
cl_context ctx = clCreateContext(
    cps,
    1,
    &device,
    NULL,
    NULL,
    &ciErrNum);

// Create the command queue
cl_command_queue myqueue = clCreateCommandQueue(
    ctx,
    device,
    0,
    &ciErrNum);
```

Step 2: Declare Buffers and Move Data

Declare buffers on the device and enqueue copies of input matrices to the device. Also declare the output buffer.

```
// We assume that A, B, C are float arrays which
// have been declared and initialized

// Allocate space for Matrix A on the device
cl_mem bufferA = clCreateBuffer(
    ctx,
    CL_MEM_READ_ONLY,
    wA*hA*sizeof(float),
    NULL,
    &ciErrNum);

// Copy Matrix A to the device
ciErrNum = clEnqueueWriteBuffer(
    myqueue,
    bufferA,
    CL_TRUE,
    0,
    wA*hA*sizeof(float),
    (void *)A,
    0,
    NULL,
    NULL);

// Allocate space for Matrix B on the device
cl_mem bufferB = clCreateBuffer(
    ctx,
    CL_MEM_READ_ONLY,
    wB*hB*sizeof(float),
    NULL,
    &ciErrNum);

// Copy Matrix B to the device
ciErrNum = clEnqueueWriteBuffer(
    myqueue,
    bufferB,
    CL_TRUE,
    0,
    wB*hB*sizeof(float),
    (void *)B,
    0,
    NULL,
    NULL);

// Allocate space for Matrix C on the device
cl_mem bufferC = clCreateBuffer(
    ctx,
    CL_MEM_WRITE_ONLY,
    hA*wB*sizeof(float),
    NULL,
    &ciErrNum);
```

Step 3: Runtime Kernel Compilation

Compile the program from the kernel array, build the program, and define the kernel.

```
// We assume that the program source is stored in the variable
// 'source' and is NULL terminated
cl_program myprog = clCreateProgramWithSource (
    ctx,
    1,
    (const char**)&source,
    NULL,
    &ciErrNum);

// Compile the program. Passing NULL for the 'device_list'
// argument targets all devices in the context
ciErrNum = clBuildProgram(myprog, 0, NULL, NULL, NULL, NULL);

// Create the kernel
cl_kernel mykernel = clCreateKernel(
    myprog,
    "simpleMultiply",
    &ciErrNum);
```

Step 4: Run the Program

Set kernel arguments and the workgroup size. We can then enqueue the kernel onto the command queue to execute on the device.

```
// Set the kernel arguments
clSetKernelArg(mykernel, 0, sizeof(cl_mem), (void *)&bufferC);
clSetKernelArg(mykernel, 1, sizeof(cl_int), (void *)&wA);
clSetKernelArg(mykernel, 2, sizeof(cl_int), (void *)&hA);
clSetKernelArg(mykernel, 3, sizeof(cl_int), (void *)&wB);
clSetKernelArg(mykernel, 4, sizeof(cl_int), (void *)&hB);
clSetKernelArg(mykernel, 5, sizeof(cl_mem), (void *)&bufferA);
clSetKernelArg(mykernel, 6, sizeof(cl_mem), (void *)&bufferB);

// Set local and global workgroup sizes
//We assume the matrix dimensions are divisible by 16
size_t localws[2] = {16,16} ;
size_t globalws[2] = {wC, hC};

// Execute the kernel
ciErrNum = clEnqueueNDRangeKernel(
    myqueue,
    mykernel,
    2,
    NULL,
    globalws,
    localws,
    0,
    NULL,
    NULL);
```

Step 5: Return Results to Host

After the program has run, we enqueue a read back of the result matrix from the device buffer to host memory.

```
// Read the output data back to the host
ciErrNum = clEnqueueReadBuffer(
    myqueue,
    bufferC,
    CL_TRUE,
    0,
    wC*hC*sizeof(float),
    (void *)C,
    0,
    NULL,
    NULL);
```

The steps outlined here show an OpenCL implementation of matrix multiplication that can be used as a baseline. In later chapters, we use our understanding of data-parallel architectures to improve the performance of particular data-parallel algorithms.

Image Rotation Example

Image rotation is a common image processing routine with applications in matching, alignment, and other image-based algorithms. The input to an image rotation routine is an image, the rotation angle θ, and a point about which rotation is done. The aim is to achieve the result shown in Figure 4.3. For the image rotation example, we use OpenCL's C++ Wrapper API.

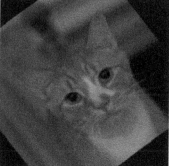

Original image　　　　　　　After rotation of 45°

FIGURE 4.3

An image rotated by 45°. The output is the same size as the input, and the out of edge values are dropped.

The coordinates of a point (x_1, y_1) when rotated by an angle θ around (x_0, y_0) become (x_2, y_2), as shown by the following equation:

$$x_2 = \cos(\theta) * (x_1 - x_0) + \sin(\theta) * (y_1 - y_0)$$
$$y_2 = -\sin(\theta) * (x_1 - x_0) + \cos(\theta) * (y_1 - y_0)$$

By rotating the image about the origin $(0, 0)$, we get

$$x_2 = \cos(\theta) * (x_1) + \sin(\theta) * (y_1)$$
$$y_2 = -\sin(\theta) * (x_1) + \cos(\theta) * (y_1)$$

To implement image rotation with openCL, we see that the calculations of the new (x, y) coordinate of each pixel in the input can be done independently. Each work-item will calculate the new position of a single pixel. In a manner similar to matrix multiplication, a work-item can obtain the location of its respective pixel using its global ID (as shown in Figure 4.4).

The image rotation example is a good example of an input decomposition, meaning that an element of the input (in this case, an input image) is decomposed into a work-item. When an image is rotated, the new locations of some pixels may be outside the image if the input and output image sizes are the same (see Figure 4.3, in

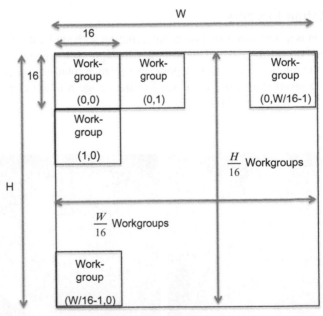

Input image workgroup configuration

FIGURE 4.4

Each element of the input image is handled by one work-item. Each work-item calculates its data's coordinates and writes image out.

which the corners of the input would not have fit within the resultant image). For this reason, we need to check the bounds of the calculated output coordinates.

```
__kernel void img_rotate(
    __global float* dest_data, __global float* src_data,
    int W, int H,                          //Image Dimensions
    float sinTheta, float cosTheta ) //Rotation Parameters
{
    //Work-item gets its index within index space
    const int ix = get_global_id(0);
    const int iy = get_global_id(1);

    //Calculate location of data to move into (ix,iy)
    //Output decomposition as mentioned
    float x0 = W/2.0f;
    float y0 = W/2.0f;
    float xoff = ix-x0;
    float yoff = iy-y0;
    int xpos = (int)(xOff*cosTheta + yOff*sinTheta + x0 );
    int ypos = (int)(yOff*cosTheta - xOff*sinTheta + y0 );

    //Bound Checking
    if((((int)xpos>=0) && ((int)xpos< W) &&
       ((int)ypos>=0) && ((int)ypos< H))
    {
        // Read (ix,iy) src_data and store at (xpos,ypos) in
        // dest_data
        // In this case, because we rotating about the origin
        // and there is no translation,
        dest_data[iy*W+ix] = src_data[ypos*W+xpos];
    }
}
```

As seen in the previous kernel code, image rotation is an *embarrassingly parallel* problem, in which each resulting pixel value is computed independently. The main steps for the host code are similar to those in Figure 4.2. For this example's host code, we can reuse a substantial amount of code from the previous matrix multiplication example, including the code that will create the context and the command queue.

To give the developer wider exposure to OpenCL, we write the host code for the image rotation example with the C++ bindings for OpenCL 1.1. The C++ bindings are also compatible with OpenCL 1.2 and provide access to the low-level features of the original OpenCL C API. The C++ bindings are compatible with standard C++ compilers, and they are carefully designed to perform no memory allocation and offer full access to the features of OpenCL, without unnecessary masking of functionality.

More details about the OpenCL 1.1 specification's C++ Wrapper API can be found at www.khronos.org/registry/cl/specs/opencl-cplusplus-1.1.pdf.

The C++ header for OpenCL is obtained by including the header `cl.hpp`. The steps are shown in a similar manner to the matrix multiplication example in order to illustrate the close correspondence between the C API and the more concise C++ bindings.

Step 1: Set Up Environment

```
// Discover platforms
cl::vector<cl::Platform> platforms;
cl::Platform::get(&platforms);

// Create a context with the first platform
cl_context_properties cps[3] = {CL_CONTEXT_PLATFORM,
    (cl_context_properties)(platforms[0])(), 0};

// Create a context using this platform for a GPU type device
cl::Context context(CL_DEVICE_TYPE_ALL, cps);

// Get device list from the context
cl::vector<cl::Device> devices =
    context.getInfo<CL_CONTEXT_DEVICES>();

// Create a command queue on the first device
cl::CommandQueue queue = cl::CommandQueue(context,
    devices[0], 0);
```

Step 2: Declare Buffers and Move Data

```
// Create buffers for the input and output data ("W" and "H"
// are the width and height of the image, respectively)
cl::Buffer d_ip = cl::Buffer(context, CL_MEM_READ_ONLY,
    W*H* sizeof(float));
cl::Buffer d_op = cl::Buffer(context, CL_MEM_WRITE_ONLY,
    W*H* sizeof(float));

// Copy the input data to the device (assume that the input
// image is the array "ip")
queue.enqueueWriteBuffer(d_ip, CL_TRUE, 0, W*H*
    sizeof(float), ip);
```

Step 3: Runtime Kernel Compilation

```
// Read in the program source
std::ifstream sourceFileName("img_rotate_kernel.cl");

std::string sourceFile(
    std::istreambuf_iterator<char>(sourceFileName),
    (std::istreambuf_iterator<char>()));

cl::Program::Sources rotn_source(1,
    std::make_pair(sourceFile.c_str(),
                   sourceFile.length()+1));
```

```
// Create the program
cl::Program rotn_program(context, rotn_source);

// Build the program
rotn_program.build(devices);

// Create the kernel
cl::Kernel rotn_kernel(rotn_program, "img_rotate");
```

Step 4: Run the Program

```
// The angle of rotation is theta
float cos_theta = cos(theta);
float sin_theta = sin(theta);

// Set the kernel arguments
rotn_kernel.setArg(0, d_op);
rotn_kernel.setArg(1, d_ip);
rotn_kernel.setArg(2, W);
rotn_kernel.setArg(3, H);
rotn_kernel.setArg(4, cos_theta);
rotn_kernel.setArg(5, sin_theta);

// Set the size of the NDRange and workgroups
cl::NDRange globalws(W,H);
cl::NDRange localws(16,16);

// Run the kernel
queue.enqueueNDRangeKernel(rotn_kernel, cl::NullRange,
    globalws, localws);
```

Step 5: Read Result Back to Host

```
// Read the output buffer back to the host
queue.enqueueReadBuffer(d_op, CL_TRUE, 0, W*H*sizeof(float), op);
```

As seen from the previous code, the C++ bindings maintain a close correspondence to the C API.

Image Convolution Example

In image processing, convolution is a commonly used algorithm that modifies the value of each pixel in an image by using information from neighboring pixels. A convolution kernel, or *filter*, describes how each pixel will be influenced by its neighbors. For example, a blurring kernel will take the weighted average of neighboring pixels so that large differences between pixel values are reduced. By using the same source image and changing only the filter, effects such as sharpening, blurring, edge enhancing, and embossing can be produced.

A convolution kernel works by iterating over each pixel in the source image. For each source pixel, the filter is centered over the pixel and the values of the filter

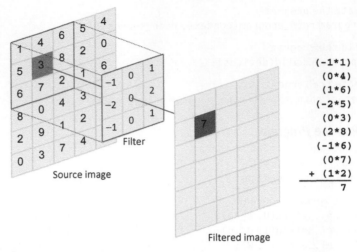

FIGURE 4.5

Applying a convolution filter to a source image.

multiply the pixel values that they overlay. A sum of the products is then taken to produce a new pixel value. Figure 4.5 provides a visual for this algorithm. Figure 4.6B shows the effect of a blurring filter and Figure 4.6C shows the effect of an edge-detection filter on the same source image seen in Figure 4.6A.

The following code performs a convolution in C. The outer two loops iterate over the source image, selecting the next source pixel. At each source pixel, the filter is applied to the neighboring pixels.

```
// Iterate over the rows of the source image
for(int i = halfFilterWidth; i < rows - halfFilterWidth; i++) {
    // Iterate over the columns of the source image
    for(int j = halfFilterWidth; j < cols - halfFilterWidth; j++) {
        sum = 0; // Reset sum for new source pixel
        // Apply the filter to the neighborhood
        for(int k = - halfFilterWidth; k <= halfFilterWidth; k++) {
            for(int l = - halfFilterWidth; l <= halfFilterWidth; l++) {
                sum += Image[i+k][j+l] *
                        Filter[k+ halfFilterWidth][l+ halfFilterWidth];
            }
        }
        outputImage[i][j] = sum;
    }
}
```

Step 1: Create Image and Buffer Objects

This example implements convolution using OpenCL images for the data type of the source and output images. Using images to represent the data has a number of advantages. For the convolution, work-items representing border pixels may read

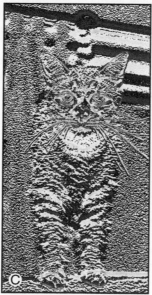

FIGURE 4.6

The effect of a blurring filter and a vertical edge-detecting filter applied to the same source image. (A) The original image. (B) Blurring filter. (C) Vertical edge-detecting filter.

out-of-bounds. Images supply a mechanism to automatically handle these accesses and return meaningful data.

The code begins by assuming that a context (context) and command queue (queue) have already been created, and that the source image (sourceImage), output image (outputImage), and filter (filter) have already been initialized on the host. The images both have dimensions width by height.

The first task is to allocate space on the device for the source image, output image, and the filter. Image declarations require a descriptor, cl_image_desc, and a format, cl_image_format. The image descriptor is used to define the size and dimensions of data, and the format is used to specify the datatype of each pixel and the channel layout of the image. The image_channel_order field of the format is where the channel layout is specified. Recall from Chapter 2 that every element of an image stores data in up to four channels, with each channel specified by RGBA, respectively. An image that will hold four values in every element should use CL_RGBA for the channel order. However, if each work-item will only access a single value (e.g., a pixel from a grayscale image or an element of a matrix), the data can be specified to only use a single channel using CL_R. This example assumes grayscale data and so only uses a single channel. The type of data is in the image_channel_data_type field of the descriptor. Integers are specified by a combination of signedness and size. For example, CL_SIGNED_INT32 is a 32-bit signed integer, and CL_UNSIGNED_INT8 is the equivalent of an unsigned character in C. Floating point data is specified by CL_FLOAT, and this is the type of data used in the example.

After creating the image format descriptor, memory objects are created to represent the images using clCreateImage(). A buffer is created for the filter and will eventually be used as constant memory.

```
// The image descriptor describes how the data will be stored in memory
// This descriptor initializes a 2D image with no pitch
cl_image_desc desc;
desc.image_type = CL_MEM_OBJECT_IMAGE2D;
desc.image_width = width;
desc.image_height = height;
desc.image_depth = 0;
desc.image_array_size = 0;
desc.image_row_pitch = 0;
desc.image_slice_pitch = 0;
desc.num_mip_levels = 0;
desc.num_samples = 0;
desc.buffer = NULL;

// The image format describes the properties of each pixel
cl_image_format format;
format.image_channel_order     = CL_R;    // single channel
format.image_channel_data_type = CL_FLOAT; // float data type
```

```
// Create space for the source image on the device
cl_mem bufferSourceImage = clCreateImage(context, CL_MEM_READ_ONLY,
&format, &desc, NULL, NULL);

// Create space for the output image on the device
cl_mem bufferOutputImage = clCreateImage(context, CL_MEM_WRITE_ONLY,
&format, &desc, NULL, NULL);

// Create space for the 7x7 filter on the device
cl_mem bufferFilter = clCreateBuffer(context, 0, filterSize*
sizeof(float), NULL, NULL);
```

Step 2: Write the Input Data

The call to `clEnqueueWriteImage()` copies an image to a device. Unlike buffers, copying an image requires supplying a three-dimensional offset and region, which define the coordinates where the copy should begin and how far it should span, respectively.

The filter is copied using `clEnqueueWriteBuffer()`, as seen in previous examples.

```
// Copy the source image to the device
size_t origin[3] = {0, 0, 0}; // Offset within the image to copy from
size_t region[3] = {width, height, 1}; // Elements to per dimension
clEnqueueWriteImage(
    queue,
    bufferSourceImage,
    CL_TRUE, origin,
    region,
    0,
    0,
    sourceImage,
    0,
    NULL,
    NULL);

// Copy the 7x7 filter to the device
clEnqueueWriteBuffer(
    queue,
    bufferFilter,
    CL_TRUE,
    0,
    filterSize*sizeof(float),
    filter,
    0,
    NULL,
    NULL);
```

Step 3: Create Sampler Object

In OpenCL, samplers are objects that describe how to access an image. Samplers specify the type of coordinate system, what to do when out-of-bounds accesses occur, and whether or not to interpolate if an access lies between multiple indices. The format of the clCreateSampler() API call is as follows:

```
cl_sampler clCreateSampler (
    cl_context context,
    cl_bool normalized_coords,
    cl_addressing_mode addressing_mode,
    cl_filter_mode filter_mode,
    cl_int *errcode_ret)
```

The coordinate system can either be normalized (i.e., range from 0 to 1) or use Pixel-based integer addresses. Setting the second argument to CL_TRUE enables normalized coordinates. Convolution does not use normalized coordinates, so the argument is set to FALSE.

OpenCL also allows a number of addressing modes to be used for handling out-of-bounds accesses. In the case of the convolution example, we use CL_ADDRESS_CLAMP_TO_EDGE to have any out-of-bounds access return the value on the border of the image, if the access went out-of-bounds. If CL_ADDRESS_CLAMP is used, the value produced by an out-of-bounds access is 0 for channels RG and B, and it returns either 0 or 1 for channel A (based on the image format). Other options are available when normalized coordinates are used.

The filter mode can be set to either access the closest pixel to a coordinate or interpolate between multiple pixel values if the coordinate lies somewhere in between.

```
// Create the image sampler
cl_sampler sampler = clCreateSampler(
    context,
    CL_FALSE,
    CL_ADDRESS_NONE,
    CL_FILTER_NEAREST,
    NULL);
```

Step 4: Compile and Execute the Kernel

The steps to create and build a program, create a kernel, set the kernel arguments, and enqueue the kernel for execution are identical to those in the previous example. Unlike the reference C version, the OpenCL code using images should create as many work-items as there are pixels in the image. Any out-of-bounds accesses due to the filter size will be handled automatically, based on the sampler object.

Step 5: Read the Result

Reading the result back to the host is very similar to writing the image, except that a pointer to the location to store the output data on the host is supplied.

```
// Read the output image back to the host
clEnqueueReadImage(
    queue,
    bufferOutputImage,
    CL_TRUE,
    origin,
    region,
    0,
    0,
    outputImage,
    0,
    NULL,
    NULL);
```

The Convolution Kernel

The kernel is fairly straightforward if the reference C code is understood—each work-item executes the two innermost loops. Data reads from the source image must be performed using an OpenCL construct that is specific to the data type. For this example, read_imagef() is used, where *f* signifies that the data to be read is of type single precision floating point. Accesses to an image always return a four-element vector (one per channel), so pixel (the value returned by the image access) and sum (resultant data that gets copied to the output image) must both be declared as a float4. Writing to the output image uses a similar function, write_imagef(), and requires that the data be formatted correctly (as a float4). Writing does not support out-of-bounds accesses. If there is any chance that there are more work-items in either dimension of the NDRange than there are pixels, bounds checking should be performed before writing the output data.

The filter is a perfect candidate for constant memory in this example because all work-items access the same element each iteration. Simply adding the keyword __constant in the signature of the function places the filter in constant memory.

```
__kernel
void convolution(
    __read_only image2d_t  sourceImage,
    __write_only image2d_t outputImage,
    int rows,
    int cols,
    __constant float* filter,
    int filterWidth,
    sampler_t sampler)
{
    // Store each work-item's unique row and column
    int column = get_global_id(0);
    int row = get_global_id(1);

    // Half the width of the filter is needed for indexing
    // memory later
    int halfWidth = (int)(filterWidth/2);
```

```
// All accesses to images return data as four-element vector
// (i.e., float4), although only the 'x' component will contain
// meaningful data in this code
float4 sum = {0.0f, 0.0f, 0.0f, 0.0f};

// Iterator for the filter
int filterIdx = 0;

// Each work-item iterates around its local area based on the
// size of the filter
int2 coords; // Coordinates for accessing the image
// Iterate over the filter rows
for(int i = -halfWidth; i <= halfWidth; i++) {
   coords.y = row + i;

   // Iterate over the filter columns
   for(int j = -halfWidth; j <= halfWidth; j++) {
      coords.x = column + j;

      float4 pixel;
      // Read a pixel from the image. A single channel image
      // stores the pixel in the 'x' coordinate of the returned
      // vector.
      pixel = read_imagef(sourceImage, sampler, coords);
      sum.x += pixel.x * filter[filterIdx++];
   }
}

// Copy the data to the output image if the
// work-item is in bounds
if(myRow < rows && myCol < cols) {
   coords.x = column;
   coords.y = row;
   write_imagef(outputImage, coords, sum);
}
}
```

COMPILING OPENCL HOST APPLICATIONS

To run a program for a GPU, an OpenCL-supported graphics driver is required. OpenCL programs using AMD's implementation can be run on x86 CPUs without the installation of any hardware drivers but still require the OpenCL runtime.

Compiling an OpenCL program is similar to compiling any application that uses dynamic libraries. Vendors distribute their own OpenCL library that must be used when compiling and linking an OpenCL executable. To compile an OpenCL program, an include path must be set to locate the OpenCL headers (cl.h or cl.hpp). The linker must know how to locate the OpenCL library (*OpenCL.lib* for Windows and *libOpenCL.a* on Linux). That's it!

Assuming that the OpenCL SDK is installed at `$(AMDAPPSDKROOT)`, an example compilation on Linux might be as follows:

```
$ g++ -o prog -I/$(AMDAPPSDKROOT)/include -L/$(AMDAPPSDKROOT)/lib/
x86_64 -lOpenCL prog.cpp
```

We see that most of the steps are similar across applications, allowing us to reuse a lot of "boiler plate" code. Applications using the C++ Wrapper API are compiled in the same manner. The C++ header file will usually be located in the same directory as the C headers.

SUMMARY

In this chapter, we discussed implementations of some well-known data-parallel algorithms. We studied the use of OpenCL buffer and image objects. We also used the C++ Wrapper API for the image rotation example.

In each example, a work-item computes the result of a single output element for the problem, although the input data requirements vary. The image rotation example is a case in which only one input element is needed. In matrix multiplication, a whole row and a whole column of the input matrices are needed by each work-item to calculate the result of one element of the output matrix. Convolution requires a neighborhood of input pixels to compute a result.

Although the examples discussed in this chapter are correct data-parallel OpenCL programs, their performance can be drastically improved. Optimizing performance based on specific hardware platforms is the goal of subsequent chapters.

Understanding OpenCL's Concurrency and Execution Model

5

INTRODUCTION

As discussed in Chapter 3, there is a wide range of devices supported by OpenCL. To achieve such wide support, it is vital that the memory and execution models for OpenCL are defined in such a way that we can achieve a high level of performance across a range of architectures without extraordinary programming effort. In this chapter, we delve deeper into these models, and in Chapter 6 we show how they map to a specific architecture that supports OpenCL.

KERNELS, WORK-ITEMS, WORKGROUPS, AND THE EXECUTION DOMAIN

OpenCL execution is centered on the concept of a kernel. A kernel is a unit of code that represents a single executing instance as written in the OpenCL C language. A kernel instance is at first sight similar to a C function: In the OpenCL C language, a kernel looks like C, it takes a parameter list, and has "local" variables (in a `private` address space, as we shall see) and standard control flow constructs. This single kernel instance is known as a work item in OpenCL terminology.

What makes the OpenCL kernel different from a C function is its parallel semantics. Any given kernel instance or work item defines just one sliver of a large parallel execution space. A kernel dispatch, initiated when the runtime processes the entry in an execution queue created by a call to `clEnqueueNDRangeKernel` on a queue object, consists of a large number of work items intended to execute together to carry out the collective operations specified in the kernel body. As the enqueue call suggests, this dispatch creates an `NDRange` (an *n*-dimensional range) worth of work items. An `NDRange` defines a one-, two-, or three-dimensional grid of work items, providing a simple and straightforward structure for parallel execution. When mapped to the hardware model of OpenCL, each work item runs on a unit of hardware abstractly known as a processing element, where a given processing element may process multiple work items in turn.

Heterogeneous Computing with OpenCL

Within a kernel dispatch, each work item is independent. In OpenCL, global synchronization between work items is not defined. This relaxed execution model allows OpenCL to scale on devices possessing a large number of cores. However, this kind of hardware actually provides a hierarchy of execution devices, particularly a hierarchy of memory structures.

To flexibly support such devices, OpenCL divides the global execution space into a large number of equally sized one-, two-, or three-dimensional sets of work items called workgroups. Within each workgroup, some degree of communication is allowed. The OpenCL specification requires that an entire workgroup can run concurrently on an element of the device hierarchy known as a compute unit. This form of concurrent execution is vital to allow synchronization. Workgroups allow for local synchronization by guaranteeing concurrent execution, but they also limit communication to improve scalability. An application that involves global communication across its execution space is challenging to parallelize to multi-core devices with OpenCL. To satisfy global communications, the compute unit will be mapped onto a single core.

By defining larger dispatches than can execute concurrently, OpenCL kernels can scale onto larger and more heavily threaded devices on which more groups and more work items can execute at once. However, for performance reasons (just as with APIs such as OpenMP and MPI), it may make more sense to only issue enough work that you know can run and more directly control optimization.

As discussed in Chapter 2, OpenCL work items attempt to express parallelism that could be expressed using Win32 or POSIX threads or a more abstract mapping to threads such as OpenMP. The design of OpenCL takes that a step further, however, because the set of work items within a workgroup can be efficiently grouped into a smaller number of hardware thread contexts. This can be viewed as a generalization of single instruction multiple data (SIMD) or pipelined vector execution where long logical vectors execute over multiple cycles, but in the OpenCL case, subvectors can maintain their own program counters until synchronization points. The best example of this is on the GPU, where as many as 64 work items execute in lock step as a single hardware thread on a SIMD unit: On AMD architectures, this is known as a *wave-front*, and on NVIDIA architectures it is called a *warp*. The result is SIMD execution via lanewise programming, an arguably simpler development model than explicit use of SIMD instructions as developers are used to when using SSE intrinsics on x86 processors. Because of this SIMD execution, it is often noted that for a given device, an OpenCL dispatch should be an even multiple of that device's SIMD width. This value can be queried through the `getInfo` functionality of the runtime as the parameter `CL_KERNEL_PREFERRED_WORK_GROUP_SIZE_MULTIPLE` to the `clGetKernelWorkGroupInfo` function.

OpenCL defines functions callable from within a kernel to obtain the position of a given work item in the execution range. Some of these functions take a dimension value, listed here as `uint dimension`. This refers to the 0th, 1st, or 2nd dimension in the iteration space as provided in the multidimensional `NDRange` parameters to the kernel enqueue:

- `uint get_work_dim()`: Returns the number of dimensions in use in the dispatch.
- `uint get_global_size(uint dimension)`: Returns the global number of work items in the dimension requested.
- `uint get_global_id(uint dimension)`: Returns the index of the current work item in the global space and in the dimension requested.
- `uint get_local_size(uint dimension)`: Returns the size of workgroups in this dispatch in the requested dimension.
- `uint get_local_id(uint dimension)`: Returns the index of the current work item as an offset from the beginning of the current workgroup.
- `uint get_num_groups(uint dimension)`: Returns the number of workgroups in the specified dimension of the dispatch. This is `get_global_size` divided by `get_local_size`.
- `uint get_group_id(uint dimension)`: Returns the index of the current work-group. That is, the global index of the first work-item in the workgroup, dividing by the workgroup size.

As an example of execution of a simple kernel, take the following trivial kernel that executes over a two-dimensional execution space, multiplies an input array by 2, and then assigns it to the output. Figure 5.1 shows how this executes in practice. We can see that the calls to `get_global_id` and `get_global_size` return different values for each work item that refer to different points in the iteration space. In this trivial example, we use the position in the space to directly map to a two-dimensional data structure. In real examples, much more complicated mappings are possible, depending on the input and output structures and the way an algorithm will process the data.

```
__kernel void simpleKernel(
    __global float *a,
    __global float *b )
{
```

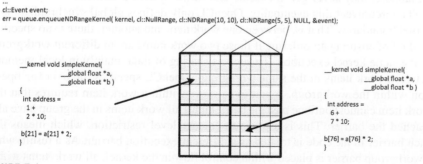

```
...
cl::Event event;
err = queue.enqueueNDRangeKernel( kernel, cl::NullRange, cl::NDRange(10, 10), cl::NDRange(5, 5), NULL, &event);
...
```

```
__kernel void simpleKernel(
    __global float *a,
    __global float *b )
{
    int address =
        1 +
        2 * 10;

    b[21] = a[21] * 2;
}
```

```
__kernel void simpleKernel(
    __global float *a,
    __global float *b )
{
    int address =
        6 +
        7 * 10;

    b[76] = a[76] * 2;
}
```

FIGURE 5.1

Executing a simple kernel showing kernel instances in the grid.

```
int address =
    get_global_id(0) +
    get_global_id(1) * get_global_size(0);

b[address] = a[address] * 2;
}
```

OPENCL SYNCHRONIZATION: KERNELS, FENCES, AND BARRIERS

In the OpenCL model at its simplest, individual work items execute independently. A write performed in one work item has no ordering guarantee with a read performed in another work item. Rather, OpenCL has both a relaxed synchronization model and a relaxed memory consistency model. Although the reality of hardware means that certain guarantees will be met, in a cross-platform API no such guarantee can be made. The solution is that OpenCL explicitly defines synchronization points where the programmer knows with certainty what the state of some part of the system is and can rely on that information to obtain expectations of behavior.

Because OpenCL runs on devices in which threading is managed by hardware, such as GPUs, in addition to operating system-managed threading models such as mainstream x86 CPUs, further care is taken to enable full concurrency. In an x86 thread, it is possible to attempt to lower a semaphore and block if the semaphore in unavailable, knowing that the operating system will remove the thread from execution and is free to schedule anything in its place with little in the way of resource constraints. On a GPU, applying the same trick in the GPU equivalent of a thread, the wavefront on AMD hardware, is problematic because the resources occupied are fixed. For example, removing one wavefront from execution does not free its resources, so it is possible to reach a situation in which a wavefront that is not yet able to fit on the device is required to free the semaphore before one that is already on the device is able to continue. Because the wavefronts on the device are waiting on that semaphore, they never get to execute and so the system deadlocks.

To circumvent this eventuality, OpenCL only defines global synchronization at kernel boundaries. That is, between one work item and another, there is no specified method of ensuring an ordering if those two work items are in different workgroups of the same kernel execution. To support sharing of data, mainly in local memory, between work items in the same workgroup, OpenCL specifies the `barrier` operation within the workgroup. A call to `barrier` within a work item requires that that work item cannot continue past the barrier until all work items in the group have also reached the barrier. This is a program-counter level restriction, which means that each barrier in the code is treated as a different execution barrier. As a result, when a workgroup barrier is placed within control flow in the kernel, all work items within the group must encounter that barrier. The net effect of this is that behavior of barriers within control flow that diverges between different work items in the group is undefined: On many devices, this leads to deadlock as work items wait for others that will never reach the barrier.

A simple example of OpenCL synchronization is shown in Figure 5.2. In this diagram, we see an initial kernel enqueue with four workgroups of eight work items each. Under the loosest interpretation of the OpenCL spec (i.e., ignoring hardware implementations), the work items in each workgroup proceed at varying rates. On issuing the barrier instruction, the most advanced work item waits for all others to catch up, only continuing after all have reached that point. Different workgroups and specifically work items in other workgroups proceed with a schedule completely unrelated to that of the first workgroup until the end of the kernel. Between kernel dispatches, all work is guaranteed to be complete and all memory consistent. Then, the next kernel launches, with the same semantics.

If we assume that the kernels enqueued as 0 and 1 are produced from the same kernel object, the following kernel code and API calls could be expected to

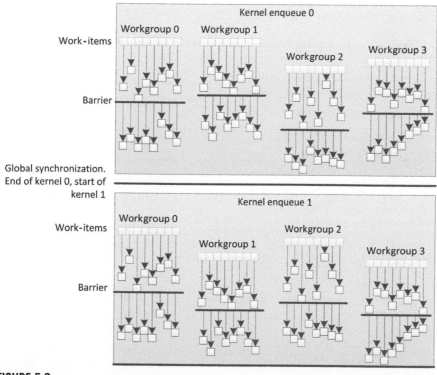

FIGURE 5.2

Synchronization behavior in OpenCL. Within a single kernel dispatch, synchronization is only guaranteed within workgroups using barriers. Global synchronization is maintained by completion of the kernel and the guarantee that on a completion event all work is complete and memory content as expected.

produce the behavior seen in Figure 5.2. In this case, the behavior we see from the work items is a simple wrapping neighborwise addition of elements in local memory, where availability of the data must be guaranteed before neighbors can be read. Note from this example that kernel arguments assigned to a kernel object are persistent and hence do not need to be repeatedly set. This is true of both the C and C++ APIs.

```
// Host code
...
  cl_mem input = clCreateBuffer(
    context,
    CL_MEM_READ_ONLY,
    10*sizeof(float),
    0,
    0);
  cl_mem intermediate = clCreateBuffer(
    context,
    CL_MEM_READ_ONLY,
    10*sizeof(float),
    0,
    0);
  cl_mem output = clCreateBuffer(
    context,
    CL_MEM_WRITE_ONLY,
    10*sizeof(float),
    0,
    0);
  clEnqueueWriteBuffer(
    queue,
    input,
    CL_TRUE,
    0,
    10*sizeof(int),
    (void *)hostInput,
    0,
    NULL,
    NULL);
  clSetKernelArg(kernel, 0, sizeof(cl_mem), (void *)&input);
  clSetKernelArg(kernel, 1, sizeof(cl_mem), (void *)&intermediate);
  clSetKernelArg(kernel, 2, 2*sizeof(float), 0);

  size_t localws[1] = {2} ;
  size_t globalws[1] = {10};

  clEnqueueNDRangeKernel(
    queue,
    kernel,
    1,
    NULL,
```

```
      globalws,
      localws,
      0,
      NULL,
      NULL);

   clSetKernelArg(kernel, 0, sizeof(cl_mem), (void *)&intermediate);
   clSetKernelArg(kernel, 1, sizeof(cl_mem), (void *)&output);

   clEnqueueNDRangeKernel(
      queue,
      kernel,
      1,
      NULL,
      globalws,
      localws,
      0,
      NULL,
      NULL);
   clEnqueueReadBuffer(
      queue,
      output,
      CL_TRUE,
      0,
      10*sizeof(float),
      (void *)&hostOutput,
      0,
      NULL,
      NULL);

...


// Kernel
__kernel void simpleKernel(
    __global float *a,
    __global float *b,
   __local float *l )
{
  l[get_local_id(0)] = a[get_global_id(0)];

  barrier(CLK_LOCAL_MEM_FENCE);

  unsigned int otherAddress =
     (get_local_id(0) + 1) % get_local_size(0);

  b[get_local_id(0)] = l[get_local_id(0)] + l[otherAddress];
}
```

QUEUING AND GLOBAL SYNCHRONIZATION

OpenCL is based on a task-parallel, host-controlled model, in which each task is data parallel. This is maintained through the use of thread-safe command queues attached to each device. Kernels, data movement, and other operations are not simply executed by the user calling a runtime function. These operations are enqueued onto a specific queue using an asynchronous enqueue operation, to be executed at some point in the future.

The commands enqueued into OpenCL's command queues can be as follows:

- Kernel execution commands
- Memory commands
- Synchronization commands

All kernel execution and synchronization commands are enqueued asynchronously. Completion of a command from the point of view of the host program is only guaranteed at a synchronization point. The following are the primary synchronization points:

- A clFinish command that blocks until an entire queue completes execution
- Waiting on the completion of a specific event
- Execution of a blocking memory operation

The last option is the simplest, often used in simple OpenCL demos. The following is a program fragment that asynchronously enqueues a sequence of commands and requires a blocking memory operation to perform synchronization with the host:

```
// Perform setup of platform, context and create buffers
...
// Create queue leaving parameters as default so queue is in-order
queue = clCreateCommandQueue( context, devices[0], 0, 0);
...

clEnqueueWriteBuffer(
    queue,
    bufferA,
    CL_TRUE,
    0,
    10 * sizeof(int),
    a,
    0,
    NULL,
    NULL);
clEnqueueWriteBuffer(
    queue,
    bufferB,
    CL_TRUE,
    0,
    10 * sizeof(int),
    b,
```

```
    0,
    NULL,
    NULL);

// Set kernel arguments
...
size_t localws[1] = {2}; size_t globalws[1] = {10};
clEnqueueNDRangeKernel(
    queue,
    kernel,
    1,
    NULL,
    globalws,
    localws,
    0,
    NULL,
    NULL);

// Perform blocking read-back to synchronize
clEnqueueReadBuffer(
    queue,
    bufferOut,
    CL_TRUE,
    0,
    10 * sizeof(int),
    out,
    0,
    0,
    0);
```

The second parameter to enqueueReadBuffer reads CL_TRUE. This parameter makes
the read buffer synchronous, such that it will block until the data has been copied
back. To correctly copy back, all activities in the queue before the copy must have
completed to correctly generate the data. Had we set that parameter to CL_FALSE, a
further synchronization operation would have been needed. The simplest approach
would have been to insert a cl finish operation on the queue:

```
clEnqueueReadBuffer(
    queue,
    bufferOut,
    CL_FALSE,
    0,
    10 * sizeof(int),
    out,
    0,
    0,
    0);
clFinish(queue);
```

Memory Consistency in OpenCL

OpenCL synchronization applies not only to completion of work but also to correct visibility of memory. OpenCL follows a relaxed memory consistency model that allows it to be more efficiently mapped to a wide range of devices. In the OpenCL model, any memory object that is shared between multiple enqueued commands is guaranteed to be consistent only at synchronization points. This means that between two commands, consistency, and hence correctness of communication, is guaranteed at the minimum between elements in an in-order queue or on a communicated event from one command that generates the event to another that waits on it.

Even in this case, memory object consistency will be maintained only within the runtime, not visibly to the host API. To achieve host API correctness, the user must use one of the discussed blocking operations. For example, clFinish will block until all operations in the specified queue have completed and hence guarantee memory consistency of any buffers used by operations in the queue.

Between devices, the same consistency issues arise. Because memory objects are associated with contexts rather than devices, it is the responsibility of the OpenCL runtime to ensure that such objects are consistent across devices when data is shared and appropriate events occur. Data is moved from one device to another such that if a kernel is to be executed on a second device, any results generated on the first will be available when necessary. The completion of an event on the first data structure is the guarantee that the data is OK to move and no separate buffer copy operation is needed.

Events

Note that the command queue is constructed ignoring the final two parameters, which are left as default. One of the properties available for this bit field is to enable out-of-order execution of the queue (CL_QUEUE_OUT_OF_ORDER_EXEC_MODE_ENABLE). Thus, although the queue in the previous example is in-order, it is possible for a queue to execute out-of-order.

An out-of-order queue has no default ordering of the operations defined in the queue. If the runtime decides that it has, for example, a DMA engine that can execute in parallel with compute units, or that the device can execute multiple kernels at once, it is at liberty to schedule those operations in parallel with no guarantee that one completes before another starts. Similarly, if the runtime has multiple queues whether on the same device or, more obviously, on multiple devices, there is no default assumption about order of execution of elements of these multiple queues.

In either case, to correctly execute such a structure requires the construction of a task graph. In OpenCL, task graph creation is through event objects. OpenCL's event model allows the construction of complicated graphs linking the tasks enqueued in any of the command queues associated with a given OpenCL context. A single event can be passed as the final parameter to the enqueue functions, and this event encapsulates the state of that enqueued command. Most important, the event registers the completion of the task along with the guarantee that all memory referenced by the task is consistent. A list of events can be passed to an enqueue function as a dependence list. This means that the command will not begin executing until all of the input events have completed. The following code is a repeat of the previous example, with an out-of-order queue and all dependencies explicitly defined. Figure 5.3 represents the same command sequence diagrammatically. As one can see in the example, a third approach for synchronizing with the host is to use an event directly. In this case, we see that we have called wait() on the read event:

```
// Perform setup of platform, context and create buffers
...
// Create queue leaving parameters as default so queue is in-order
queue = clCreateCommandQueue( context, devices[0], 0, 0);
...

cl_event writeEventA;
cl_event writeEventB;
cl_event kernelEvent;
cl_event readEvent;

clEnqueueWriteBuffer(
    queue,
    bufferA,
    CL_TRUE,
    0,
```

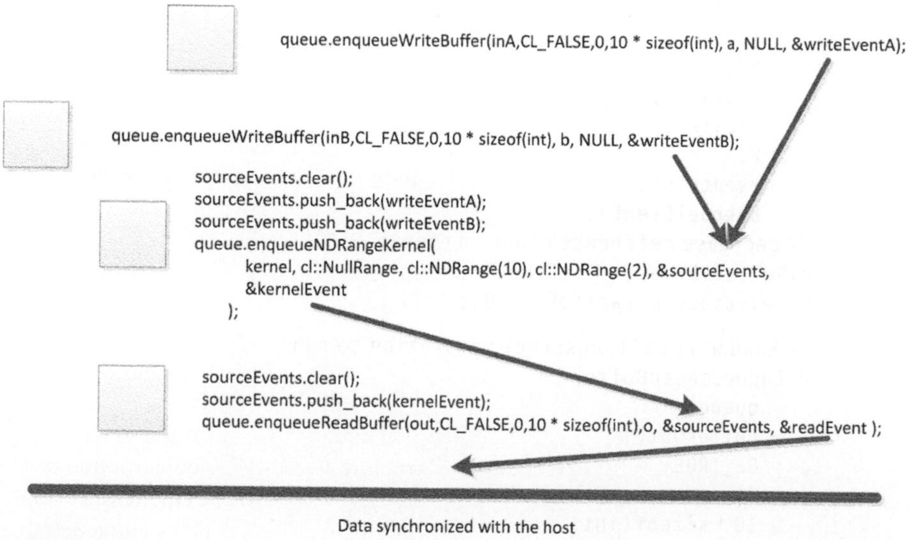

```
queue.enqueueWriteBuffer(inA,CL_FALSE,0,10 * sizeof(int), a, NULL, &writeEventA);

queue.enqueueWriteBuffer(inB,CL_FALSE,0,10 * sizeof(int), b, NULL, &writeEventB);

sourceEvents.clear();
sourceEvents.push_back(writeEventA);
sourceEvents.push_back(writeEventB);
queue.enqueueNDRangeKernel(
    kernel, cl::NullRange, cl::NDRange(10), cl::NDRange(2), &sourceEvents,
    &kernelEvent
);

sourceEvents.clear();
sourceEvents.push_back(kernelEvent);
queue.enqueueReadBuffer(out,CL_FALSE,0,10 * sizeof(int),o, &sourceEvents, &readEvent );
```

Data synchronized with the host

FIGURE 5.3

One enqueued command can depend on a set of enqueued commands through the events passed to the respective enqueue functions.

```
            10 * sizeof(int),
            a,
            0,
            NULL,
            &writeEventA);
    clEnqueueWriteBuffer(
            queue,
            bufferB,
            CL_TRUE,
            0,
            10 * sizeof(int),
            b,
            0,
            NULL,
            &writeEventB);

    // Set kernel arguments

    ...
    size_t localws[1] = {2}; size_t globalws[1] = {10};

    // Wait on both writes before executing the kernel
    cl_event eventList[2];
    eventList[0] = writeEventA;
    eventList[1] = writeEventB;
    clEnqueueNDRangeKernel(
            queue,
            kernel,
            1,
            NULL,
            globalws,
            localws,
            2,
            eventList,
            &kernelEvent);
    // Decrease reference count on events
    clReleaseEvent(writeEventA);
    clReleaseEvent(writeEventB);

    // Read will wait on kernel completion to run
    clEnqueueReadBuffer(
            queue,
            bufferOut,
            CL_TRUE,
            0,
            10 * sizeof(int),
            out,
            1,
            &kernelEvent,
            &readEvent);
```

```
clReleaseEvent(kernelEvent);

// Block until the read has completed
clWaitForEvents(1, &readEvent);
clReleaseEvent(readEvent);
```

Command Queues to Multiple Devices

Understanding the synchronization capabilities and the host memory model of OpenCL is necessary for the management of multiple command queues. Multiple queues can be mapped to the same device to overlap execution of different commands or overlap commands and host–device communication. If we have multiple devices in a system (e.g., a CPU and a GPU or multiple GPUs), each device needs its own command queue.

Figure 5.4 shows an OpenCL context with two devices. Separate command queues are created to access each device. The following code shows how two command queues can be created within the same context. It is important to note that synchronization using OpenCL events can only be done for commands within the same context. If separate contexts were created for different devices, then synchronization using events would not be possible, and the only way to share data between devices would be to use `clFinish` and then explicitly copy data between buffer objects.

```
cl_uint num_devices;
cl_device_id devices[2];
cl_context ctx;

//Obtain devices of both CPU and GPU types
```

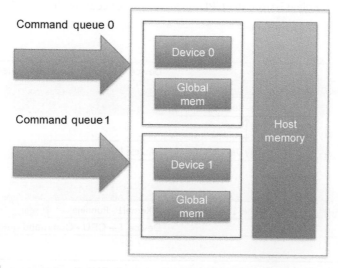

FIGURE 5.4

Multiple command queues created for different devices declared within the same context.

```
err_code = clGetDeviceIDs(
    NULL,
    CL_DEVICE_TYPE_CPU,
    1,
    &devices[0],
    &num_devices);
err_code = clGetDeviceIDs(
    NULL,
    CL_DEVICE_TYPE_GPU,
    1,
    &devices[1],
    &num_devices);
//Create a context including two devices
ctx = clCreateContext(0, 2, devices, NULL, NULL, &err);
cl_command_queue queue_cpu, queue_gpu;

//Create queues to each device
queue_cpu = clCreateCommandQueue(context, devices[0], 0, &err);
queue_gpu = clCreateCommandQueue(context, devices[1], 0, &err);
```

Multiple device programming with OpenCL can be summarized with two execution models usually seen in parallel programming for heterogeneous devices:

- Two or more devices work in a pipeline manner such that one device waits on the results of another, shown in Figure 5.5.
- A model in which multiple devices work independently of each other, shown in Figure 5.6.

In the following code, the wait list orders execution such that the kernel on the GPU queue will complete before the CPU queue begins executing the kernel:

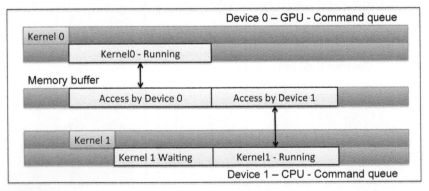

FIGURE 5.5

Multiple devices working in a cooperative manner on the same data. The CPU queue will wait until the GPU kernel is finished.

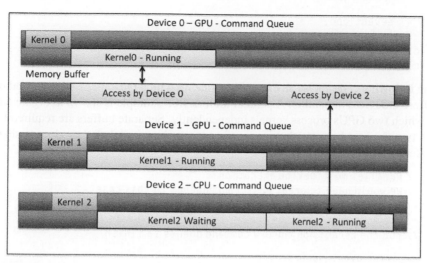

FIGURE 5.6

Multiple devices working in a parallel manner. In this scenario, both GPUs do not use the same buffers and will execute independently. The CPU queue will wait until both GPU devices are finished.

```
//! A collaborative - pipelined model of multidevice execution
//! The enqueued kernel on the GPU command queue waits for the kernel on
the CPU
//! command queue to finish executing
cl_event event0_cpu, event1_gpu;

// Starts as soon as enqueued
err = clEnqueueNDRangeKernel(
    queue_gpu,
    kernel1_gpu,
    2,
    NULL,
    global,
    local,
    0,
    NULL,
    &event_gpu);
// Starts after event_gpu is on CL_COMPLETE
err = clEnqueueNDRangeKernel(
    queue_cpu,
    kernel2_cpu,
    2,
    NULL,
    global,
    local,
    1,
```

```
        &event_gpu,
        &event_cpu);
clFlush(queue_cpu);
clFlush(queue_gpu);
```

The following code shows an execution model in which the kernels are executed on different devices in parallel. A parallel multidevice example is shown in Figure 5.6, in which two GPUs process kernels independently. Separate buffers are required for the two devices because they can only execute in parallel if they do not share buffers.

```
// Parallel multidevice execution
// We would need to create 3 command queues in this case
// 2 queues for 2 GPUs and 1 queue for the CPU
// The enqueued kernel on the CPU command queue waits
// for the kernels on the GPU command queues to finish

cl_event event_gpu[2];

// Both the GPU devices can execute concurrently as soon as they have
// their respective data since they have no events in their waitlist
err = clEnqueueNDRangeKernel(
    queue_gpu_0,
    kernel_gpu,
    2,
    NULL,
    global,
    local,
    0,
    NULL,
    &event_gpu[0]);
err = clEnqueueNDRangeKernel(
    queue_gpu_1,
    kernel_gpu,
    2,
    NULL,
    global,
    local,
    0,
    NULL,
    &event_gpu[1]);
// The CPU will wait till both GPUs are done executing their kernels
// Two events in the CPU's waitlist
err = clEnqueueNDRangeKernel(
    queue_cpu,
    kernel_cpu,
    2,
    NULL,
    global,
```

```
            local,
            2,
            event_gpu,
            NULL);

    clFlush(queue_gpu_0);
    clFlush(queue_gpu_1);
    clFlush(queue_cpu);
```

Event Uses beyond Synchronization

Due to the asynchronous nature of the OpenCL API, there is no good way for individual API calls to return error conditions or profiling data that relates to the execution of the OpenCL command rather than the setup of the queue performed by the enqueue function. Whereas the API calls can return error conditions relating to their parameters, error conditions relating to the execution of the OpenCL command itself can be queried through the event the command returns. Indeed, completion can be considered a condition similar to any other.

Event queries are performed through the getInfo function on an event. The following concepts can be queried through getInfo:

- CL_EVENT_COMMAND_QUEUE: Returns the command queue associated with the event (useful if events are being passed around a complicated program).
- CL_EVENT_CONTEXT: Returns the context associated with the event.
- CL_EVENT_COMMAND_TYPE: Returns the command associated with the event. This can be one of a list of types, including CL_COMMAND_NDRANGE_KERNEL and CL_COMMAND_READ_BUFFER.
- CL_EVENT_COMMAND_EXECUTION_STATUS: Returns the status of the command associated with the event. CL_COMPLETE is the event we wait on with event.wait(), but the command can be queued, submitted, or running as well. A negative integer value in this field is the method by which error codes that only arise when the command tries to execute are returned.

If the context was created with profiling enabled, event.getProfilingInfo allows the developer to obtain timing information from the command. Profiling with events is discussed in Chapter 13.

User Events

User events are OpenCL's method for allowing the user to enqueue commands that depend on the completion of some arbitrary task. The user event can be passed to OpenCL enqueue functions like any other event, but the execution status of the event is set explicitly.

For example, to ensure that a buffer is not overwritten by an asynchronous OpenCL read operation until the buffer is no longer in use, we could do something such as the following:

```
    cl_event userEvent = clCreateUserEvent( context 0 );
    clEnqueueReadBuffer(
```

```
        queue,
        bufferOut,
        CL_TRUE,
        0,
        10 * sizeof(int),
        out,
        1,
        &userEvent,
        0);

// Do other things
...

// Make sure that the host pointer bufferOut is safe to overwrite
// at this point because it has been used on the host side
clSetUserEventStatus( userEvent, CL_COMPLETE );

// Now the read buffer operation can continue because
// its dependencies are satisfied
```

Event Callbacks

OpenCL allows a user to define callbacks invoked when events reach specific states. The callback function will be invoked for a specified execution status of a command in the queue. Event callbacks can be used to enqueue new commands. Callbacks can also be used to invoke host functions such as specialized CPU libraries. The clSetEventCallback function call is used to set a callback for an event:

```
// Function call to set an event callback
cl_int clSetEventCallback (
    //OpenCL event
    cl_event event,
    //Event Status which invokes callback
    cl_int command_exec_callback_type,
    //Function pointer - parameter type shown
    void (CL_CALLBACK *pfn_event_notify)
        (cl_event event,
         cl_int event_command_exec_status,
         void *user_data),
    //Pointer to user data which is used by callback
    void *user_data )
```

A usage scenario of OpenCL callbacks (Figure 5.7) includes applications in which the host CPU interacts tightly with a device such as a GPU. In such applications, usually the host would have to wait while the device is executing. This could reduce the system's efficiency. An alternative method would be to set a callback to a stub host function. The host could improve its efficiency by doing other work instead of spinning while waiting on the GPU.

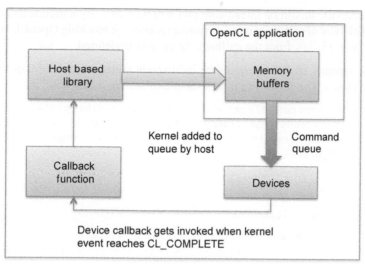

FIGURE 5.7

Using callbacks to enqueue data to device.

The location of the clSetEventCallback is key in the following code segment. The function call is required after the clEnqueueNDRangeKernel because the clSetEvent Callback function requires a valid event object that gets populated by the runtime.

The following code will return with an invalid event error code because the runtime has not populated an event with valid information when the callback is being set up:

```
cl_event completionEvent;
// Wrong location to set callback in
errcode = clSetEventCallback(
    completionEvent,
    CL_COMPLETE,
    myCallback,
    (void *)&ipargs);
// clSetEventCallback will return an invalid event error code
errcode = clEnqueueNDRangeKernel(command_queue,
    kernel,
    2,
    0,
    globalworksize,
    localworksize,
    &completionEvent);
```

Callbacks should be used with caution for the following reasons, as highlighted by the OpenCL specification:

- There is no guarantee that the callback functions registered for multiple execution status for the same event will be called in the exact order that the execution status of a command changes.

- The callback should be thread-safe and will be called asynchronously.
- The behavior of calling expensive system routines, or blocking OpenCL API calls such as `clFinish` from the callback function is undefined.

For these reasons, callbacks should be lightweight stubs, which call more complicated functions. The following is an example of setting a callback:

```
// The callback can only get a single void* user_data pointer.
// As a work around, a programmer can pass multiple
// arguments by wrapping them within a structure as shown
struct arg_block{
      data_type arg0;
      data_type arg1;
};
cl_event completionEvent;

//! Simple example showing declaration of a callback
//! The callback function can only have the signature shown below
void CL_CALLBACK
callbackFunction(
    cl_event event,
    cl_int cmd_exec_status,
    void *user_data) {
    //Use this function to invoke a host Library
    arg_block * ipargs = (arg_block * )user_data;
    //Call host function
    host_function(arg_block.arg0, arg_block.arg1);
}

//!Start Device computation
errcode = clEnqueueNDRangeKernel(
    command_queue,
    kernel,
    2,
    0,
    globalworksize,
    localworksize,
    0,
    NULL
    &completionEvent);

// Set the callback such that callbackFunction is called when
// completionEvent indicates that the kernel
// has completed (CL_COMPLETE)
errcode = clSetEventCallback(
    completionEvent,
    CL_COMPLETE,
    callbackFunction,
    (void *)&ipargs);
```

One of the primary benefits of using the event-handling capabilities of OpenCL is that application-level behavior and synchronization requirements can be handled in a consistent manner on both CPU and GPU for multiple vendor implementations. This restricts device-specific tuning to only the compute kernels.

Native Kernels

An alternative to callbacks that is more cleanly integrated into the OpenCL execution model is to use native kernels. Native kernels allow standard C functions compiled with a traditional compiler rather than the OpenCL compiler flow to be executed within the OpenCL task graph, be triggered by events, and trigger further events.

The difference between enqueuing a native kernel and enqueuing a kernel is that rather than taking a `cl_kernel` object as an argument, the native kernel enqueue function, `clEnqueueNativeKernel`, takes a function pointer to a standard C function. The argument list is provided separately along with its size. Because OpenCL uses buffer and image objects, these are passed as kernel arguments, and it is useful to be able to pass these to native functions. This process is called unboxing, and it is handled by passing in a list of memory objects, in the argument `mem_list`, and a list of pointers, `args_mem_loc`, mapping into `args` where the unboxed memory pointers will be placed.

To illustrate the point, consider the following example, in which a native function expects an argument list containing five values, where the 0 and 2 indexes are set to integers 5 and 8, respectively, and the 1, 3, and 4 indexes are two buffer objects and an image object. This is shown in Figure 5.8. The corresponding code is as follows:

```
cl_command_queue queue = clCreateCommandQueue(...);
cl_mem buffer1         = clCreateBuffer(...);
cl_mem buffer2         = clCreateBuffer(...);
cl_mem image           = clCreateImage2D(...);

// initialize buffers, images, and so on

size_t cb_args = 5;
num_mem_objects = 3;
void *args[5] = { (void *)5, NULL, (void *)8, NULL, NULL };

cl_mem mem_list[3] = { buffer1, buffer2, image};
void * args_mem_loc[3] = { &args[1], &args[3], &args[4] };
```

Finally, given a native function void `foo(void * args)`, we can call `clEnqueueNativeKernel`:

```
clEnqueueNativeKernel(
    queue,
    foo,
```

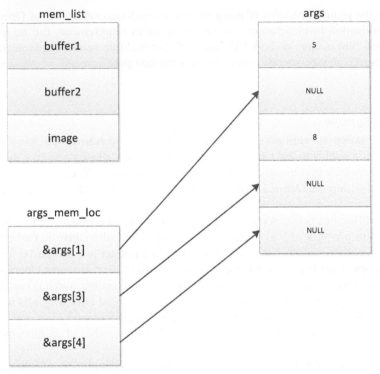

FIGURE 5.8

Example showing OpenCL memory objects mapping to arguments for `clEnqueue NativeKernel`.

```
args,
cb_args,
num_mem_objects,
mem_list,
args_mem_loc,
0,
NULL,
NULL);
```

Command Barriers and Markers

An alternative method of synchronizing in an out-of-order queue is similar to the approach for synchronizing within a workgroup. In both cases, a barrier operation causes anything executing from the queue before the barrier to complete until activities after the queue can continue. A barrier includes no state and does not support an event of its own but sits in a queue guaranteeing ordering. A barrier is conceptually similar to calling `clWaitForEvents` from the host, but is managed internally to the runtime. Barriers are enqueued using the `clEnqueueBarrier WithWaitList` command, that takes a list of events to wait on. If no events are provided the barrier waits for completion of all preceeding commands in the command queue.

Markers are similar to barriers and are enqueued with the matching `clEnqueue MarkerWithWaitList` command. The difference between a barrier and a marker is that the marker does not block the execution of subsequent commands in the queue but simply triggers an event when its dependencies are satisfied.

Between these synchronization commands and the more general use of events, OpenCL provides the ability to produce sophisticated and complicated task graphs enabling highly complicated behaviors.

THE HOST-SIDE MEMORY MODEL

OpenCL devices such as GPUs and other accelerators frequently operate with memory systems separate from the main memory associated with the computer's primary CPUs. In addition, OpenCL's concurrency model supports a relaxed consistency in which global synchronization of memory is only defined on the completion of events and local synchronization on barrier operations. To support both of these features, OpenCL's memory objects are defined to be in a separate space from the host CPU's memory. Any movement of data in and out of OpenCL memory objects from a CPU pointer must be performed through API functions. It is important to note that OpenCL's memory objects are defined on a context and not on a device. That is, in general, moving data in and out of a buffer need not move data to any specific device. It is the job of the runtime to ensure that data is in the correct place at the correct time.

OpenCL's memory objects are divided into two types, where specific placement, layout, and format of these two types are defined by parameters. The two types of objects defined in the OpenCL specification are buffers and images.

Buffer objects are one-dimensional arrays in the traditional CPU sense and similar to memory allocated through `malloc` in a C program. Buffers can contain any scalar data type, vector data type, or user-defined structure. The data stored in a buffer is sequential, such that the OpenCL kernel can access it using pointers in a random access manner familiar to a C programmer.

Image objects take a different approach. Because GPUs are designed for processing graphics workloads, they are heavily optimized for accessing image data. This works in three main ways:

- GPU cache hierarchies and data flow structures are designed to optimize access to image-type data.

- GPU drivers optimize data layouts to support the hardware in providing efficient access to the data, particularly when using two-dimensional access patterns.
- Image access hardware supports sophisticated data conversions that allow data to be stored in a range of compressed formats.

The data layout transformations involved in optimizing image access make it difficult to define pointer access to this data because the relationship of one memory location to another becomes opaque to the developer. As a result, image structures are completely opaque not only to the developer but also to the kernel code, accessible only through specialized access functions.

Buffers

Buffer objects map very easily to the standard array representation that people expect in the host C program. Consider the following host code, which is legal C:

```
float a[10], b[10];
for( int i = 0; i < 10; ++i ){
    *(a+i) = b[i];
}
```

The example shows that we can access *a* and *b* either through pointers or using array access syntax. This is important because it implies that data is allocated sequentially, such that the *i*th element a[i] of array a is stored at location (a + i).

We can use sizeof operations on array elements to calculate offsets into arrays cast to pointers of different types. In low-level code, it is useful to have these features, and it is a natural expectation for a C-derived language. For example, the following OpenCL kernel code, taken from the Bullet physics SDK, allows us to perform flexible output into a vertex buffer by parameterizing with base pointer and strides. The position and normal arrays we receive are float4 in structure, and the output is a structure containing the position and normal information as well as other content that the kernel need not know about.

```
__kernel void OutputToVertexArray(
    const int startNode,
    const int numNodes,
    __global float *g_vertexBuffer,
    const int positionOffset,
    const int positionStride,
    const __global float4* g_vertexPositions,
    const int normalOffset,
    const int normalStride,
    const __global float4* g_vertexNormals ){

    int nodeID = get_global_id(0);
    float4 position = g_vertexPositions[nodeID + startNode];
    float4 normal = g_vertexNormals[nodeID + startNode];
```

```
int positionDestination =
    nodeID * positionStride + positionOffset;
g_vertexBuffer[positionDestination]   = position.x;
g_vertexBuffer[positionDestination+1] = position.y;
g_vertexBuffer[positionDestination+2] = position.z;

int normalDestination = nodeID * normalStride + normalOffset;
g_vertexBuffer[normalDestination]   = normal.x;
g_vertexBuffer[normalDestination+1] = normal.y;
g_vertexBuffer[normalDestination+2] = normal.z;
}
```

Manipulating Buffer Objects

Buffer objects are similar to malloc'd arrays, so their creation is relatively simple. At the simplest level, creation requires a size, a context in which to create the buffer, and a set of creation flags:

```
cl_mem clCreateBuffer(
    cl_context context,
    cl_mem_flags flags,
    size_t size,
    void *host_ptr,
    cl_int *err)
```

The function returns a buffer object, where the error code is returned through a variable passed by reference as the last parameter. The flags allow for various combinations of read-only/write-only data and allocation options. For example, in the following code, we create a read-only buffer that will be stored directly in a source array a, which is of the same size as the buffer. Note that memory in OpenCL is only guaranteed to be consistent at completion events of enqueued operations. As a result, when CL_MEM_USE_HOST_PTR is used, the runtime is still able to copy the data to the device, execute, and return it on completion because the data is guaranteed to have been synchronized after the kernel completion event. Any error value will be returned in err, which can be any of a range of error conditions defined in the specification. CL_SUCCESS is returned by any of the OpenCL functions when they complete successfully.

```
cl_int err;
int a[16];
cl_mem newBuffer = clCreateBuffer(
    context,
    CL_MEM_READ_ONLY | CL_MEM_USE_HOST_PTR,
    16*sizeof(int),
    a,
    &err);
if( err != CL_SUCCESS ) {
    // Do whatever error test is necessary
}
```

After creation, access to buffer objects is achieved through access functions. These functions are intended, like the rest of the OpenCL API, to be used asynchronously. That is, if we call clEnqueueReadBuffer, we cannot expect to be able to read the data from the target host array until we know—through the event mechanism, a clFinish call, or by passing CL_TRUE to clEnqueueReadBuffer to make it a blocking call—that the read has completed. Thus, for example, the following host code sequence does not guarantee that the two printf calls A and B generate different values even if outputBuffer's content would suggest that it should. The printf of C is the only point in the code where the printed value is guaranteed to be that copied from outputBuffer.

```
int returnedArray[16];
cl_buffer outputBuffer;
cl_event readEvent;

// Some code that fills returned Array with 0s and invokes kernels
// that generates a result in outputBuffer

printf( "A: %d\n", returnedArray[3] );
clEnqueueReadBuffer(
    commandQueue,
    outputBuffer,
    CL_FALSE,
    0,
    sizeof(int)*16,
    returnedArray,
    0,
    0,
    &readEvent );
printf( "B: %d\n", returnedArray[3] );
clWaitForEvents(1, &readEvent);
printf( "C: %d\n", returnedArray[3] );
```

This is a vital point about the OpenCL memory model. Changes to memory are not guaranteed to be visible, and hence memory is not guaranteed to be consistent, until an event reports that the execution has completed. This works both ways: In a transfer between a host buffer and a device buffer, you cannot reuse a host buffer until you know that the event associated with the asynchronous copy moving data into the device buffer has completed. Indeed, a careful reading of the OpenCL specification suggests that because buffers are associated with the context and not a device, a clEnqueueWriteBuffer enqueue, even on completion, does not guarantee to have moved the data to the device, only that it be moved out of the host pointer:

> If blocking_write is CL_TRUE, the OpenCL implementation copies the data referred to by ptr and enqueues the write operation in the command-queue. The memory pointed to by ptr can be reused by the application after the clEnqueue-WriteBuffer call returns

> *OpenCL 1.2 specification section 5.2.2*

However, unlike other API calls in OpenCL, the read and write buffer calls allow us to specify synchronous execution. Had we replaced the previous call with

```
clEnqueueReadBuffer(
    commandQueue,
    outputBuffer,
    CL_TRUE,
    0,
    sizeof(int)*16,
    returnedArray,
    0,
    0,
    &readEvent );
```

execution of the host thread would stall at the read buffer call until all execution had completed and the copy had been correctly performed.

OpenCL also supports of sub-buffer objects that allow us to divide a single buffer into multiple smaller buffers that may overlap and that can be read, written, copied, and used in much the same way as their parent buffer objects. Note that overlapping sub-buffers and the combination of sub-buffers and their parent buffer objects constitutes aliasing, and behavior is undefined in these circumstances.

Images

Images differ from buffers in three ways. Images are

- opaque types that cannot be viewed directly through pointers in device code;
- multidimensional structures; and
- limited to a range of types relevant to graphics data rather than being free to implement arbitrary structures.

Image objects exist in OpenCL to offer access to special function hardware on graphics processors that is designed to support highly efficient access to image data. These special function units do not always support the full range of access modes necessary to enable buffer access, but they may provide additional features such as filtering in hardware in a highly efficient manner. Filtering operations enable efficient transformations of image data based on collections of pixels. These operations would require long instruction sequences with multiple read operations and can be very efficiently performed in dedicated hardware units.

Image data is accessed through specialized access functions in the kernel code, as discussed later. Access to images from the host is not significantly different from access to buffers, except that all functions are expanded to support addressing in multiple dimensions. Thus, for example, clEnqueueReadImage is more like clEnqueueReadBufferRect than clEnqueueReadBuffer.

The major difference between buffers and images from the host is in the formats images can support. Whereas buffers support the basic OpenCL types and structures made from them, Image formats are more subtle.

Image formats are a combination of a channel order and a channel type. Channel order defines the number of channels and the order in which they occur—for example, CL_RGB, CL_R, or CL_ARGB. Channel type is selected from a wide range of storage formats from CL_FLOAT to less storage-hungry formats such as CL_UNORM_SHORT_565, which packs into a single 16-bit word in memory. When accessed from kernel code, reading from any of these formats results in upconversion to a standard OpenCL C type. The list of image formats can be queried by the API call clGetSupportedImageFormats.

Images offer an additional feature that enables optimizations in the runtime system and hardware that buffers may often not support. Whereas image data can be mapped to the host using the clEnqueueMapImage API call, and hence image data must have a certain format when viewed through the mapped host pointer, the semantics of the map operation allow for format conversion. This feature of OpenCL data structures enables the runtime system to perform transformations on data that it controls.

Image objects cannot be accessed through pointers on the device and cannot be both read and write within the same kernel. As a result, the transformations that the runtime system performs can be entirely opaque to the kernels executing on the OpenCL device: Transformations can significantly improve performance without affecting code correctness. This feature of images also removes the possibility of aliased data, allowing the hardware to cache images in situations in which buffers cannot be safely cached.

Take one common optimization as an example. Any given multidimensional data structure, of which an image is an example, must be mapped to a single dimensional memory address at some point. The obvious method, and indeed the method applied to multidimensional arrays in most programming languages, is a dictionary order in either column-major or row-major pattern. That is, (x,y) comes before $(x+1,y)$, which comes long before $(x,y+1)$, and so on. The long distance in memory between (x,y) and $(x,y+1)$ means that an access of consecutive addresses in the y-dimension stride inefficiently through memory hitting a large number of cache lines. In contrast, the fact that (x,y) is adjacent to $(x+1,y)$ means consecutive accesses in x stride efficiently (and cause memory accesses to coalesce).

Z-order or Morton order memory layouts apply a mapping that preserves spatial locality of data points. Figure 5.9 shows that the data is stored in order $(0,0), (1,0), (0,1), (1,1), (2,0)$ and so on. By storing data according to its position in a Z-ordered mapping, we may hit the same cache line repeatedly when performing a vertical read. If we go further by laying out our computational work in a two-dimensional layout (as we see with the quads created in the graphics pipeline), we further improve this data locality. This sort of optimization is only possible transparently (and hence different optimizations can be performed on different architectures) if we offer the kernel programmer no guarantees about the relative locations of memory elements.

We can go a step further with this approach. If we are executing on an architecture that does not have vector registers and does not perform vector reads from memory, we might wish float4 a = read_imagef(sourceImage, imageSampler, location)

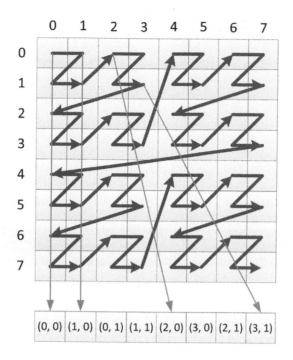

FIGURE 5.9

Applying the Z-order mapping to a two-dimensional memory space.

to compile down to four scalar reads instead of a single vector read. In these circumstances, it might be a more efficient use of the memory system to read from the same offset into four separate arrays instead of four times from the single array because the data in each separate array would exhibit better locality on each individual read operation.

THE DEVICE-SIDE MEMORY MODEL

On OpenCL devices, the memory space is classified into four primary categories:

- Global memory
- Local memory
- Constant memory
- Private memory

These memory spaces are visualized in Figure 5.10. As discussed in Chapter 3, OpenCL is designed to run on a range of architectures. The purpose of arranging a memory hierarchy of this form is to allow OpenCL to perform efficiently on such architectures. The actual meaning of each memory space in terms of a hardware mapping is very much implementation dependent. However they are mapped to hardware, as a

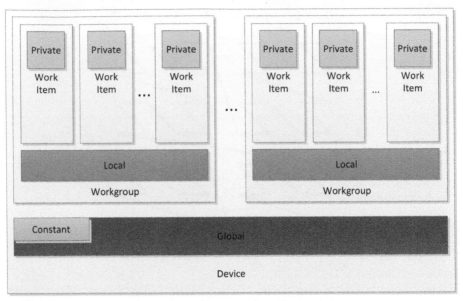

FIGURE 5.10

The OpenCL memory spaces available on an OpenCL device.

programming construct, these memory spaces are disjoint. Furthermore, as shown in Figure 5.10, local and private are divided into disjoint blocks across compute units and work items. By defining separate layers of address space in this way, the mapping to hardware can efficiently use anything from relaxed memory consistency models with programmatically controlled scratchpad buffers as seen on most GPU devices to fully coherent memory systems such as x86-based architectures.

The default address space for function arguments and local variables within a function or block is private. Pointer arguments to functions can be placed in one of the other address spaces depending on where the data comes from or where it is to be used. Note that the pointer itself is always in the private address space wherever the data lies.

The address spaces are strictly disjoint when used through pointers. Casting from one address space to another is not legal because this would imply either that the data lives at a globally accessible address or that the compiler would have to generate a copy to go with the cast, which is not feasible in practice. Image arguments to functions always live in the global address space, so we discuss images in those terms.

Device-Side Relaxed Consistency

OpenCL's relaxed consistency model applies within the kernel as well as between dispatches. Writes to memory are not guaranteed to be visible until the end of the kernel execution unless fence operations are used. As a result, we have a hierarchy of consistency:

- Within a work item, memory operations are ordered predictably: Any two reads and writes to the same address will not be reordered by hardware or the compiler.
- Between work items and within a workgroup, memory is only guaranteed to be consistent at a barrier operation.
- Between workgroups, there are no guarantees about memory consistency until completion of the kernel execution—that is, when the event reports completion.

Given the previous hierarchy, there is no requirement for the compiler to make anything but the last write to a given address visible outside a given work item. To allow some level of communication between work items within and between workgroups, OpenCL provides a set of fence operations. Even with these fences, there are no guarantees of ordering between work items.

Fences come in read, write, and read/write versions:

- `read_mem_fence( cl_mem_fence_flags flags )`
- `write_mem_fence( cl_mem_fence_flags flags )`
- `mem_fence( cl_mem_fence_flags flags )`

In each case, the fence is parameterized with flags specifying the address space it is fencing. The value of these flags is some combination of `CLK_LOCAL_MEM_FENCE` and `CLK_GLOBAL_MEM_FENCE`. The fence ensures that loads and/or stores issued before the fence will complete before any loads and/or stores issued after the fence. No synchronization is implied by the fences alone. The `barrier` operation supports a read/write fence in one or both memory spaces as well as blocking until all work items in a given workgroup reach it.

An alternative approach to ensuring that memory operations are correctly communicated between work items is to use atomic operations. These are particularly useful because they guarantee not only that a write update occurs but also that a read and write combined with some operation on the data occur without interruption from another work item. However, they are only defined on integer data due to the complexity (both in implementation and in comprehension) of performing floating point atomics in most hardware. Atomic operations may be arithmetic operations, such as `int atomic_add( volatile __global int *p, int val )`, and data-only, such as `int atomic_xchg (volatile __global int *p, int val)`. In all cases, the atomic operation returns the original data that was at the memory location. Note that if the return value is ignored, the compiler is at liberty to use nonreturning atomic operations, which are far more efficient on many architectures.

Global Memory

Global memory, defined in OpenCL C code by a pointer with the type qualifier `__global` (or `global`), or by one of the image types `image2d_t` or `image3d_t`, refers to data in a memory space consistently addressable by all compute units in the device. The two types of object differ in their scope and use cases.

The `__global` address space qualifier refers to a pointer referencing data in a buffer object. As noted previously, a buffer can carry any scalar data type, vector data type, or user-defined structure. Whatever the type of buffer, it is accessed at the end of a pointer and can be read/write accessible as well as read-only. Thus, for example, the following trivial operation code is an example of valid use of a buffer:

```
typedef struct AStructure {
    float a;
    float b;
} AStructure;

__kernel void aFunction( __global AStructure *inputOutputBuffer ) {
    __global AStructure* inputLocation =
        inputOutputBuffer + get_global_id(0);
    __global AStructure* outputLocation =
        inputOutputBuffer + get_global_size(0) + get_global_id(0);

    outputLocation->a = inputLocation->a * -1;
    outputLocation->b = (*inputLocation).b + 3.f;
}
```

Image objects, although conceptually in the __global memory space, are treated differently from buffers and are not mappable to __global pointers. Image objects can be one-dimensional, two-dimensional or three-dimensional and created using the image1d_t, image2d_t or image3d_t type qualifiers. Unlike buffers, images can be either read-only or write-only but never both within the same kernel. This is a result of the design of GPU hardware supporting very high-performance caching and filtering. Within kernel code, we specify which form of access we are using with the __read_only and __write_only access qualifiers on kernel image parameters.

Images are opaque memory objects. Although we can read or write the data based on addresses, we do not really know the relative memory locations of two different values in the image. As a result, and to support parameterization of the style of read, rather than accessing images through pointers, we use a set of built-in functions: read_imagef, read_imagei, read_imageui, write_imagef, and so on. Each of the image read functions takes three parameters:

```
float4 read_imagef(
    image2d_t image,
    sampler_t sampler,
    float2 coord)
```

The final address parameter can optionally be an int2 (or int4 if the image is of type image3d_t), and the precise meaning of the returned data depends on the image format. The OpenCL specification lists these options in full.

The first and third parameters to the read functions are self-explanatory, being the image object itself and the coordinate of the read. The second parameter is more complicated. This is a sampler object that defines how the image is interpreted by the hardware or runtime system. The sampler can be defined either by declaring a constant variable of sampler_t type within the OpenCL C source or by passing as a kernel parameter a sampler created in host code using the `clCreateSampler` function. The following is an example of the use of a constant-variable-declared sampler:

```
__constant sampler_t sampler =
    CLK_NORMALIZED_COORDS_TRUE | CLK_FILTER_LINEAR;
__kernel void samplerUser(
    __read_only image2d_t sourceImage,
    __global float *outputBuffer ) {

    float4 a = read_imagef(
        sourceImage,
        sampler,
        (float2)(
            (float)(get_global_id(0)),
            (float)(get_global_id(1))) );
    outputBuffer[
        get_global_id(1) * get_global_size(0) +
        get_global_id(0)] = a.x + a.y + a.z + a.w;
}
```

The value returned in the float4 vector depends on the image format specified on image creation. A `CL_R` image, for example, would only contain data in the x channel with 1.0 in the w (alpha) channel.

The write functions take a similar set of parameters, replacing the sampler with the value to write:

```
float4 write_imagef(image2d_t image, float2 coord, float4 color)
```

Local Memory

A subset of the architectures supported by OpenCL, including many of the GPUs and the Cell broadband engine, possess small scratchpad memory buffers distinct from the primary DRAM and caching infrastructure. Local memory in these cases is disjoint from global memory and often accessed using separate memory operations. As a result, data must be copied in and out of it programmatically. Depending on the architecture, this occurs either through DMA transfers (most efficiently accessed using the `async_work_group_copy` function) or by memory-to-memory copies. Local memory is also supported in CPU implementations, but it sits in standard cacheable memory; in such cases, use of local memory can still be beneficial because it encourages cache-aware programming.

Local memory is most useful because it provides the most efficient method of communication between work items in a workgroup. Any allocated local memory buffer can be accessed at any location by an entire workgroup and hence writes to the local array will be visible to other work items. Remember that OpenCL work items are conceptually, if not literally, executed independently.

Local memory is defined by the `__local` address space qualifier and can be defined either locally in the kernel or as a parameter. Both examples are shown in the following code:

```
__kernel void localAccess(
    __global float* A,
    __global float* B,
    __local float* C )
{
    __local float aLocalArray[1];

    if( get_local_id(0) == 0 ) {
        aLocalArray[0] = A[0];
    }
    C[get_local_id(0)] = A[get_global_id(0)];

    barrier( CLK_LOCAL_MEM_FENCE );

    float neighborSum = C[get_local_id(0)] + aLocalArray[0];

    if( get_local_id(0) > 0 )
        neighborSum = neighborSum + C[get_local_id(0)-1];

    B[get_global_id(0)] = neighborSum;
}
```

Figure 5.11 shows a diagrammatic representation of the data flow in the previous code sample. Note that data will be read from global memory and written to the two local arrays C and aLocalArray at unpredictable times as the work items execute independently in an undefined order. The reality will be slightly more predictable on

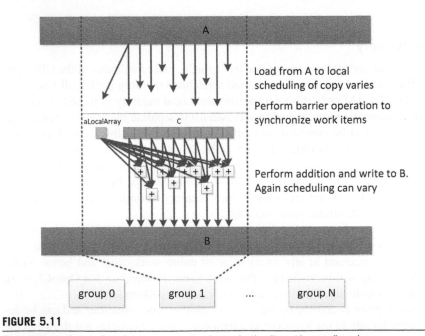

FIGURE 5.11

The pattern of data flow for the example shown in the "localAccess" code.

a given device because implementations will map to hardware in predictable ways. For example, on the AMD GPUs, execution occurs in lock-step over a wide SIMD vector, meaning that the read and write operations will have an ordering guarantee over the entire vector in the same way that they would over a single work item. However, this feature does not apply generally. In the general case, we must insert the barrier operation: Only at this barrier can we guarantee that all writes to local arrays, and the global memory reads that fed them, will have been completed across the workgroup such that the data is visible to all work items. Beyond this barrier, the data can be used by the entire workgroup as shown in the lower part of the diagram.

aLocalArray is at function scope lexically but is visible to the entire workgroup. That is, there is only one 32-bit variable in local memory per workgroup, and any work item in the group using the name aLocalArray has access to the same 32-bit value. In this case, after the barrier we know that work item 0 has written to aLocalArray and hence all work items in the group can now read from it.

The alternative method for creating local arrays is through a kernel parameter, as we see for array C. This version is created by a runtime API call. To allocate the memory, we call clSetKernelArg as we would for passing a global array to the kernel, but we leave the final pointer field as 0. We therefore allocate a per-workgroup amount of memory based on the third parameter but with no global object to back it up so it sits in local memory:

```
ciErrNum = clSetKernelArg(
    kernel object,
    parameter index,
    size in bytes,
    0);
```

Constant Memory

The constant address space, described by the __constant qualifier, intends to cleanly separate small sets of constant values from the global address space such that the runtime can allocate caching resources or efficient constant memory banks if possible. Data allocated in the constant address space is passed to the kernel using clSetKernelArg and can be accessed through a pointer from within the kernel. Architectures differ in how they treat this data. For example, the AMD Radeon™ HD 6970 is designed to support three types of constant data:

- Direct address: The address of the data is constant and can be embedded into the instruction. This is very fast, 16 bytes/cycle/core, because data can be placed in hardware constant buffers.
- Same index: The address is the same across an entire wavefront; 4 bytes/cycle/core.
- Varying index: Treated as global memory and may be cached through L1.

OpenCL defines a limited number of constant arguments for each device that, along with the constant buffer size, can be queried with CL_DEVICE_MAX_CONSTANT_ARGS and CL_DEVICE_MAX_CONSTANT_BUFFER_SIZE arguments to clDeviceInfo arguments.

To pass a __constant buffer to a kernel, the buffer must be allocated using the CL_MEM_READ_ONLY flag.

Private Memory

Private memory refers to all variables not declared with an address space qualifier, all variables within nonkernel functions, and all function arguments that are not pointers. In principle, private data may be placed in registers, but due to either a lack of capacity spilling or an inability for the hardware to dynamically index register arrays, data may be pushed back into global memory. The amount of private memory allocated directly impacts on the number of registers used by the kernel.

Like local memory, a given architecture will have a limited number of registers. The performance impact of using too large a number will vary from one architecture to another.

x86 CPUs have a relatively small number of registers. However, due to large caches, the operations of pushing these registers to memory on the stack and returning them to registers later often incur little overhead. Variables can be efficiently moved in and out of scope, keeping only the most frequently used data in registers.

GPUs do not generally have the luxury of using a cache in this way. Many devices do not have read/write caches, and those that do may be limited in size and hence spilling registers from a large number of work items would rapidly lead to filling this cache, leading to stalling on a miss when the data is required again. Spilling to DRAM on such a device causes a significant performance degradation and is best avoided.

When not spilling registers, the capacity of the register bank of a GPU trades against the number of active threads in a similar manner to that of LDS. The AMD Radeon HD 6970 architecture has 256 kB of registers on each compute unit. This is 256 four-vector (128-bit) registers per work item in a 64-wide wavefront. If we use 100 registers per work item, only two waves will fit on the hardware, which is not enough to cover anything more than instruction latency. If we use 49 registers per work item, we can fit five waves, which helps with latency hiding.

Moving data into registers may appear to improve performance, but if the cost is that one fewer wavefront can execute on the core, less latency hiding occurs and we may see more stalls and more wasted GPU cycles.

SUMMARY

In this chapter, we discussed the consistency, concurrency, and synchronization of OpenCL programs. OpenCL follows a relaxed execution and consistency model to aid efficient implementation on as wide a range of architectures as possible. In later chapters, we consider how the execution model maps to some specific architectures and then discuss case studies that give some idea of how to optimize an OpenCL program to use the hardware efficiently.

Dissecting a CPU/GPU OpenCL Implementation

6

INTRODUCTION

In Chapter 3, we discussed trade-offs present in different architectures, many of which support the execution of OpenCL programs. The design of OpenCL is such that the model maps capably to a wide range of architectures, allowing for tuning and acceleration of kernel code. In this chapter, we discuss OpenCL's mapping to a real system in the form of a high-end AMD CPU combined with an AMD Radeon HD7970 GPU. Although AMD systems have been chosen to illustrate this mapping and implementation, each respective vendor has implemented a similar mapping for NVIDIA GPUs, Intel/ARM CPUs, and any OpenCL-compliant architecture.

OPENCL ON AN AMD BULLDOZER CPU

AMD's OpenCL implementation is designed to run on both AMD GPUs and AMD's x86 CPUs in an integrated manner. All host code executes as would be expected on the general-purpose x86 CPUs in a machine, along with operating system and general application code. However, AMD's OpenCL implementation is also capable of compiling and executing OpenCL C code on x86 devices using the queuing mechanisms provided by the OpenCL runtime.

OpenCL can run on each of the eight cores of an AMD FX-8150 chip within the larger system. Figure 6.1 shows a diagram of the FX-8150 design.

In Figure 6.2, OpenCL is mapped onto this architecture. The entire chip is consumed by the OpenCL runtime as a single device that is obtained using clGetDeviceIDs and is passed to clCreateContext and clBuildProgram. The CPU device requires the CL_DEVICE_TYPE_CPU flag to be passed to the device types parameter of clGetDeviceIDs.

By treating the entire CPU as a single device, parallel workloads can be spread across the CPU cores from a single queue, efficiently using the parallelism present in the system. It is possible to split the CPU into multiple devices using the device fission extension that is discussed in a later chapter.

The OpenCL CPU runtime creates a thread to execute on each core of the CPU as a work pool to process OpenCL kernels as they are generated. These threads are

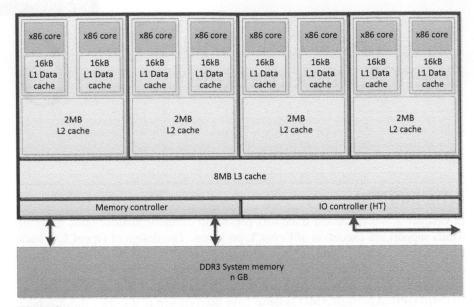

FIGURE 6.1

AMD FX-8150 CPU eight cores in four dual-core modules and a large level 3 cache.

passed work by a core management thread for each queue that has the role of removing the first entry from the queue and setting up work for the worker threads. Any given OpenCL kernel may comprise thousands of workgroups for which arguments must be appropriately prepared, memory allocated, and, if necessary, initialized and work queues generated.

OpenCL utilizes barriers and fences to support fine-grained synchronization. On a typical CPU-based system, in which the operating system is responsible for managing interthread communication, the cost of interacting with the operating system is a barrier to achieving efficient scaling of parallel implementations. In addition, running a single workgroup across multiple cores could create cache-sharing issues. To alleviate these issues, the OpenCL CPU runtime executes a workgroup within a single operating system thread. The OpenCL thread will run each work item in the workgroup in turn before moving onto the next work item. After all work items in the workgroup have finished executing, the worker thread will move on to the next workgroup in its work queue. As such, there is no parallelism between multiple work items within a workgroup, although between workgroups multiple operating system threads allow parallel execution when possible.

In the presence of barrier synchronization, OpenCL work items within a single workgroup execute concurrently. Each work item in the group must complete the section of the code that precedes the barrier operation, wait for other work items

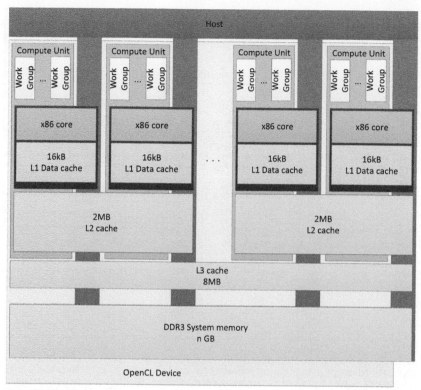

FIGURE 6.2

The OpenCL mapping to the FX8150 chip. Note that the host runs on the same cores that represent the OpenCL device's compute units.

to reach the barrier, and then continue execution. At the barrier operation, one work item must terminate and another continue; however, it is impractical for performance reasons to let the operating system handle this with *thread preemption* (i.e., interrupting one thread to allow another to run). Indeed, as the entire workgroup is running within a single thread, preemption would not be meaningful. In AMD's OpenCL CPU runtime, barrier operations are supported using `setjmp` and `longjmp`. `setjmp` stores system state and `longjmp` restores it by returning to the system state at the point where `setjmp` was called (Gummaraju *et al.*, 2010). The runtime provides custom versions of these two functions because they need to work in cooperation with the hardware branch predictor and maintain proper program stack alignment.

An example of using a barrier in kernel `foo()` is shown in Figure 6.3. Note that although a CPU thread eventually executes multiple workgroups, it will complete one workgroup at a time before moving on to the next. When a barrier is involved, it will execute every work item of that group up to the barrier, then every work item

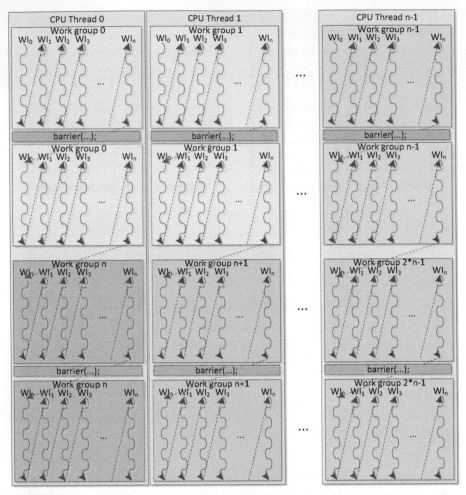

FIGURE 6.3

An OpenCL worker thread processes an entire workgroup one work item at a time. At a barrier or the end of the kernel, the thread transitions to the next work item.

after the barrier, hence providing correct barrier semantics and re-establishing concurrency, if not parallelism, between work items in a single workgroup.

```
__kernel foo(){
    ...
    barrier(CLK_GLOBAL_MEM_FENCE);
    ...
}
```

The AMD Bulldozer microarchitecture includes 128-bit vector registers and operations from various Streaming SIMD Extension (SSE) and Advanced Vector Extension (AVX) versions.[1] OpenCL C includes a set of vector types: float2, float4, int4, and other data formats. Mathematical operations are *overloaded*[2] on these vector types, enabling the following operations:

```
float4 a = input_data[location];
float4 b = a + (float4)(0.f, 1.f, 2.f, 3.f);
output_data[location] = b;
```

These vector types are stored in vector registers and operations on them compile to SSE and AVX instructions on the AMD Bulldozer architecture. This offers an important performance optimization. Vector load and store operations, as we also see in our low-level code discussions, improve the efficiency of memory operations. Currently, access to SIMD vectors is entirely explicit within a single work item: We will see how this model differs on AMD GPU devices when we discuss a GPU in the next section.

The AMD Bulldozer design does not provide dedicated hardware for scratchpad memory buffers. CPUs typically provide multiple levels of memory caching in order to hide main memory access latency. The data localization provided by local memory supports efficient mapping onto the CPU cache hierarchy and allows the kernel developer to improve cache performance even in the absence of a true hardware scratchpad. To improve cache locality, local memory regions are allocated as an array per CPU thread and reused for each workgroup executed by that thread. For a sequence of workgroups, barring any data races or memory conflicts, there is then no need for this local memory to generate further cache misses and, as an additional benefit, there is no overhead from repeated calls to memory allocation routines. Figure 6.4 shows how we would map local memory to the AMD CPU cache.

Work item data stored in registers is backed into a work item stack in main memory during the setjmp call. This memory is carefully laid out to behave well in the cache, reducing cache contention and hence conflict misses and improving the utilization of the cache hierarchy. In particular, the work item stack data is staggered in memory to reduce the chance of conflicts, and data is maintained in large pages to ensure contiguous mapping to physical memory and to reduce pressure on the CPU's translation lookaside buffer.[3]

---

[1] SSE and AVX are a SIMD instruction set extensions to the x86 architecture. Both AMD and Intel have introduced multiple generations of SSE instruction set extensions since 1999 and have supported AVX since 2011.

[2] Overloading is a form of polymorphism that supports reuse of the same function name over multiple parameter types, simplifying code such that only intent is required in the function name rather than intent and parameter type.

[3] A translation lookaside buffer is a hardware table on the CPU that caches virtual to physical memory address translations.

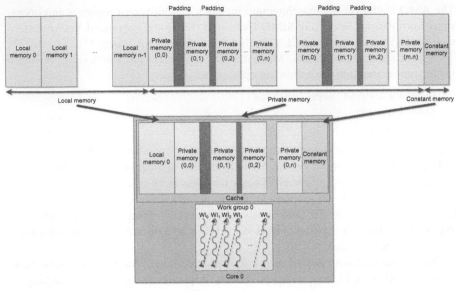

FIGURE 6.4

In the CPU implementation of OpenCL, regions of local, private, and constant memory are stored contiguously for each workgroup and work item. This data will be loaded into the cache hierarchy as contiguous blocks, maintaining cache locality as much as possible while a given workgroup is executing.

OPENCL ON THE AMD RADEON HD7970 GPU

A GPU is a significantly different target for OpenCL code compared with the CPU. The reader must remember that a graphics processor is primarily designed to render three-dimensional graphics efficiently. This goal leads to significantly different prioritization of resources and hence a significantly different architecture from that of the CPU. On current GPUs, this difference comes down to a few main features, of which the following three were discussed in Chapter 3:

- Wide single instruction multiple data (SIMD) execution: A far larger number of execution units execute the same instruction on different data items.
- Heavily multithreading: Support for a large number of concurrent thread contexts on a given GPU compute core.
- Hardware scratchpad memory: Physical memory buffers purely under the programmer's control.

The following are additional differences that are more subtle but interesting because they create opportunities to provide improvements in terms of latency of work dispatch and communication:

- Hardware synchronization support: Supporting fine-grained communication between concurrent hardware threads.

- Hardware managed tasking and dispatch: Work queue management and load balancing in hardware.

Hardware synchronization support reduces the overhead of synchronizing execution of multiple thread contexts on a given SIMD core, enabling fine-grained communication at low cost.

GPUs provide extensive hardware support for task dispatch because of their deep roots in the three-dimensional graphics world. Gaming workloads involve managing complicated task graphs arising from interleaving of work in a graphics pipeline. As shown in the high-level diagram of the AMD Radeon HD7970 in Figure 3.11, the architecture consists of a command processor and group generator at the front that passes constructed groups to a pair of hardware schedulers. These two schedulers arrange compute workloads onto the 32 cores spread throughout the device, each of which contains one scalar unit and four vector units. For graphics workloads, AMD includes a further set of hardware accelerator blocks below the command processor:

- Tesselator: Tessellation is the process of generating smaller triangles from larger ones to scale model complexity at runtime.
- Geometry assembler: Packages geometric information for processing by shaders.
- Rasterizer: Transforms vector data into a raster format.
- Hierarchical Z processor: Maintains a hierarchical representation of the scene depth to reduce load by providing the ability to reject pixels early based on depth.

Together, these units allow the hardware to schedule workloads as shown in Figure 6.5. To obtain the high degrees of performance acceleration associated with

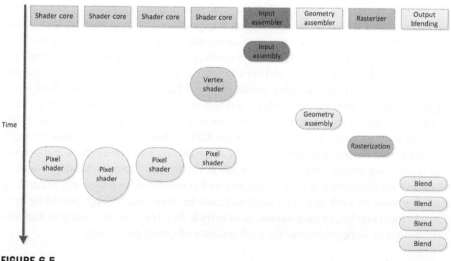

FIGURE 6.5

A hardware-managed schedule for the set of tasks performed on a small unit of GPU work. When many of these work loads are scheduled together, the hardware can be very efficiently utilized.

GPU computing, scheduling must be very efficient. Thread scheduling overhead needs to remain low because the chunks of work assembled by the input assembly may be very small—for example, a single triangle consisting of a few pixels. This amount of work alone would not keep the machine utilized, but remember that the full graphics pipeline is very quickly assembling, rasterizing and shading a large number of triangles concurrently. We can see a simplified version of such a schedule in Figure 6.5. Note that the unutilized compute time depicted by whitespace in the figure will fill out easily when multiple triangles are being processed concurrently. This presents a good example of why the GPU is designed for high-throughput processing and, hence, why workloads need to map properly to the underlying hardware to attain good performance.

For OpenCL, much of this rasterization and assembly hardware is not necessary because dispatches are predefined with large sizes and need only be assembled into appropriate workgroups and hardware threads to launch on the device. However, to allow a deeply pipelined command processor and work generator to work efficiently and to reach high performance levels on a GPU, we need to:

- Provide a lot of work for each kernel dispatch.
- Batch jobs together.

By providing a sufficient amount of work in each kernel, we ensure that the group generation pipeline is kept occupied so that it always has more work to give to the wave schedulers and the schedulers always have more work to push onto the SIMD units. In essence, we wish to create a large number of threads to occupy the machine: As discussed previously, the GPU is a throughput machine.

The second point refers to OpenCL's queuing mechanism. When the OpenCL runtime chooses to process work in the work queue associated with the device, it scans through the tasks in the queue with the aim of selecting an appropriately large chunk to process. From this set of tasks, it constructs a command buffer of work for the GPU in a language understood by the command processor at the front of the GPU's pipeline. This process consists of (1) constructing a queue, (2) locating it somewhere in memory, (3) telling the device where it is, and (4) asking the device to process it. Such a sequence of operations takes time, incurring a relatively high latency for a single block of work. In particular, as the GPU runs behind a driver running in kernel space, this process requires a number of context switches into and out of kernel space to allow the GPU to start running. As in the case of the CPU, where context switches between threads would become a significant overhead, switching into kernel mode and preparing queues for overly small units of work is inefficient. There is a fairly constant overhead for dispatching a work queue and further overhead for processing depending on the amount of work in it. This overhead must be overcome through providing very large kernel launches, or long sequences of kernels. In either case the goal is to increase the amount of work performed for each instance of queue processing.

Threading and the Memory System

Figure 6.6 shows an approximation of the memory hierarchy of a system containing an AMD FX8150 CPU and an AMD Radeon HD7970 GPU. The CPU cache hierarchy in this setup is arranged to reduce latency of a single memory access

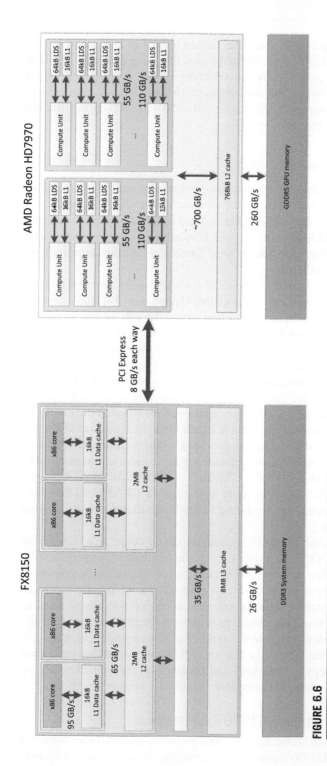

FIGURE 6.6

Approximate bandwidth numbers for the various levels of memory hierarchy on both the AMD FX8150 CPU and the AMD Radeon HD7970 GPU. Note particularly the low bandwidth of the PCI express bus compared with the other levels, particularly the caches, on both sides of the interface.

stream: Any significant latency will cause that stream to stall and reduce execution efficiency. Because the design of the GPU cores uses threading and wide SIMD to maximize throughput at the cost of latency, the memory system is similarly designed to maximize bandwidth to satisfy that throughput, with some latency cost.

The limited caching associated with high-bandwidth GDDR5 on the Radeon design is made possible by the following:

- Local data shares (LDS)
- A high level of on-chip multithreading

LDS allows for high bandwidth and low latency programmer-controlled read/write access. This form of programmable data reuse is less wasteful and also more area/power efficient than hardware-controlled caching. The reduced waste data access (data that is loaded into the cache but not used) means that the LDS can have a smaller capacity than an equivalent cache. In addition, the reduced need for control logic and tag structures result in a smaller area per unit capacity.

Hardware-controlled multithreading in the GPU cores allows the hardware to cover latency to memory. To perform a memory access, a thread running on a SIMD unit is temporarily removed from that unit and placed into a separate memory controller. The thread does not resume on the SIMD until the memory access returns. To reach high levels of performance and utilization, a sufficiently large number of threads must be running. Four or more wavefronts per SIMD unit or 16 per core (Compute Unit) may be necessary in many applications. Each SIMD unit can maintain up to 10 wavefronts, with 40 active across the compute unit. To enable fast switching, wavefront state is maintained in registers, not cache. Each wavefront in flight is consuming resources and so increasing the number of live wavefronts to cover latency must be balanced against register and LDS use.

The caches that are present in the system provide a filtering mechanism to combine complicated gathered read and scattered write access patterns in vector memory operations into the largest possible units. The large vector reads that result from well-structured memory accesses are far more efficient for a DRAM-based system, requiring less temporal caching than the time-distributed smaller reads arising from the most general CPU code.

The diagram in Figure 6.6 shows the PCI Express bus as the connection between the CPU and GPU devices. All traffic between the CPU, and hence main memory, and the GPU must go through this pipe. Because PCI Express bandwidth is significantly lower than access to DRAM and even lower than the capabilities of on-chip buffers, this can become a significant bottleneck on a heavily communication-dependent application. In an OpenCL application, we need to minimize the number and size of memory copy operations relative to the kernels we enqueue. It is difficult to achieve good performance in an application that is expected to run on a discrete GPU if that application has a tight feedback loop involving copying data back and forth across the PCI Express bus. Chapter 7 will discuss data movement optimization tradeoffs in more detail.

Instruction Execution on the HD7970 Architecture

The idea of programming a SIMD architecture using a lanewise model was discussed previously. Within each HD7970 compute unit or core the instruction scheduler may schedule up to 5 instructions on each cycle onto the scalar unit, one of the SIMD units, memory unit or other hardware special function devices.

In previous devices, such as the HD6970 architecture presented in the earlier edition of the book, control flow was managed automatically by a branch unit. This design led to a very specialized execution engine that looked somewhat different from other vector architectures on the market. The HD7970 design is more explicit in integrating scalar and vector code instruction-by-instruction, much as an x86 CPU will when integrating SSE or AVX operations.

The SIMD engine executes 64-wide logical SIMD entities called wavefronts. Each wavefront utilizes a single instruction decode and has its own instruction stream and can be viewed as a separate hardware thread context. The 64 work items within the wavefront execute over four clock cycles over a 16-lane hardware SIMD unit. Different wavefronts execute at different points in their instruction streams. All branching is performed at wavefront granularity.

Any possibility of sub-wavefront (divergent) branching requires restricting of ISA into a sequence of mask and unmask operations. The result is a very explicit sequence of instruction blocks that execute until all necessary paths have been covered. Such execution divergence creates inefficiency as only part of the vector unit is active at any given time, however being able to support such control flow improves the programmability by removing the need for the programmer to manually vectorize code. Very similar issues arise when developing for competing architectures such as NVIDIA's GTX580 design and are inherent in software production for wide vector architectures, whether manually-, compiler-, hardware-vectorized or somewhere in between.

The following is an example of code designed to run on the HD7970 compute unit (see the Southern Islands ISA specification [cite]SI-ISA[/cite]). Let's take a very simple kernel that will diverge on a wavefront of any width greater than one:

```
kernel void foo(const global int* in, global int *out)
{
  if( get_global_id(0) == 0 ) {
    out[get_global_id(0)] = in[get_global_id(0)];
  } else {
    out[get_global_id(0)] = 0;
  }
}
```

While this is a trivial kernel, it will allow us to see how the compile maps this to ISA, and indirectly how that ISA will behave on the hardware. When we compile this for the HD7970 we get the following:

```
shader main
  asic(SI_ASIC)
  type(CS)
  s_buffer_load_dword s0, s[4:7], 0x04
  s_buffer_load_dword s1, s[4:7], 0x18
```

```
s_waitcnt lgkmcnt(0)
s_min_u32 s0, s0, 0x0000ffff
v_mov_b32 v1, s0
v_mul_i32_i24 v1, s12, v1
v_add_i32 v0, vcc, v0, v1
v_add_i32 v0, vcc, s1, v0
s_buffer_load_dword s0, s[8:11], 0x00
s_buffer_load_dword s1, s[8:11], 0x04
v_cmp_eq_i32 s[4:5], v0, 0
s_and_saveexec_b64 s[4:5], s[4:5]
v_lshlrev_b32 v1, 2, v0
s_cbranch_execz label_0016
s_waitcnt lgkmcnt(0)
v_add_i32 v1, vcc, s0, v1
s_load_dwordx4 s[8:11], s[2:3], 0x50
s_waitcnt lgkmcnt(0)
tbuffer_load_format_x v1, v1, s[8:11], 0 offen
        format:[BUF_DATA_FORMAT_32,BUF_NUM_FORMAT_FLOAT]
label_0016:
s_andn2_b64 exec, s[4:5], exec
v_mov_b32 v1, 0
s_mov_b64 exec, s[4:5]
v_lshlrev_b32 v0, 2, v0
s_waitcnt lgkmcnt(0)
v_add_i32 v0, vcc, s1, v0
s_load_dwordx4 s[0:3], s[2:3], 0x58
s_waitcnt vmcnt(0) & lgkmcnt(0)
tbuffer_store_format_x v1, v0, s[0:3], 0 offen
        format:[BUF_DATA_FORMAT_32,BUF_NUM_FORMAT_FLOAT]
s_endpgm
end
```

This code may be viewed, like OpenCL code, to represent a single lane of execution: a single work item. However, unlike the higher level language, here we see a combination of scalar operations, (prefixed with s_) intended to execute on the scalar unit of the GPU core that we see in Figure 6.7, and vector operations (prefixed with v_) that execute across one of the vector units.

If we look at the structure of the code carefully, we see:

A vector comparison operation, across the entire wavefront we compare the local id with the constant 0.

```
v_cmp_eq_i32 s[4:5], v0, 0
```

then manipulates the execution mask by anding with the result of the comparison and updating the scalar register with the current value of the mask. In addition this operation ensures that the scalar condition code (SCC) register is set: this is what will trigger the conditional branch.

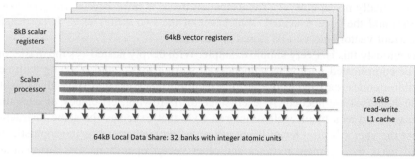

FIGURE 6.7

The compute unit/core on the Radeon HD7970 architecture. The compute unit consists of a scalar processor and four 16-lane SIMD units. Each SIMD unit executes a 64-element wavefront over four cycles. 64kB of vector registers are partitioned between the four SIMD cores allowing high throughput access.

```
s_and_saveexec_b64 s[4:5], s[4:5]
```

The aim of this is that if any lane of the wavefront was due to enter the if, the conditional branch will not happen. If the conditional branch does not happen, the code will enter the if part of the conditional. If no lane needs to enter the if part, the scalar unit will execute the branch and control will pass to the else part.

```
s_cbranch_execz label_0016
```

If the if branch is executed, a vector load (a load from the t, or texture, buffer, showing the graphics heritage of the ISA: tbuffer_load_format_x) pulls the expected data into a vector register, v1. Note that the tbuffer_store operation was factored out by the compiler so we only see it once in the compiled code while we saw two in the original OpenCL C source.

  In the else branch the behavior is as we expect: those lanes that did not execute the if branch should execute here. Specifically, the execution mask is replaced by the current mask NANDed with the original, stored mask and made active:

```
s_andn2_b64 exec, s[4:5], exec
```

And then v1 is loaded with 0, which is what we expect from the OpenCL C source.

```
v_mov_b32 v1, 0
```

There is no branch to skip the else branch. It appears that in this case the compiler has decided that, as there is no load to perform in the else branch, the overhead of simply masking out the operations and treating the entire section as predicated execution is an efficient solution, such that the else branch will **always** execute and simply usually not update v1. The execution mask is refreshed (s_mov_b64 exec, s[4:5]) and the code executed. Whichever of the two writes to v1 is correct for the current vector lane will be stored to memory.

Obviously this is a very simple example. With deeply nested ifs the mask code can be complicated with long sequences of storing masks and ANDing with new condition codes, narrowing the set of executing lanes at each stage until finally scalar branches are needed. At each stage of narrowing, efficiency of execution decreases and as a result well structured code that executes the same instruction across the vector is vital for efficient use of the architecture. It is the sophisticated set of mask management routines and other vector operations that differentiates this ISA from a CPU ISA like SSE, not an abstract notion of having many more cores.

A diagram of the SIMD unit that executes this code is shown in Figure 6.7. Each SIMD unit contains a 32-ported LDS with a four-operation latency and atomic units on its interface. These atomic units mean that non-returning atomic operations can be executing on the LDS at the same time as arithmetic operations executing within the ALUs, offering further parallelism. Two wavefronts from different SIMD units on the same core may be coalesced together over the 32 banks of the LDS unit. Reads or writes from one or both wavefronts active on the LDS interface may collide, and colliding reads or writes are replayed over multiple cycles until all operations are complete. For reads, this can cause the ALUs to stall.

The Shift from VLIW Execution

Earlier AMD architectures described in the previous edition of the book suffered from a more complicated, harder to read ISA. This was in part due to a decoupled scalar unit with a high latency of execution, and partly due to the use of a VLIW execution. While on the HD7970 instructions may be dynamically scheduled across the four SIMD units in a compute unit, on earlier devices these four (or, indeed, five) SIMD units executed in lock-step from a compiler-generated instruction schedule. In general this change should lead to fewer bubbles in the instruction schedule, however it does lead to one important difference in the mapping of OpenCL from what we will have seen in the past. The use of OpenCL builtin vector types was previously advised as a way to increase the arithmetic intensity of a function and to pack more arithmetic operations close together to fill a VLIW packet.

For example on the HD6970 architecture we might see the following instruction in its ISA:

```
17      y: ADD _____ , R1.x, PV16.x
        z: ADD T0.z, R1.x, -PV16.x
18      x: MOV R1.x, R0.w
        y: MOV R1.y, R0.w
        z: MOV R1.z, R0.w
        w: MUL_e _____ , R4.x, PV17.y
```

This is a pair of instruction packets, each containing up to four operations. The first one is only half full: this is where vector operations came in. In addition, the four banks of the register file that we see in Figure 6.7 were accessed from the four VLIW slots (with some flexibility) — such that vector variables were optimally stored. The architectural change to the four dynamically scheduled SIMD units we see in Figure 6.7 means that the extra arithmetic instructions may not be necessary, rather that this may be seen as purely an arithmetic intensity question. More significantly, use of an OpenCL short vector consumes multiple consecutive registers, and with no gain in terms of register packing efficiency this may lead to overuse of the register file. Note that four wavefronts are active in the space that would previously have been occupied by one: with extra intermediate registers to match.

Resource Allocation

Each SIMD unit on the GPU includes a fixed amount of register and LDS storage space. There are 256 kB of registers on each compute unit. These registers are split into four banks such that there are 256 registers per SIMD unit, each 64-lanes wide and 32-bits per lane. These registers will be divided based on the number of wavefronts executing on the SIMD unit. There are 64 kB of LDS on each compute unit, accessible as a random access 32-bank SRAM. The LDS is divided between the number of workgroups executing on the compute unit, based on the local memory allocation requests made within the kernel and through the OpenCL runtime parameter-passing mechanism.

When executing a single kernel on each compute unit, as is the standard mapping when running an OpenCL program, we might see a resource bottleneck, as seen in Figure 6.8. In this diagram, we see two workgroups each containing two wavefronts, where each work item (and hence wavefront scaled up) needs 42 vector registers,

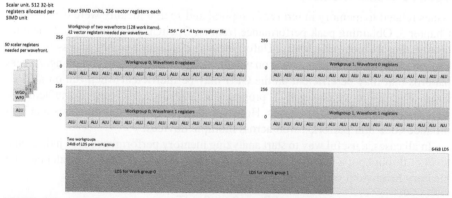

FIGURE 6.8

Allocating the resources of a single compute unit to OpenCL workloads. Given a workgroup of 128 work items that requires 24 kB of LDS and where each work item requires 42 vector registers and 50 scalar registers, we can fit two workgroups, and hence four wavefronts, on each SIMD unit: We are limited by the availability of LDS while register capacity is largely unused.

a share in 50 scalar registers and the workgroup needs 24 kB of LDS. This allocation of four wavefronts per compute unit is limited by the LDS requirements of the workgroup and is below the minimum number of wavefronts we need to run on the device to keep the device busy as with only one wavefront per SIMD unit we have no capacity to switch in a replacement when the wavefront is executing scalar code or memory operations. If we can increase the number of wavefronts running on the SIMD unit to four or more, we have a better chance of keeping the scalar and vector units busy during control flow and, particularly, memory latency, where the more threads running, the better our latency hiding. Because we are LDS limited in this case, increasing the number of wavefronts per workgroup to three would be a good start if this is practical for the algorithm. Alternatively, reducing the LDS allocation would allow us to run a third workgroup on each compute unit, which is very useful if one wavefront is waiting on barriers or memory accesses and hence not on the SIMD unit at the time.

Each wavefront runs on a single SIMD unit and stays there until completion. Any set of wavefronts that are part of the same workgroup stay together on a single compute unit. The reason for this should be clear when seeing the amount of state storage required by that group: In this case, we see 24 kB of LDS and 84 kB of registers per workgroup. This would be a significant amount of data to have to flush to memory and move to another core. As a result, when the memory controller is performing a high-latency read or write operation, if there is not another wavefront with ALU work to perform ready to be scheduled onto the SIMD unit, hardware will lie idle.

MEMORY PERFORMANCE CONSIDERATIONS IN OPENCL
OpenCL Global Memory

Issues related to memory in terms of temporal and spatial locality were discussed in Chapter 3. Obtaining peak performance from an OpenCL program depends heavily on utilizing memory efficiently. Unfortunately, efficient memory access is highly dependent on the particular device on which the OpenCL program is running. Access patterns that may be efficient on the GPU may be inefficient when run on a CPU. Even when we move an OpenCL program to GPUs from different manufacturers, we can see substantial differences. However, there are common practices that will produce code that performs well across multiple devices.

In all cases, a useful way to start analyzing memory performance is to judge what level of throughput a kernel is achieving. A simple way to do this is to calculate the memory bandwidth of the kernel:

$$EB = (B_r + B_w)/T$$

where

EB is the effective bandwidth;
B_r is the number of bytes read from global memory;

B_w is the number of bytes written to global memory; and

T is the time required to run the kernel.

T can be measured using profiling tools such as the AMD Stream Profiler (which is discussed in Chapter 13). B_r and B_w can often be calculated by multiplying the number of bytes each work item reads or writes by the global number of work items. Of course, in some cases, this number must be estimated because we may branch in a data-dependent manner around reads and writes.

Once we know the bandwidth measurement, we can compare it with the peak bandwidth of the execution device and determine how far away we are from peak performance: The closer to peak, the more efficiently we are using the memory system. If our numbers are far from peak, then we can consider restructuring the memory access pattern to improve utilization.

Spatial locality is an important consideration for OpenCL memory access. Most architectures on which OpenCL runs are vector based at some level (whether SSE-like vector instructions or automatically vectorised from a lane-oriented input language such as AMD IL or NVIDIA PTX), and their memory systems benefit from issuing accesses together across this vector. In addition, localized accesses offer caching benefits.

On most modern CPUs, there is a vector instruction set; the various versions of SSE and the AVX are good examples. For efficient memory access, we want to design code such that full, aligned, vector reads are possible using these instruction sets. Given the small vector size, the most efficient way to perform such vector reads is to give the compiler as much information as possible by using vector data types such as `float4`. Such accesses make good use of cache lines, moving data between the cache and registers as efficiently as possible. However, on these CPUs, caching helps cover some of the performance loss from performing smaller, unaligned, or more randomly addressed reads. Figures 6.9 and 6.10 provide a simple example of the difference between a single contiguous read and a set of four random reads. Not only do the narrower reads hit multiple cache lines (creating more cache misses if they do not hit in the cache) but they also cause less efficient transfers to be passed through the memory system.

GPU memory architectures differ significantly from CPU memory architectures, as discussed in Chapter 3. GPUs use multithreading to cover some level of memory latency and are biased in favor of ALU capability rather than caching and sophisticated out-of-order logic. Given the large amounts of compute resources available on typical GPUs, it becomes increasingly important to provide high bandwidth to the memory system if we do not want to starve the GPU. Many modern GPU architectures, particularly high-performance desktop versions such as the latest AMD Radeon and NVIDIA GeForce designs, utilize a wide-SIMD architecture. Imagine the loss of efficiency in Figure 6.10 scaled to a 64-wide hardware vector, as we see in the AMD Radeon HD7970 architecture.

Efficient access patterns differ even among these architectures. For an x86 CPU with SSE, we would want to use 128-bit `float4` accesses, and we would want as

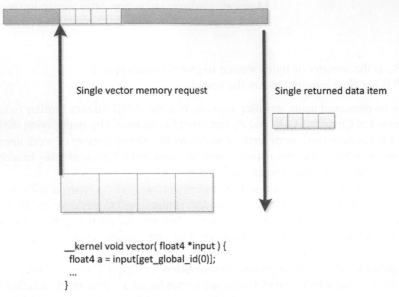

Contiguous data in memory

Single vector memory request   **Single returned data item**

```
__kernel void vector( float4 *input ) {
    float4 a = input[get_global_id(0)];
    ...
}
```

FIGURE 6.9

Using vector reads, we give more opportunities to return data efficiently through the memory system.

Contiguous data in memory

Four smaller requests

Four separate returned data items
Less efficient use of memory system

```
__kernel void vector( __global float *input, int a, int b, int c ) {
    float4 a = (float4)(
        input[get_global_id(0)*4],
        input[get_global_id(0)*4+a],
        input[get_global_id(0)*4+b],
        input[get_global_id(0)*4+c])
    ...
}
```

FIGURE 6.10

If we transfer the same four floats as in Figure 6.9 but with a more random pattern, we return smaller chunks of memory through the memory system less efficiently.

many accesses as possible to fall within cache lines to reduce the number of cache misses. For the AMD Radeon HD7970 GPU architecture consecutive work items in a wavefront will issue a memory request simultaneously. These requests will be delayed in the memory system if they cannot be efficiently serviced. For peak efficiency the work items in a wavefront should issue 32-bit reads such that the reads form a contiguous 256-byte memory region so that the memory system can create a single large memory request. To achieve reasonable portability across different architectures, a good general solution is to compact the memory accesses as effectively as possible, allowing the wide vector machines (AMD and NVIDIA GPUs) and the narrow vector machines (x86 CPUs) to both use the memory system efficiently. To achieve this, we should access memory across a whole workgroup starting with a base address aligned to workgroupSize * loadSize, where loadSize is the size of the load issued by each work item, and which should be reasonably sized—preferably 128 bits on x86 CPUs and AMD GPU architectures and expanding to 256 bits on AVX-supported architectures.

Further complications arise when dealing with the specifics of different memory systems, such as reducing conflicts on the off-chip links to DRAM. For example, let us consider the way in which the AMD Radeon architecture allocates its addresses. Figure 6.11 shows that the low 8 bits of the address are used to select the byte within the memory bank; this gives us the cache line and sub-cache line read locality. If we try to read a column of data from a two-dimensional array, we already know that we are inefficiently using the on-chip buses. It also means that we want multiple groups running on the device simultaneously to access different memory channels and banks. Each memory channel is an on-chip memory controller corresponding to a link to an off-chip memory (Figure 6.12). We want accesses across the device to be spread across as many banks and channels in the memory system as possible, maximizing concurrent data access. However, a vector memory access from a single wavefront that hits multiple memory channels (or banks) occupies those channels, blocking access from other wavefronts and reducing overall memory throughput. Optimally, we want a given wavefront to be contained with a given channel and bank, allowing multiple wavefronts to access multiple channels in parallel. This will allow data to stream in and out of memory efficiently.

To avoid using multiple channels, a single wavefront should access addresses from within a 64-word region, which is achievable if all work items read 32 bits from consecutive addresses. The worst possible situation is if each work item in multiple

31:x	bank	channel	7:0 address

FIGURE 6.11

The meaning of the bits comprising the address of a global memory byte on the Radeon architecture. The precise share of the bits varies from one device to another. For example, devices with 8 channels will use 3 channel selection bits. The HD7970 architecture has 12 channels and uses a more complicated computation.

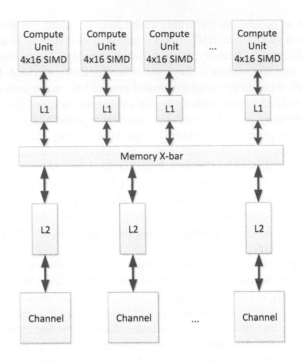

FIGURE 6.12

The HD7970 memory system showing how multiple SIMD cores can collide on the same channels, and hence banks, through the crossbar.

wavefronts reads an address with the same value above bit 8: Each one hits the same channel and bank, and accesses are serialized, achieving a small fraction of peak bandwidth. More details on this subject for AMD architectures can be found in AMD's OpenCL programming guide (Advanced Micro Devices, Incorporated, 2012). Similar information is provided to cover the differences in competing architectures from the respective vendors—for example, NVIDIA's CUDA programming guide (NVIDIA Corporation, 2012).

Local Memory as a Software-Managed Cache

Most OpenCL-supporting devices have some form of cache support. Due to their graphics-oriented designs, many GPUs have read-only data caches that enable some amount of spatial reuse of data.

The easiest way to guarantee the use of caches on a wide range of devices is to use Images (discussed in Chapter 5). Images map data sets to the texture read hardware and, assuming that complicated filtering and two-dimensional access modes are not needed, improve memory efficiency on the GPU. However, GPU caches are small compared with the number of active thread contexts reading data. Programmer-controlled scratchpad memory in the local address space is an efficient approach for caching data with less overhead from wasted space than hardware-controlled caches, better power efficiency, and higher performance for a given area. It is also useful as a way to exchange data with other work items in the same workgroup with a very low and, barring collisions, guaranteed access latency.

Figure 5.11 shows a simple example of this approach. The code loads a range of data from A into C and then accesses multiple values from it, avoiding a second read from DRAM. At the same time, the code loads a single value from aLocalArray just once and reuses it across all work items in the group, thereby considerably reducing the memory traffic. The amount of automatic cache reuse varies from one architecture to another. Given that we have knowledge of the underlying memory access patterns, we can control how much reuse of data is present in the application.

Of course, there are trade-offs when considering how best to optimize data locality. In some cases, the overhead of the extra copy instructions required to move data into local memory and then back out into the ALU (possibly via registers) will sometimes be less efficient than simply reusing the data out of cache. Moving data into local memory is most useful when there are large numbers of reads and writes reusing the same locations, when the lifetime of a write is very long with a vast number of reads using it, or when manual cache blocking offers a way to correct for conflict misses that can often be problematic in two-dimensional data access patterns.

In the case of read/write operations, the benefit of local memory becomes even more obvious, particularly given the wide range of architectures with read-only caches. Consider, for example, the following relatively naive version of a prefix sum code:

```
void localPrefixSum(
    __local unsigned *prefixSums,
    unsigned numElements ) {

    // Run through levels of tree halving sizes of the element set
    // performing reduction phase
    int offset = 1;
    for( int level = numElements/2; level > 0; level /= 2 ) {
        barrier(CLK_LOCAL_MEM_FENCE);

        for( int sumElement = get_local_id(0);
             sumElement < level;
             sumElement += get_local_size(0) ) {

            int ai = offset*(2*sumElement+1)-1;
            int bi = offset*(2*sumElement+2)-1;

            prefixSums[bi] = prefixSums[ai] + prefixSums[bi];
        }

        offset *= 2;
    }
```

```
    barrier(CLK_LOCAL_MEM_FENCE);

    // Need to clear the last element
    if( get_local_id(0) == 0 ) {
        prefixSums[ numElements-1 ] = 0;
    }

    // Push values back down the tree
    for( int level = 1; level < numElements; level *= 2 ) {
        offset /= 2;
        barrier(CLK_LOCAL_MEM_FENCE);

        for( int sumElement = get_local_id(0);
            sumElement < level;
            sumElement += get_local_size(0) ) {

          int ai = offset*(2*sumElement+1)-1;
          int bi = offset*(2*sumElement+2)-1;

          unsigned temporary = prefixSums[ai];
          prefixSums[ai] = prefixSums[bi];
          prefixSums[bi] = temporary + prefixSums[bi];
        }
    }
}
```

Although the previous code is not optimal for many architectures, it does effectively share data between work items using a local array. The data flow of the first loop (`level = numElements>>1 to 0`) is shown in Figure 6.13. Note that each iteration of the loop updates a range of values that a different work item will need to use on the next iteration. Note also that the number of work items collaborating on the calculation decreases on each iteration. The inner loop masks excess work items off to avoid diverging execution across the barrier. To accommodate such behavior, we insert barrier operations to ensure synchronization between the work items and so that we can guarantee that the data will be ready for the execution of the next iteration.

The prefix sum code discussed previously uses local memory in a manner that is inefficient on most wide SIMD architectures, such as high-end GPUs. As mentioned in the discussion on global memory, memory systems tend to be banked to allow a large number of access ports without requiring multiple ports at every memory location. As a result, scratchpad memory hardware (and caches, similarly) tends to be built such that each bank can perform multiple reads or concurrent reads and writes (or some other multiaccess configuration), whereas multiple reads will be spread over multiple banks. This is an important consideration when we are using wide SIMD hardware to access memory. The HD7970 GPU can issue four vector instructions on a cycle and can process local memory operations from two of the four SIMD units. As each SIMD unit is 16 lanes wide, up to 32 local reads or writes may be issued every cycle and the local memory, or LDS, has 32 banks. If each bank supports a single access port, then we can only achieve this throughput if all accesses target

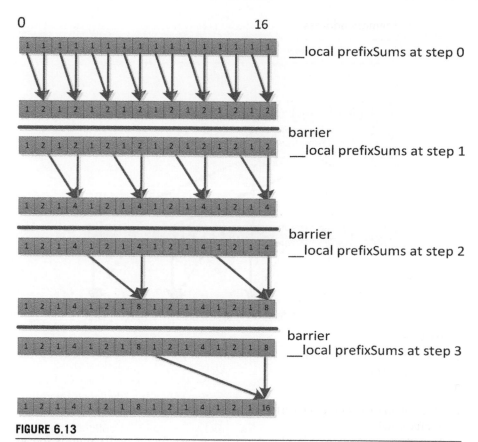

FIGURE 6.13

The accumulation pass of a prefix sum over 16 elements operating in local memory using eight work items. The accumulation phase would be followed by a propagation phase that pushes results back down the tree to give a correct prefix value in each location.

different memory banks because each bank can only provide one value. Similar rules arise on competing architectures; NVIDIA's Fermi architecture, for example, also has a 32-banked local memory.

The problem for local memory is not as acute as that for global memory. In global memory, we saw that widely spread accesses would incur latency because they might cause multiple cache line misses. In local memory, at least on architectures with true scratchpads, the programmer knows when the data is present because he or she put it there manually. The only requirement is that the 16 accesses we issue as part of that read or write instruction hit different banks.

Figure 6.14 shows a simplification for comparison—step 1 of the prefix sum in Figure 6.13 accessing a local memory with eight memory banks, where each work item can perform a single local memory operation per cycle. In this case, our local memory buffer can return up to eight values per cycle from memory.

Memory address:

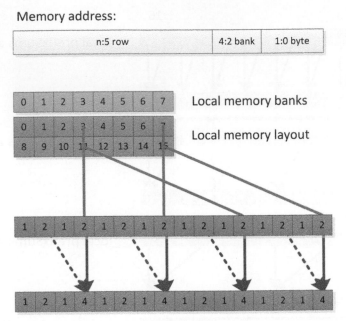

FIGURE 6.14

Step 1 of Figure 6.13 showing behavior with a local memory of eight banks and one access per work item per cycle.

What result do we obtain when performing the set of accesses necessary for step 1 of the prefix sum?

Note that our 16-element local memory (necessary for the prefix sum) is spread over two rows. Each column is a bank, and each row is an address within a bank. Assuming (as is common in many architectures) that each bank is 32 bits wide, and assuming, for simplicity, that the current wavefront is not competing with one from another SIMD unit, our memory address would break down as shown at the top of Figure 6.14. Two consecutive memory words will reside in separate banks. As with global memory, a SIMD vector that accesses consecutive addresses along its length will efficiently access the local memory banks without contention. In Figure 6.14, however, we see a different behavior. Given the second access to local memory, the read from `prefixSums[bi]` in

```
prefixSums[bi] = prefixSums[ai] + prefixSums[bi];
```

tries to read values from locations 3, 7, 11, and 15. As shown in Figure 6.14, 3 and 11 both sit in bank 3; 7 and 15 both sit in bank 7. There is no possible way to read two rows from the same bank simultaneously, so these accesses will be serialized on GPUs by the hardware, incurring a read delay. For good performance, we might wish to restructure our code to avoid this conflict. One useful technique is to add *padding* to the addresses, and an example of this is shown in Figure 6.15. By shifting

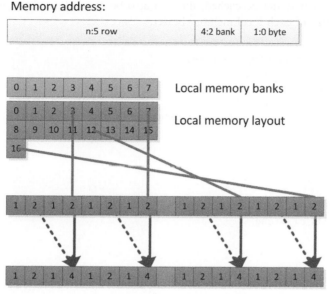

FIGURE 6.15

Figure 6.15 with padding added in the data structures showing how it removes the conflict in this case.

addresses after the first set (aligning to banks), we can change evenly strided accesses to avoid conflicts. Unfortunately, this adds address computation overhead, which can be more severe than the bank conflict overhead; hence, this trade-off is an example of architecture-specific tuning.

Local memory should be carefully rationed. Any device that uses a real scratch-pad region that is not hardware managed will have a limited amount of local memory. In the case of the AMD Radeon HD7970 GPU, this space is 64 kB, following OpenCL minimum requirements. It is important to note that this 64 kB is shared between all workgroups executing simultaneously on the core. Also, because the GPU is a latency hiding throughput device that utilizes multithreading on each core, the more workgroups that can fit, the better the hardware utilization is likely to be. If each workgroup uses 16 kB, then only four can fit on the core. If these workgroups contain a small number of wavefronts (one or two), then there will only barely be enough hardware threads to cover latency. Therefore, local memory allocation will be needed to balance efficiency gains from sharing and efficiency losses from reducing the number of hardware threads to one or two on a multithreaded device.

The OpenCL API includes calls to query the amount of local memory the device possesses, and this can be used to parameterize kernels before the programmer compiles or dispatches them. The first call in the following code queries the type of the local memory so that it is possible to determine if it is dedicated or in global memory (which may or may not be cached; this can also be queried), and the second call returns the size of each local memory buffer:

```
cl_int err;
cl_device_local_mem_type type;
err = clGetDeviceInfo(
    deviceId,
    CL_DEVICE_LOCAL_MEM_TYPE,
    sizeof(cl_device_local_mem_type),
    &type,
    0 );
cl_ulong size;
err = clGetDeviceInfo(
    deviceId,
    CL_DEVICE_LOCAL_MEM_SIZE,
    sizeof( cl_ulong ),
    &size,
    0 );
```

SUMMARY

The aim of this chapter was to show a very specific mapping of OpenCL to an architectural implementation. In this case, it was shown how OpenCL maps slightly differently to a CPU architecture and a GPU architecture. The core principles of this chapter apply to competing CPU and GPU architectures, but significant differences in performance can easily arise from variation in vector width (32 on NVIDIA GPUs, 32/64 on AMD GPUs, and much smaller on CPUs), variations in thread context management, and instruction scheduling. It is clear that in one book we cannot aim to cover all possible architectures, but by giving one example, it is hoped that further investigation through vendor documentation can lead to efficient code on whatever OpenCL device is being targeted.

References

Advanced Micro Devices, Incorporated. (2012). *The AMD Accelerated Parallel Processing—OpenCL Programming Guide*. Sunnyvale, CA: Advanced Micro Devices, Inc.

AMD Southern Islands Instruction Set Architecture http://developer.amd.com/tools/hc/amdappsdk/assets/AMD_Southern_Islands_Instruction_Set_Architecture.pdf

Gummaraju, J., Morichetti, L., Houston, M., Sander, B., Gaster, B. R., & Zheng, B. *Twin Peaks: A Software Platform for Heterogeneous Computing on General-Purpose and Graphics Processors*. Association for Computing Machinery. (2010). *PACT 2010: Proceedings of the Nineteenth International Conference on Parallel Architectures and Compilation Techniques: September 11–15, 2010, Vienna, Austria*. Association for Computing Machinery.

NVIDIA Corporation. (2012). *NVIDIA CUDA C Programming Guide*. Santa Clara, CA: NVIDIA Corporation.

Data Management

When programming with OpenCL for a discrete GPU, the overhead of transferring data between the host and the device needs to be considered carefully since this communication can dominate overall program execution time. Data transfer time can rival the performance benefits afforded by data-parallel execution on GPUs, and it is not uncommon for data transfer to be on the same order of time as kernel execution. As we move to shared-memory CPU–GPU systems (APUs), the performance issues involved with proper data management and communication are equally critical. This chapter introduces many of the key concepts and presents details required to understand data transfers and data accesses within discrete and shared-memory heterogeneous systems.

MEMORY MANAGEMENT

Modern operating systems provide the abstraction of **virtual memory** to user processes (Peter Denning—Virtual Memory, 1970). Virtual memory hides the true storage medium and makes data byte addressable regardless of where it actually resides. Operating systems provide each process a separate virtual memory address space, allowing them to execute with the entire virtual address space at their disposal. The most important aspect of virtual memory for this discussion is that it allows a process to execute without the need to have all of its code and data resident in the CPU main memory (i.e., DRAM).

The virtual address space of a process is divided into fixed-size blocks, called **pages**. In the physical memory system, the **physical address** space (the range of actual memory locations) is likewise divided into equally sized **frames** so that a frame is capable of storing a page. Virtual pages can be mapped to any frame in main memory, mapped to a location on disk, or not yet be allocated. However, the CPU requires a page to be in a main memory frame when it is being accessed or executed. When a process executes an instruction using a virtual memory address, a hardware unit called the **Memory Management Unit** (**MMU**) intervenes and provides the mapping of the virtual address to the physical address. If the physical address of a page is not in main memory, a **page fault** occurs, and the process is suspended while the page is retrieved and a virtual-to-physical mapping is created. This technique is known as **demand paging** and is completely transparent to the user process (except

Heterogeneous Computing with OpenCL

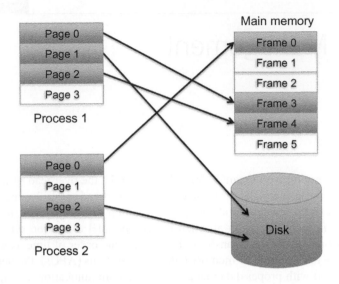

FIGURE 7.1

An illustration of demand paging for two user processes.

for the time it takes to service the page fault). Figure 7.1 shows an example of demand paging.

Virtual memory has implications on data transfer performance in OpenCL, since transferring data from the CPU to the GPU when using a discrete GPU uses **Direct Memory Access (DMA)** over the PCI-Express bus. DMA is an efficient way to access data directly from a peripheral device without CPU intervention. DMA requires that the data is resident in main memory and will not be moved by the operating system. When the operating system does not have the discretion to move a page, the page is said to be **pinned** (or **page-locked**).

The PCI-Express protocol allows any device connected to the bus, such as a GPU, to transfer data to or from the CPU's main memory. When performing DMA transfers, a device driver running on the CPU supplies a physical address, and the **DMA engine** on the GPU can then perform the transfer and signal to the CPU when it has completed. Once the transfer completes, the pages can then be unmapped from memory.

Modern x86 systems use an **I/O Memory Management Unit (IOMMU)** as an interface between the PCI-Express bus and the main memory bus (AMD IOMMU Architectural Specification; Intel Virtualization Technology for Directed I/O Architecture Specification). The IOMMU performs the same role for peripheral devices as the MMU does for x86 cores, mapping virtual I/O addresses to physical addresses. The major benefit of utilizing an IOMMU for a GPU is that it allows the device to perform DMA transfers from noncontiguous physical address locations and allows access to physical locations that may be out of the range of addresses supported by the device. A block diagram of system with an IOMMU is shown in Figure 7.2.

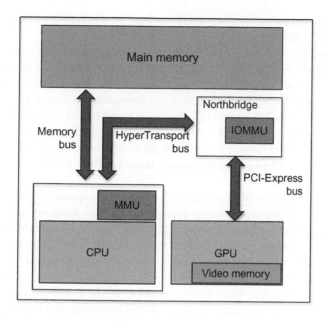

FIGURE 7.2

A system containing an IOMMU.

DATA TRANSFER IN A DISCRETE ENVIRONMENT

In a machine with an x86 CPU and a GPU, an OpenCL call to transfer data from the host to the device (e.g., clEnqueueWriteBuffer) is done using the DMA unit on the GPU. As described previously, DMA requires that the pages that are being accessed need to be pinned in memory. Therefore, to transfer data from the CPU to the GPU, the OpenCL runtime must take the following steps:

1. Pin the memory pages containing the source data or copy the source data to pre-pinned memory pages.
2. Ensure that memory space has been allocated for the data on the GPU.
3. Pin the destination pages in the GPU memory system.
4. Initiate the DMA transfer from the CPU memory to the GPU memory.

Optimizations

To help speed up the process of transferring data, OpenCL allows flags to be passed to clCreateBuffer. The OpenCL specification is intentionally ambiguous in defining the meanings of flags passed to the runtime in clCreateBuffer. Vendors interpret the flags passed by the developer as possible optimizations to the data's location that can be applied by the runtime. While performance portability is not achievable, these flags have obvious mappings to behavior.

As discussed above, pinning memory pages requires operating system intervention and so some overhead is incurred in addition to the actual data transfer. To amortize this overhead, the developer can request to the runtime that the buffer be created and pinned for its lifetime. Using this approach, the cost of performing pinning is only incurred once instead of before each transfer. For version 2.7 of AMD's OpenCL APP SDK and NVIDIA's CUDA Toolkit 4.2, the flag CL_ALLOC_HOST_PTR passed to clCreateBuffer is interpreted by the runtime to create pinned memory on the host. Figure 7.3 shows the performance benefits of pre-pinning memory for repeated data transfers.

The trade-off with creating pinned buffers is that the operating system is no longer free to evict the pages containing the buffer data from memory, and system performance can degrade if there is not enough physical memory for other programs to use. Using pinned memory for optimized transfers also makes programs less portable. For example, creating a large pinned buffer may be fine on a server with large amounts of physical RAM installed, yet it could cause the program to crash on a laptop or another system that has a small amount of RAM available. Further, even if RAM is not a concern for a single program, if multiple users on a system all run programs with pinned memory, they could quickly fill up the system RAM.

Zero-Copy Buffers

In addition to using DMA transfers, GPUs also have the ability to access data directly from CPU main memory during kernel execution. This reduces the overhead of the data transfer but limits access performance to the speed of the PCI-Express bus. The

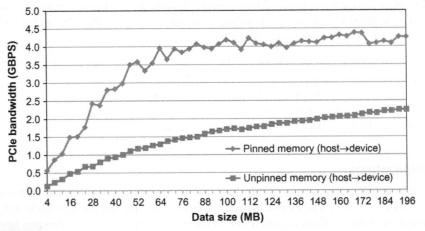

FIGURE 7.3

A comparison of data transfer rate using pinned and non-pinned buffers.

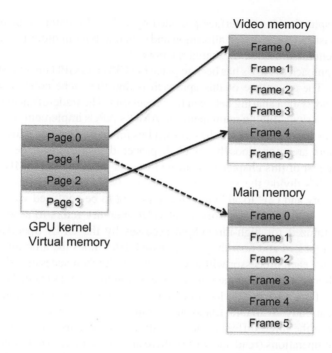

FIGURE 7.4

By default, pages of a kernel's virtual address space map to video memory on the GPU. Zero-copy buffers map CPU main memory into a kernel's virtual address space, allowing the data to be accessed without requiring a data transfer. The dashed line represents a (slower) access to CPU main memory over the PCI-Express bus. (For color version of this figure, the reader is referred to the online version of this chapter.)

term **zero-copy buffer** is used to describe an OpenCL buffer that physically resides in host memory but is accessed during kernel execution by the device. Figure 7.4 shows an example of the virtual address space of a GPU kernel that uses both GPU video memory and zero-copy memory from the CPU.

The best scenario to use zero-copy buffers is when the data is small and does not warrant the overhead of a transfer or when a buffer will only be sparsely read or written. Later in the chapter, an example application is presented that highlights the trade-offs of using zero-copy buffers.

DATA PLACEMENT IN A SHARED-MEMORY ENVIRONMENT

In shared-memory, heterogeneous systems-on-a-chip (e.g., AMD Fusion, Intel Ivy Bridge), the PCI-Express link is no longer needed, as both the CPU and the GPU access the same main memory. There are two major benefits of using shared-memory in a heterogeneous system: (1) we remove the overhead associated with expensive data transfers, and (2) a common virtual address space can be presented to both devices. Despite the clean interface provided by a shared-memory system, the programmer must carefully design allocation and data mapping in order to reap the performance benefits provided by shared memory.

Intel's approach to APUs has been to place the CPU and GPU under a shared last-level cache. The advantage of this approach is that the cache coherence protocol naturally handles data sharing between the processors. The trade-off is that both processors share a single link to main memory. AMD's APUs implement separate paths to memory so that each processor has its own bus for accessing data. However, since the processors are more loosely coupled, proper data placement becomes more critical. The rest of this chapter is dedicated to data placement in AMD APUs.

AMD APUs divide the system memory into two logical regions: (1) regular system memory and (2) "local" video memory (not to be confused with OpenCL's terminology). In Fusion processors, local video memory refers to a portion of the memory optimized for high-throughput accesses by the GPU. Specifying where buffers are allocated and how they are accessed determines the amount of memory bandwidth that each processor will have to work with when accessing shared memory. Data allocated in system memory has the option to be set as cached or uncached by the CPU. Data allocated in local memory is always uncached by the CPU. The GPUs on currently available Llano and Trinity Fusion devices have read-only caches. Given the three different memory allocation options, two processors, and two types of operations (read and write), there are a total of 12 bandwidth considerations that the programmer must consider when placing data. It should also be noted that both cached and uncached system memory require pinning data so that it is accessible by the GPU, which has the same trade-offs as described previously.

In AMD's current Llano and Trinity APUs, the GPU accesses local memory with high bandwidth using the Radeon Memory Bus (RMB), and accesses system memory with lower bandwidth using the Fusion Compute Link (FCL). The RMB addresses memory directly (via the IOMMU) and is noncoherent with the CPU cache hierarchy. The FCL, on the other hand, is the bus used to access data that is coherent in the CPU cache hierarchy. In order to maintain coherent state, the FCL interacts with the MMU and is therefore slower than the RMB. The CPU accesses system memory through the standard memory bus, with writes to local and uncached memory going through a **Write Combining** (**WC**) unit. The job of the WC unit is to coalesce multiple write accesses into the fewest number of memory transactions possible, reducing unnecessary memory traffic. A diagram of the different paths to memory is shown in Figure 7.5.

In addition to determining the cache behavior of memory, the virtual-to-physical mapping of program data also plays a major role in performance. In Fusion processors, the GPU and CPU each have their own set of page tables, and each has its own **Address Translation Cache** (more commonly referred to as a **Translation Lookaside Buffer**), which is a cached version of the page tables. For the GPU, the IOMMU plays the role of the MMU and performs virtual-to-physical address translation. When data is stored in local memory, the GPU page tables contain the valid virtual-to-physical mapping, and the IOMMU will have to be consulted by the

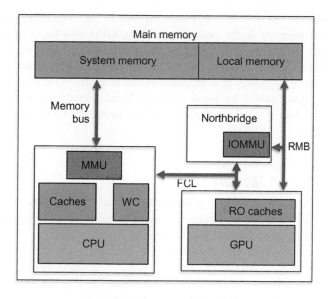

FIGURE 7.5

Diagram of the different paths to memory in a Fusion system.

CPU before it can access the data. Similarly, when data is stored in system memory, the CPU page tables contain the valid mapping, and the MMU will need to be consulted by the GPU. Currently, Fusion systems rely on the OpenCL driver to fill in the GPU page tables when a kernel is scheduled, since the address ranges that will be accessed are known in advance. The synchronization between page tables implemented by Fusion allows data to be referenced by a single pointer that can be shared by both the CPU and the GPU.

Local Memory

When data is allocated in local memory, the GPU maintains the valid virtual-to-physical mappings in its page tables. This allows the GPU to read and write to local memory at the full speed of the RMB, without having to involve the CPU.

For the CPU to access local memory, it must first request the virtual-to-physical mapping from the GPU IOMMU. This additional step increases the latency for an access. Since writes are combined in the WC unit, this path from CPU to local memory still provides decent performance. When the CPU needs to read from local memory, accesses are uncached and only a single inflight access is permitted. Only a single inflight access from the CPU is permitted since uncached writes need to be verified as having completed before read accesses are issued to the cache hierarchy.

By default, clCreateBuffer allocates buffers in local memory. Allocating a buffer in local memory is the best choice if the GPU will be accessing a large amount of data. Since reads to system memory are so slow, it often makes sense to create a buffer in local memory separate from the host pointer (i.e., do not use CL_MEM_USE_HOST_PTR). If a separate buffer is used, clEnqueueWriteBuffer performs a DMA transfer to local memory, local memory is used for kernel execution, and then clEnqueueReadBuffer performs a DMA transfer back to system memory.

Cacheable System Memory

For a buffer allocated in cacheable system memory, the CPU uses the standard memory path through the cache hierarchy. Accesses by the CPU can thus achieve high performance on reads and writes for this type of buffer.

If the GPU accesses a buffer in cacheable system memory, it must first obtain the virtual-to-physical mappings from the CPU MMU. The GPU must then snoop the cache hierarchy to retrieve the latest value of the data. These operations impact memory bandwidth for read and write operations by the GPU.

When the flag CL_MEM_ALLOC_HOST_PTR is passed to clCreateBuffer, the buffer is allocated in system memory. If the buffer is mapped to a pointer using clEnqueueMapBuffer, the data is set as cacheable. The flag CL_MEM_USE_HOST_PTR will leave existing data in cacheable system memory and use this space to create the buffer. This option is the best to use if the data will mostly be accessed by the CPU, and only sparingly by the GPU.

Uncached System Memory

Uncached system memory avoids using the cache hierarchy and provides a middle ground between cacheable and local memory. CPU writes to uncached memory still occur at full speed, since the cache hierarchy is simply ignored. CPU reads, however, must maintain memory consistency by first flushing outstanding writes in the WC unit back to main memory. This additional step reduces memory bandwidth when the CPU reads uncached data.

Uncached memory relieves the GPU from having to snoop the CPU cache hierarchy, which improves read and write bandwidth when compared to using cacheable memory.

Creating a buffer in uncached system memory is achieved by calling clCreateBuffer with the CL_MEM_ALLOC_HOST_PTR and CL_MEM_READ_ONLY flags from the OpenCL program. The CL_MEM_READ_ONLY flag tells the OpenCL runtime that the buffer is read-only with respect to the GPU, so the CPU will not need to read output data from the buffer. This allows fast GPU reads and writes, and fast CPU writes.

EXAMPLE APPLICATION—WORK GROUP REDUCTION

This section covers the implementation of a **reduction** algorithm to illustrate the performance benefits of using different OpenCL buffers. A reduction is any algorithm that converts a large data set into a smaller data set using an operator on each element. A simple reduction example is to compute the sum of the elements in an array.

```
float sum_array(float * a, int No_of_elements)
{
    float sum = 0.0f;
    for (int i = 0; i < No_of_elements; i++)
    sum += a[i];
    return sum;
}
```

With OpenCL, the common way to parallelize a reduction is to divide the input data set between different work groups on a GPU, where each work group is responsible for computing a single element. Within a work group, the reduction is performed over multiple stages. At each stage, work-items sum an element and its neighbor that is one stride away. The stride grows at each stage and the number of participating work items decreases. This methodology of reducing a data set is known as a **reduction tree** and is shown in Figure 7.6. The OpenCL kernel is shown below.

```
// A simple reduction tree kernel where each work group reduces a set
// of elements to a single value in local memory and writes the
// resultant value to global memory.
__kernel void reduction_kernel(
unsigned int N, // number of elements to reduce
```

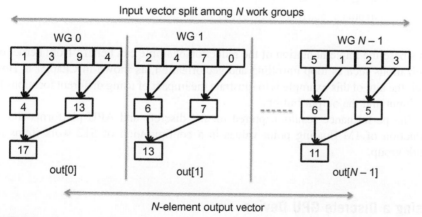

FIGURE 7.6

A sum reduction tree implemented in OpenCL.

```
__global float* input,
__global float* output,
__local float* sdata)
{
// Get index into local data array and global array
unsigned int localId = get_local_id(0);
unsigned int globalId = get_global_id(0);
unsigned int groupId = get_group_id(0);
unsigned int wgSize = get_local_size(0);

// Read in data if within bounds
sdata[localId] = (i<N) ? input[globalId]: 0;

// Synchronize since all data needs to be in
// local memory and visible to all work items
barrier(CLK_LOCAL_MEM_FENCE);

// Each work item adds two elements in parallel.
// As stride increases, work items remain idle.
for(int offset = wgSize ; offset > 0; offset >>= 1)
{
    if (localId < offset && localId + offset < wgSize)
    {
       sdata[localId] += sdata[localId + offset];
    }
    barrier(CLK_LOCAL_MEM_FENCE);
}
barrier(CLK_LOCAL_MEM_FENCE);

// Only one work item needs to write out result of the work
//group's reduction
if ( tid == 0 )
    output[groupId] = sdata[0];
}
```

This baseline implementation of the reduction example can benefit from kernel optimizations such as loop unrolling and vectorization, as shown in Chapter 8. However, the aim of this example is to illustrate the impact of using different locations for the input and the output buffers.

The performance results captured for the discrete and APU platforms show a reduction of 1M floating point values in a configuration of 512 work items per work group.

Using a Discrete GPU Device

The following cases describe various buffer allocation options for the reduction example with a discrete GPU. The experiments were performed on a Radeon 7850 GPU and a Tesla M2070 GPU. The results are presented in Tables 7.1 and 7.2.

Table 7.1 Breakdown of the Execution Times of the Reduction Application for Various Data Allocation Options on a Radeon 7850 GPU

Buffer Allocation	Write to Device (ms)	Kernel Execution (ms)	Read from Device (ms)	Total Time (ms)
Case 1: Default buffers	2.01	0.13	0.13	2.27
Case 2: Pinned staging buffers	0.70	0.13	0.05	0.88
Case 3: Zero-copy host buffers	N/A	0.90	N/A	0.90
Case 4: Pinned input, zero-copy output	0.71	0.13	N/A	0.84

Case 1 Using device buffers

In this case, the input and the output buffers of the reduction kernel are allocated in the video memory of the device. This is the most common scenario and has the overhead of two data transfers: writing data to the GPU before execution and reading back the results after execution. When data is transferred to the device, the OpenCL kernel can utilize the high bandwidth of the GPU's video memory.

Case 2 Using pinned staging buffers

This case is similar to Case 1, except that pinned buffers on the CPU are used to make transfers more efficient. The input data is first transferred to a pre-pinned buffer on the CPU. The transfer to the GPU is then more efficient, as the DMA transfer takes place without any additional overhead. Execution then occurs with the buffers in video memory. Finally, after execution completes, the output data is transferred to a pinned output buffer on the CPU.

Case 3 Using zero-copy buffers

By creating the input and output buffers as zero-copy buffers, the kernel accesses are performed directly in CPU main memory, and the overhead of data transfers with the GPU is avoided. Although the transfer overhead is avoided, memory performance is limited by the interconnect (PCI-Express) bandwidth during execution. Zero-copy buffers are implemented as buffer copies on the Tesla 2070, so the results are not included in Table 7.2.

Case 4 Combination

Recall that for GPU execution, zero-copy buffers are beneficial when the overhead of data transfer is higher than the cost of direct access of CPU memory by the GPU kernel. This is usually the case when a small amount of data is read or written. Intuition says that since the input buffer is large and every element is used, it will benefit from being allocated in device memory, and since the output buffer is small,

Table 7.2 Breakdown of the Execution Times of the Reduction Application for Regular and Pinned Buffers on an NVIDIA Tesla M2070 GPU

Buffer Allocation	Write to Device (ms)	Kernel Execution (ms)	Read From Device (ms)	Total Time (ms)
Case 1: Default buffers	1.30	0.37	0.01	1.67
Case 2: Pinned staging buffers for device I/O	0.70	0.37	<0.01	1.08

it should benefit from the zero-copy approach. Recall that in the reduction code, the output buffer is only written to once by a single work item in each work group.

Case 2 in Table 7.1 shows that if it is possible to use pinned staging buffers, they can greatly improve the rate of data transfer. Case 3 shows that although zero-copy buffers avoid the overhead of data transfer, the slower access to CPU main memory can have a large impact on kernel execution time. Since a reduction example starts with a large amount of input data and generates a small amount of output data, Case 4 provides the best overall performance.

Although Case 4 provides the shortest total execution time, it should be noted that if the output buffer were used in future computation on the device, the zero-copy approach would result in slow accesses by the device. In such scenarios, creating the output buffer in video memory on the GPU would likely provide better results.

Table 7.2 shows that pinned buffers also achieved a large speedup with the Tesla 2070 GPU. Notice that both GPUs were able to saturate the PCI-Express bus during pinned transfers.

Using an APU

The following cases describe a similar set of experiments using a Llano APU with various allocation options for input and output buffers. The longer kernel execution duration is related to the smaller number of compute units on the GPU device of the Llano APU as compared to the Radeon 7850 discrete GPU. The GPU on the Llano APU is also an implementation of the older Evergreen architecture.

Recall that in an APU, the CPU and GPU share a single memory. However, in AMD APUs, there are two regions of memory that have different performance characteristics: regular system memory, and local memory, which is optimized for GPU accesses.

Case 1 Using local memory buffers
By default, OpenCL buffers are allocated in local memory, and transfers still need to be used to copy data to these buffers from system memory. However, since the PCI-Express bus is avoided, transfer time is faster than with the discrete GPU.

Case 2 Using pinned staging buffers

As in the discrete case, using pinned buffers greatly reduce the amount of time for the data transfers. As with Case 1, the data ends up in local memory, so the kernel execution time remains the same.

Case 3 Using zero-copy buffers

In this case, the benefit of the APU platform is clearly seen. There is very little degradation (none in this case) in kernel performance when using zero-copy host buffers during kernel execution. This should be compared against the discrete platform, where a 7X degradation in execution performance is seen when using the zero-copy buffers during execution.

Case 1 in Table 7.3 shows that the overhead of data transfer in an APU is much lower than the corresponding case for a discrete GPU. As with the discrete example, Case 2 shows that APUs also benefit from pinned staging buffers. However, the biggest benefit is shown in Case 3, where the use of zero-copy buffers eliminates data transfer overhead with minimal performance degradation.

Table 7.3 Breakdown of the Execution Times of the Reduction Application for Various Data Allocation Options on an A8-3850 APU

Buffer Allocation	Write to Device (ms)	Kernel Execution (ms)	Read From Device (ms)	Total Time (ms)
Case 1: Default buffers	0.96	1.40	0.15	2.52
Case 2: Pinned host buffers	0.27	1.40	0.03	1.70
Case 3: Zero-copy buffers	N/A	1.40	N/A	1.40

References

AMD IOMMU Architectural Specification (2011). http://support.amd.com/us/Processor_TechDocs/48882.pdf.

Intel Virtualization Technology for Directed I/O Architecture Specification (2011). http://download.intel.com/technology/computing/vptech/Intel(r)_VT_for_Direct_IO.pdf.

Peter J. Denning—Virtual Memory. (1970). *ACM Computing Surveys* 2: 153–189.

OpenCL Case Study: Convolution

INTRODUCTION

In Chapter 4, we introduced a basic convolution example using OpenCL images. Images provided the benefit of automatically handling out-of-bounds accesses (by clamping or wrapping accesses), which simplified the coding that would have been required for the cases in which the convolution filter accessed data outside of the image. Thus, image support may reduce control flow overhead and provide caching and data access transformations that improve memory system performance. When targeting GPUs, the automatic caching mechanism provided for images is much better than not caching. In many circumstances, however, it can be outperformed by efficient use of local memory. In this chapter, we use a convolution filter to provide some intuition on how to make good use of local memory. We encourage the reader to compare the two different implementation choices and judge which would be best for a particular use case.

CONVOLUTION KERNEL

The OpenCL convolution kernel can be naturally divided into three sections: (1) the caching of input data from global to local memory, (2) performing the convolution, and (3) the writing of output data back to global memory. This chapter focuses on the first task, optimizing data caching for the underlying memory system. Loop unrolling is also discussed in the context of performing the convolution. The write back stage is straightforward and will not be discussed in detail. During the discussion, a 7×7 filter is considered when concrete examples facilitate the discussion of optimizations, although the principles should generalize to different filter configurations. Optimizations for the OpenCL kernel are presented inline throughout the chapter, along with any relevant host code. The complete reference implementations are provided in Code Listings.

Selecting Workgroup Sizes

Recall that when performing a convolution, each work-item accesses surrounding pixels based on the size of the filter. The filter *radius* is the number of pixels in each direction that are accessed, not including the current pixel. For example, a 7×7 filter accesses three additional pixels in each direction, so the radius is 3. From Figure 4.5, it is easy to see that adjacent output points have two-dimensional locality for data accesses. Each work region also involves a wide data halo of padding pixels due to the size of the input filter. This tells us that for efficiency, we should use two-dimensional access regions, and a square minimizes the ratio of the halo dimensions to the output data size and hence the input:output efficiency. For this example, we consider a mapping of work-items using a single work-item per output approach, leaving multi-output optimizations to be considered in a histogram example in Chapter 9. Figure 8.1 shows the padding pixels required for a given work region and hence an OpenCL workgroup.

In OpenCL, work-item creation and algorithm design must be considered simultaneously, especially when local memory is used. For convolution, the size of the workgroups and the algorithm for caching data to local memory are closely related. There are two obvious approaches for caching data. The first approach is to create the same number of work-items as there are data elements to be cached in local memory. That is, create as many work-items as there are in the combined number of output and padding pixels. Using this approach, each element would simply copy one pixel from global to local memory, and then the work-items representing the border pixels would sit idle during the convolution. The limitations of this approach are that larger filter sizes will not allow many output elements to be computed per workgroup, and when targeting GPUs, wavefronts may be fragmented, causing ALU cycles to be wasted. Alternatively, the second approach is to create as many work-items as will be performing the convolution. In this approach, there will be fewer work-items than pixels to be cached, so some work-items will have to copy multiple elements and none will sit idle during the convolution. This approach is obviously much better suited for large filters because the number of padding elements will not limit the number of work-items that generate output pixels. For this example, the second approach to work-item creation is used because it is better suited for OpenCL targeting GPUs.

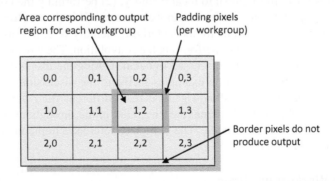

FIGURE 8.1

Workgroups have a unique output region for which they produce values. Each workgroup caches values from the source image corresponding to its output location as well as padding pixels determined by the filter radius.

Taking this optimization approach a step further, we might like to create fewer work-items than output pixels in a group. The reader can easily infer such an approach from the algorithm discussed and may like to experiment with this trade-off. Finding the optimal combination can mean exploring a large design space.

Selecting an efficient workgroup size requires consideration of the underlying memory architecture. For the AMD 6970 GPU sixteen consecutive work-items issuing 128-bit reads on an aligned address can come closest to fully utilizing the memory bus bandwidth. The most favorable memory transactions on NVIDIA platforms come from 32 work-items issuing a combined request that is 128 bytes in size and 128-byte aligned (NVIDIA, 2009). This means 32 work-items will access consecutive 4-byte elements, beginning at a 128 byte aligned address boundary, which is the most ideal access pattern. Transactions of 64 and 32 bytes are also supported. For this example, creating workgroups of either 32 or 16 items in width offers us a good chance for creating efficient memory requests regardless of platform. The Y-dimension of the workgroup does not affect memory access performance. On AMD GPUs, the workgroup size limit is 256 work-items, so choosing a width of 32 produces a height of 8, and a width of 16 produces a height of 16. With NVIDIA, larger workgroup sizes are possible, although the "ideal" size is really determined by the interplay between hardware resources. The workgroup size that performs best will be a trade-off between the efficiency of the memory accesses and the efficiency of the computation. For the code and analysis presented in this chapter, we use 16×16 workgroups to perform the convolution.

When performing reads from global to local memory, each workgroup needs to copy twice the filter radius additional work-items in each dimension. For a 7×7 filter, this would mean an additional six pixels in each dimension. When computing the NDRange size, one filter radius of border pixels around the image (i.e., 3 for a 7×7 filter) will not compute output values because they would cause out-of-bounds accesses for the filter.[1] For an image with dimensions `imageWidth` and `imageHeight`, only `(imageWidth-2*filterRadius) x (imageHeight-2*filterRadius)` work-items are needed in each dimension, respectively. Because the image will likely not be an exact multiple of the workgroup size, additional workgroups must be created in both the X- and Y-dimensions (Figure 8.2). These last workgroups in each dimension may not be fully utilized, and this must be accounted for in the OpenCL kernel. A function that takes a value (e.g., the image width) and rounds it up to a multiple of another value (e.g., the workgroup width) is shown here:

```
// This function takes a positive integer and rounds it up to
// the nearest multiple of another provided integer
unsigned int roundUp(unsigned int value, unsigned int multiple) {
```

---

[1]The algorithm could be modified to have the border pixels produce output values by detecting out-of-bounds accesses and returning valid values.

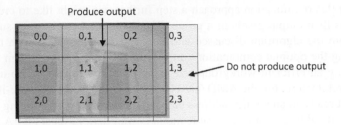

FIGURE 8.2

The last workgroups in each dimension may contain out-of-bounds pixels. The work-items representing these locations will need to be handled in the kernel.

```
// Determine how far past the nearest multiple the value is
unsigned int remainder = value % multiple;

// Add the difference to make the value a multiple
if(remainder != 0) {
    value += (multiple-remainder);
}

return value;
}
```

The code to compute the NDRange size for an image with dimensions `imageWidth` and `imageHeight` is as follows:

```
// Selected workgroup size is 16x16
int wgWidth = 16;
int wgHeight = 16;

// When computing the total number of work-items, the
// padding work-items do not need to be considered
int totalWorkItemsX = roundUp(imageWidth-paddingPixels,
    wgWidth);
int totalWorkItemsY = roundUp(imageHeight-paddingPixels,
    wgHeight);

// Size of a workgroup
size_t localSize[2] = {wgWidth, wgHeight};
// Size of the NDRange
size_t globalSize[2] = {totalWorkItemsX, totalWorkItemsY};
```

Caching Data to Local Memory

Caching data in local memory first requires allocating space in local memory—either statically by hard coding the values into the OpenCL kernel or dynamically by specifying a size and passing it as a kernel argument. Because the program will have to cache a different amount of data based on the filter size, the following dynamically allocates local memory space and passes it as the seventh argument (the argument at index 6) to the OpenCL kernel:

```
int localWidth = localSize[0] + paddingPixels;
int localHeight = localSize[1] + paddingPixels;
size_t localMemSize = (localWidth * localHeight *
    sizeof(float));
...
// Dynamically allocate local memory (per workgroup)
clSetKernelArg(kernel, 6, localMemSize, NULL);
```

The process of copying data from global memory to local memory often requires the most thought and is often the most error-prone operation when writing a kernel. The work-items first need to determine where in global memory to copy from and then ensure that they do not access a region that is outside of their working area or out of bounds for the image. The following code identifies each work-item locally and globally and then performs the copy from global memory to local memory. Figure 8.3 provides an illustration of the variables used to perform the copy in this example:

```
__kernel
void convolution(__global float* imageIn,
                 __global float* imageOut,
                 __constant float* filter,
                        int rows,
                        int cols,
                        int filterWidth,
                 __local float* localImage,
                        int localHeight,
                        int localWidth) {
    // Determine the amount of padding for this filter
    int filterRadius = (filterWidth/2);
    int padding = filterRadius * 2;
```

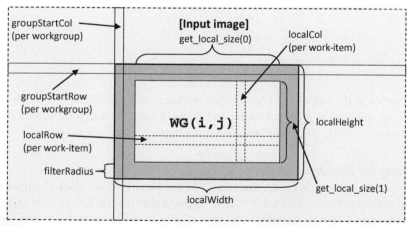

FIGURE 8.3

Illustration of the variables required for identifying a work-item's read location within the input image.

```
// Determine where each workgroup begins reading
int groupStartCol = get_group_id(0)*get_local_size(0);
int groupStartRow = get_group_id(1)*get_local_size(1);

// Determine the local ID of each work-item
int localCol = get_local_id(0);
int localRow = get_local_id(1);

// Determine the global ID of each work-item. work-items
// representing the output region will have a unique
// global ID
int globalCol = groupStartCol + localCol;
int globalRow = groupStartRow + localRow;

// Cache the data to local memory

// Step down rows
for(int i = localRow; i < localHeight; i +=
    get_local_size(1)) {

    int curRow = groupStartRow+i;

    // Step across columns
    for(int j = localCol; j < localWidth; j +=
        get_local_size(0)) {

        int curCol = groupStartCol+j;

        // Perform the read if it is in bounds
        if(curRow < rows && curCol < cols) {
            localImage[i*localWidth + j] =
            imageIn[curRow*cols+curCol];
        }
    }
}
barrier(CLK_LOCAL_MEM_FENCE);

// Perform the convolution
...
```

The barrier at the end of the copy is required because work-items will finish with their data transfers at different times, and no work-item in the group should begin the convolution step until all transfers are complete.

Aligning for Memory Accesses

Performance on both NVIDIA and AMD GPUs benefits from data alignment in global memory. Particularly for NVIDIA, aligning accesses on 128-byte boundaries and accessing 128-byte segments will map ideally to the memory hardware. However, in this example, the 16-wide workgroups will only be accessing 64-byte segments, so data should be aligned to 64-byte addresses. This means that the first column that each workgroup accesses should begin at a 64-byte aligned address.

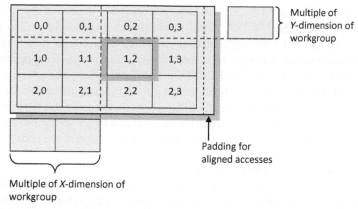

Multiple of
Y-dimension of
workgroup

Padding for
aligned accesses

Multiple of *X*-dimension of
workgroup

FIGURE 8.4

The first padding pixel read by each workgroup will be a multiple of the workgroup size in each dimension. Padding the image and sizing the *X*-dimension of the workgroup appropriately ensures aligned accesses.

In this example, the choice to have the border pixels not produce values determines that the offset for all workgroups will be a multiple of the workgroup dimensions (i.e., for a 16 × 16 workgroup, workgroup <N, M> will begin accessing data at column N*16). An example of the offset of each workgroup is presented in Figure 8.4. To ensure that each workgroup aligns properly, the only requirement then is to pad the input data with extra columns so that its width becomes a multiple of the *X*-dimension of the workgroup.

Manually padding a data array on the host can be complicated, time-consuming, and sometimes infeasible. To avoid such tedious data fixup, OpenCL has introduced a command called clEnqueueWriteBufferRect() to copy a host array into the middle of a larger device buffer. When creating the buffer, the number of columns used to determine the size should be the number of elements required to provide the desired alignment. For a 16 × 16 workgroup, the number of columns should be rounded up to the nearest multiple of 16. The call to clEnqueueWriteBufferRect()that copies the host data into the padded device buffer is listed here:

```
// Pad the number of columns (assuming 16x16 workgroup)
int deviceWidth = roundUp(imageWidth, 16);
// No padding needed for rows
int deviceHeight = imageHeight;

// Copy the input data on the host to the padded buffer
// on the device
clEnqueueWriteBufferRect(queue, d_inputImage, CL_TRUE,
    buffer_origin, host_origin, region,
    deviceWidth*sizeof(float), 0, imageWidth*sizeof(float),
    0, inputImage, 0, NULL, NULL);
```

The grid cells: 0,0 0,1 0,2 0,3 / 1,0 1,1 1,2 1,3 / 2,0 2,1 2,2 2,3

By aligning data to a 64-byte boundary, performance improved by 10% on a Radeon 6970 GPU. The NVIDIA Fermi architecture automatically caches memory transactions on-chip in L1 memory, and because nonaligned reads get turned into an additional access (which is usually used in the following read anyway), negligible performance gains can be achieved on a GTX 480. On the GT200 series architecture, automatic caching is not supported, so memory alignment plays a more significant role. Using the NVIDIA Visual Profiler and a GTX 285 GPU, we see that aligning to a 64-byte address boundary results in fewer memory transactions, each of a larger size, producing an 8% improvement in memory performance over the original version of the code.

Improving Efficiency with Vector Reads

AMD 5000-series and 6000-series GPUs are optimized for 128-bit read operations per SIMD lane and therefore see performance gains from performing vector reads (i.e., reading float4 data allows us to come closer to achieving peak memory bandwidth than reading float data). The 7000 series GPU will not benefit substantially from vector reads. Additionally, if a filter has radius of 8 or less (i.e., the filter is at most 17×17), a 16×16 workgroup can copy all of the padding and output pixels with only a single float4 read per work-item.

The first step is to resize the local memory allocation to include the extra pixels required to support the float4 data type:

```
int localWidth = roundUp(localSize[0]+padding, 4);
int localHeight = localSize[1]+padding;
size_t localMemSize = (localWidth*localHeight*sizeof(float));
```

The code to perform the vector transfer of data from global memory to local memory is listed next. To employ a vector read and still use scalar data for the convolution, the input image is given the type float4, and the local memory cache is given the data type float. When the read is performed, a temporary __local float4 pointer is set to the desired location in local memory and is used to read the data. By using float4 as the data type of the input image, the width (number of columns) of the image is divided by four because each column stores four values. The number of rows in the image does not change.

```
__kernel
void convolution_read4(__global float4* imageIn,
                       __global float* imageOut,
                       __constant float* filter,
                               int rows,
                               int cols,
                               int filterWidth,
                       __local float* localImage,
                               int localHeight,
                               int localWidth) {
```

```
// Vector pointer that will be used to cache data
// scalar memory
__local float4* localImage4;

// Determine the amount of padding for this filter
int filterRadius = (filterWidth/2);
int padding = filterRadius * 2;

// Determine where each workgroup begins reading
int groupStartCol = get_group_id(0)*get_local_size(0)/4;
int groupStartRow = get_group_id(1)*get_local_size(1);

// Flatten the localIds 0-255
int localId = get_local_id(1)*get_local_size(0) +
    get_local_id(0);
// There will be localWidth/4 work-items reading per row
int localRow = (localId / (localWidth/4));
// Each work-item is reading 4 elements apart
int localCol = (localId % (localWidth/4));

// Determine the row and column offset in global memory
// assuming each element reads 4 floats
int globalRow = groupStartRow + localRow;
int globalCol = groupStartCol + localCol;

// Set the vector pointer to the correct scalar location
// in local memory
localImage4 = (__local float4*)
    &localImage[localRow*localWidth+localCol*4];
// Perform all of the reads with a single load
if(globalRow < rows && globalCol < cols/4 &&
    localRow < localHeight) {
    localImage4[0] = imageIn[globalRow*cols/4+globalCol];
}
barrier(CLK_LOCAL_MEM_FENCE);

// Perform the convolution
...
```

On the AMD Radeon 6970, a significant performance gain is achieved by using vector reads. Compared to the initial implementation of the algorithm, a 42% improvement in memory performance was seen when using the `float4` data type with aligned memory accesses. The memory hardware on NVIDIA GPUs benefits less from 128-bit reads, and the extra register pressure can decrease overall performance; thus, even though the overall number of memory transactions decreased using the vector type, a slight performance degradation was seen in this example.

Performing the Convolution

Now that the data is stored in local memory, it can be efficiently accessed to perform the convolution. The following code provides an implementation of the algorithm that corresponds to the C version in Chapter 4. Each work-item represents an output location and applies the filter by performing multiply-accumulate operations in a neighborhood around its location. No output is produced for pixels that would need to access out-of-bounds locations in the original image due to the filter size. For a 7×7 filter, the first valid output pixel will be located at index (3,3), and issue accesses to the padding pixels beginning at index (0,0). Because we want all work-items to produce output data, the work-item with global index (0,0) will produce the output value at (3,3). In other words, each work-item's output value will be offset from its global ID by the filter radius in both the X and Y directions. The following code performs the convolution:

```
// Only allow work-items mapping to valid locations in
// the output image to perform the convolution
if(globalRow < rows - padding && globalCol < cols - padding) {

    // Each work-item will filter around its start location
    // (starting from the filter radius left and up)
    float sum = 0.0f;
    int filterIdx = 0;

    // The convolution loop
    for(int i = localRow; i < localRow+filterWidth; i++) {
        int offset = i*localWidth;
        for(int j = localCol; j < localCol+filterWidth; j++) {
            sum += localImage[offset+j] * filter[filterIdx++];
        }
    }

    // Write the data out
    imageOut[(globalRow+filterRadius)*cols +
        (globalCol+filterRadius)] = sum;
}
}
```

Improving Performance with Loop Unrolling

Unlike the 7970 GPU, the AMD 6970 GPU is a VLIW (Very Long Instruction Word) architecture where the compiler is tasked with packing multiple instructions to keep the ALU Units busy. Using the AMD APP Profiler, we are able to see that the ALU packing in the VLIW units for this kernel is low (only 43%). This means that less than half of the ALU units are being utilized, and it is a sign that the compiler cannot find sufficient instructions to fill the VLIW units. For the convolution kernel, the tight computation loops are the likely culprit. If we know that the filter size will be static (i.e., at compile time), we can unroll the inner loop to increase the ratio of ALU to branching instructions.

```
// Only allow work-items mapping to valid locations in
// the output image to perform the convolution
if(globalRow < rows - padding && globalCol < cols - padding) {

    // Each work-item will filter around its start location
    //(starting from the filter radius left and up)
    float sum = 0.0f;
    int filterIdx = 0;

    // Inner loop unrolled
    for(int i = localRow; i < localRow+filterWidth; i++) {
        int offset = i*localWidth+localCol;
        sum += localImage[offset++] * filter[filterIdx++];
        sum += localImage[offset++] * filter[filterIdx++];
        sum += localImage[offset++] * filter[filterIdx++];
        sum += localImage[offset++] * filter[filterIdx++];
        sum += localImage[offset++] * filter[filterIdx++];
        sum += localImage[offset++] * filter[filterIdx++];
        sum += localImage[offset++] * filter[filterIdx++];
    }

    // Write the data out
    imageOut[(globalRow+filterRadius)*cols +
        (globalCol+filterRadius)] = sum;
    }
}
```

On an AMD Radeon 6970, using a 7×7 filter and a 600×400 image, unrolling the innermost loop provided a $2.4\times$ speedup and increased the ALU packing efficiency to 79%. The GTX 285 and 480 saw similar performance gains—$2.6\times$ and $2.2\times$ speedups, respectively.

Completely unrolling both inner and outer loops of the convolution increases the code size and may not be possible for large filtering kernels. However, in general, loop unrolling produces a substantial speedup on both AMD and NVIDIA GPU devices. With a 7×7 filter, the Radeon 6970 achieved a $6.3\times$ speedup over the non-unrolled version. The GTX 285 and 480 saw speedups of $3.2\times$ and $2.9\times$, respectively, over the non-unrolled version.

Using the memory optimizations and loop unrolling described in this chapter, both the Radeon 6970 and the GTX 480 are able to perform the convolution at a rate of approximately 2 billion pixels per second while using a 7×7 filter.

CONCLUSIONS

This chapter discussed a classical computational kernel, convolution, that is used in many machine vision, statistics, and signal processing applications. We presented how to approach optimization of this OpenCL kernel when targeting either AMD or NVIDIA GPUs. We explored the benefits of different memory optimizations and showed that performance is heavily dependent on the underlying memory architecture of the different devices. However, for all devices considered, significant performance improvements were obtained in the computational portions of the algorithm by giving up the generality of the double convolution loops and unrolling for specific kernel sizes. In general, many performance optimizations will depend on the specifics of the underlying device hardware architecture. To obtain peak performance, the programmer should be equipped with this information.

CODE LISTINGS
Host Code

```
#define WGX 16
#define WGY 16

// Uncomment each of these to run with the corresponding
// optimization
#define NON_OPTIMIZED
//#define READ_ALIGNED
//#define READ4

// This function takes a positive integer and rounds it up to
// the nearest multiple of another provided integer
unsigned int roundUp(unsigned int value, unsigned int multiple) {

        // Determine how far past the nearest multiple the value is
        unsigned int remainder = value % multiple;

        // Add the difference to make the value a multiple
        if(remainder != 0) {
                value += (multiple-remainder);
        }

        return value;
}
int main(int argc, char** argv) {

        // Set up the data on the host

        // Rows and columns in the input image
        int imageHeight;
        int imageWidth;

        // Homegrown function to read a BMP from file
        float* inputImage = readImage("input.bmp", &imageWidth,
           &imageHeight);

        // Size of the input and output images on the host
        int dataSize = imageHeight*imageWidth*sizeof(float);

        // Pad the number of columns
```

```
#ifdef NON_OPTIMIZED
    int deviceWidth = imageWidth;
#else // READ_ALIGNED || READ4
    int deviceWidth = roundUp(imageWidth, WGX);
#endif
    int deviceHeight = imageHeight;
    // Size of the input and output images on the device
    int deviceDataSize = imageHeight*deviceWidth*sizeof(float);

    // Output image on the host
    float* outputImage = NULL;
    outputImage = (float*)malloc(dataSize);
    for(int i = 0; i < imageHeight; i++) {
        for(int j = 0; j < imageWidth; j++) {
            outputImage[i*imageWidth+j] = 0;
        }
    }

    // 45 degree motion blur
    float filter[49] =
        {0,       0,      0,      0,      0, 0.0145,      0,
         0,       0,      0,      0, 0.0376, 0.1283, 0.0145,
         0,       0,      0, 0.0376, 0.1283, 0.0376,      0,
         0,       0, 0.0376, 0.1283, 0.0376,      0,      0,
         0, 0.0376, 0.1283, 0.0376,      0,      0,      0,
    0.0145, 0.1283, 0.0376,      0,      0,      0,      0,
         0, 0.0145,      0,      0,      0,      0,      0};
    int filterWidth = 7;
    int filterRadius = filterWidth/2;
    int paddingPixels = (int)(filterWidth/2) * 2;

    // Set up the OpenCL environment

    // Discovery platform
    cl_platform_id platform;
    clGetPlatformIDs(1, &platform, NULL);

    // Discover device
    cl_device_id device;
    clGetDeviceIDs(platform, CL_DEVICE_TYPE_ALL, 1, &device,
        NULL);

    // Create context
    cl_context_properties props[3] = {CL_CONTEXT_PLATFORM,
        (cl_context_properties)(platform), 0};
    cl_context context;
    context = clCreateContext(props, 1, &device, NULL, NULL,
        NULL);

    // Create command queue
    cl_command_queue queue;
```

```
    queue = clCreateCommandQueue(context, device, 0, NULL);

    // Create memory buffers
    cl_mem d_inputImage;
    cl_mem d_outputImage;
    cl_mem d_filter;
    d_inputImage = clCreateBuffer(context, CL_MEM_READ_ONLY,
        deviceDataSize, NULL, NULL);
    d_outputImage = clCreateBuffer(context, CL_MEM_WRITE_ONLY,
        deviceDataSize, NULL, NULL);
    d_filter = clCreateBuffer(context, CL_MEM_READ_ONLY,
        49*sizeof(float),NULL, NULL);

    // Write input data to the device
#ifdef NON_OPTIMIZED
    clEnqueueWriteBuffer(queue, d_inputImage, CL_TRUE, 0,
    deviceDataSize,
        inputImage, 0, NULL, NULL);
#else // READ_ALIGNED || READ4
    size_t buffer_origin[3] = {0,0,0};
    size_t host_origin[3] = {0,0,0};
    size_t region[3] = {deviceWidth*sizeof(float),
        imageHeight, 1};
    clEnqueueWriteBufferRect(queue, d_inputImage, CL_TRUE,
        buffer_origin, host_origin, region,
        deviceWidth*sizeof(float), 0, imageWidth*sizeof(float), 0,
        inputImage, 0, NULL, NULL);
#endif

    // Write the filter to the device
    clEnqueueWriteBuffer(queue, d_filter, CL_TRUE, 0,
        49*sizeof(float), filter, 0, NULL, NULL);

    // Read in the program from file
    char* source = readSource("convolution.cl");

    // Create the program
    cl_program program;

    // Create and compile the program
    program = clCreateProgramWithSource(context, 1,
        (const char**)&source, NULL, NULL);
    cl_int build_status;
    build_status = clBuildProgram(program, 1, &device, NULL, NULL,
        NULL);

    // Create the kernel
    cl_kernel kernel;
#if defined NON_OPTIMIZED || defined READ_ALIGNED
    // Only the host-side code differs for the aligned reads
    kernel = clCreateKernel(program, "convolution", NULL);
```

```
#else // READ4
   kernel = clCreateKernel(program, "convolution_read4", NULL);
#endif

   // Selected workgroup size is 16x16
   int wgWidth = WGX;
   int wgHeight = WGY;

   // When computing the total number of work-items, the
   // padding work-items do not need to be considered
   int totalWorkItemsX = roundUp(imageWidth-paddingPixels,
      wgWidth);
   int totalWorkItemsY = roundUp(imageHeight-paddingPixels,
      wgHeight);

   // Size of a workgroup
   size_t localSize[2] = {wgWidth, wgHeight};
   // Size of the NDRange
   size_t globalSize[2] = {totalWorkItemsX, totalWorkItemsY};

   // The amount of local data that is cached is the size of the
   // workgroups plus the padding pixels
#if defined NON_OPTIMIZED || defined READ_ALIGNED
   int localWidth = localSize[0] + paddingPixels;
#else // READ4
   // Round the local width up to 4 for the read4 kernel
   int localWidth = roundUp(localSize[0]+paddingPixels, 4);
#endif
   int localHeight = localSize[1] + paddingPixels;

   // Compute the size of local memory (needed for dynamic
   // allocation)
   size_t localMemSize = (localWidth * localHeight *
      sizeof(float));

   // Set the kernel arguments
   clSetKernelArg(kernel, 0, sizeof(cl_mem), &d_inputImage);
   clSetKernelArg(kernel, 1, sizeof(cl_mem), &d_outputImage);
   clSetKernelArg(kernel, 2, sizeof(cl_mem), &d_filter);
   clSetKernelArg(kernel, 3, sizeof(int), &deviceHeight);
   clSetKernelArg(kernel, 4, sizeof(int), &deviceWidth);
   clSetKernelArg(kernel, 5, sizeof(int), &filterWidth);
   clSetKernelArg(kernel, 6, localMemSize, NULL);
   clSetKernelArg(kernel, 7, sizeof(int), &localHeight);
   clSetKernelArg(kernel, 8, sizeof(int), &localWidth);

   // Execute the kernel
   clEnqueueNDRangeKernel(queue, kernel, 2, NULL, globalSize,
      localSize, 0, NULL, NULL);

   // Wait for kernel to complete
```

```
        clFinish(queue);

        // Read back the output image
#ifdef NON_OPTIMIZED
        clEnqueueReadBuffer(queue, d_outputImage, CL_TRUE, 0,
            deviceDataSize, outputImage, 0, NULL, NULL);
#else // READ_ALIGNED || READ4
        // Begin reading output from (3,3) on the device
        // (for 7x7 filter with radius 3)
        buffer_origin[0] = 3*sizeof(float);
        buffer_origin[1] = 3;
        buffer_origin[2] = 0;

        // Read data into (3,3) on the host
        host_origin[0] = 3*sizeof(float);
        host_origin[1] = 3;
        host_origin[2] = 0;

        // Region is image size minus padding pixels
        region[0] = (imageWidth-paddingPixels)*sizeof(float);
        region[1] = (imageHeight-paddingPixels);
        region[2] = 1;

            // Perform the read
        clEnqueueReadBufferRect(queue, d_outputImage, CL_TRUE,
            buffer_origin, host_origin, region,
            deviceWidth*sizeof(float), 0, imageWidth*sizeof(float), 0,
            outputImage, 0, NULL, NULL);
#endif

        // Homegrown function to write the image to file
        storeImage(outputImage, "output.bmp", imageHeight,
            imageWidth);

        // Free OpenCL objects
        clReleaseMemObject(d_inputImage);
        clReleaseMemObject(d_outputImage);
        clReleaseMemObject(d_filter);
        clReleaseKernel(kernel);
        clReleaseProgram(program);
        clReleaseCommandQueue(queue);
        clReleaseContext(context);

        return 0;
}
```

Kernel Code

```
    __kernel
    void convolution(__global float* imageIn,
                    __global float* imageOut,
```

```
            __constant float* filter,
                    int rows,
                    int cols,
                    int filterWidth,
            __local float* localImage,
                    int localHeight,
                    int localWidth) {

// Determine the amount of padding for this filter
int filterRadius = (filterWidth/2);
int padding = filterRadius * 2;

// Determine the size of the workgroup output region
int groupStartCol = get_group_id(0)*get_local_size(0);
int groupStartRow = get_group_id(1)*get_local_size(1);

// Determine the local ID of each work-item
int localCol = get_local_id(0);
int localRow = get_local_id(1);

// Determine the global ID of each work-item. work-items
// representing the output region will have a unique global
// ID
int globalCol = groupStartCol + localCol;
int globalRow = groupStartRow + localRow;

// Cache the data to local memory

// Step down rows
for(int i = localRow; i < localHeight; i +=
    get_local_size(1)) {

    int curRow = groupStartRow+i;

    // Step across columns
    for(int j = localCol; j < localWidth; j +=
        get_local_size(0)) {

        int curCol = groupStartCol+j;

        // Perform the read if it is in bounds
        if(curRow < rows && curCol < cols) {
            localImage[i*localWidth + j] =
                imageIn[curRow*cols+curCol];
        }
    }
}
barrier(CLK_LOCAL_MEM_FENCE);

// Perform the convolution
if(globalRow < rows-padding && globalCol < cols-padding) {

    // Each work-item will filter around its start location
```

```
        //(starting from the filter radius left and up)
        float sum = 0.0f;
        int filterIdx = 0;

        // Not unrolled
        for(int i = localRow; i < localRow+filterWidth; i++) {
            int offset = i*localWidth;
            for(int j = localCol; j < localCol+filterWidth; j++){
                sum += localImage[offset+j] *
                    filter[filterIdx++];
            }
        }

        /*
        // Inner loop unrolled
        for(int i = localRow; i < localRow+filterWidth; i++) {
            int offset = i*localWidth+localCol;
            sum += localImage[offset++] * filter[filterIdx++];
            sum += localImage[offset++] * filter[filterIdx++];
            sum += localImage[offset++] * filter[filterIdx++];
            sum += localImage[offset++] * filter[filterIdx++];
            sum += localImage[offset++] * filter[filterIdx++];
            sum += localImage[offset++] * filter[filterIdx++];
            sum += localImage[offset++] * filter[filterIdx++];
        }
        */

        // Write the data out
        imageOut[(globalRow+filterRadius)*cols +
            (globalCol+filterRadius)] = sum;
    }

    return;
}
__kernel
void convolution_read4(__global float4* imageIn,
                       __global float* imageOut,
                       __constant float* filter,
                                int rows,
                                int cols,
                                int filterWidth,
                       __local float* localImage,
                                int localHeight,
                                int localWidth) {

    // Vector pointer that will be used to cache data
    // scalar memory
    __local float4* localImage4;

    // Determine the amount of padding for this filter
    int filterRadius = (filterWidth/2);
    int padding = filterRadius * 2;
```

```
// Determine where each workgroup begins reading
int groupStartCol = get_group_id(0)*get_local_size(0)/4;
int groupStartRow = get_group_id(1)*get_local_size(1);

// Flatten the localIds 0-255
int localId = get_local_id(1)*get_local_size(0) +
    get_local_id(0);
// There will be localWidth/4 work-items reading per row
int localRow = (localId / (localWidth/4));
// Each work-item is reading 4 elements apart
int localCol = (localId % (localWidth/4));

// Determine the row and column offset in global memory
// assuming each element reads 4 floats
int globalRow = groupStartRow + localRow;
int globalCol = groupStartCol + localCol;

// Set the vector pointer to the correct scalar location
// in local memory
localImage4 = (__local float4*)
    &localImage[localRow*localWidth+localCol*4];

// Perform all of the reads with a single load
if(globalRow < rows && globalCol < cols/4 &&
    localRow < localHeight) {

    localImage4[0] = imageIn[globalRow*cols/4+globalCol];
}
barrier(CLK_LOCAL_MEM_FENCE);

// Reassign local IDs based on each work-item processing
// one output element
localCol = get_local_id(0);
localRow = get_local_id(1);

// Reassign global IDs for unique output locations
globalCol = get_group_id(0)*get_local_size(0) + localCol;
globalRow = get_group_id(1)*get_local_size(1) + localRow;
// Perform the convolution
if(globalRow < rows-padding && globalCol < cols-padding) {

    // Each work-item will filter around its start location
    // (starting from half the filter size left and up)
    float sum = 0.0f;
    int filterIdx = 0;

    // Not unrolled
    for(int i = localRow; i < localRow+filterWidth; i++) {
        int offset = i*localWidth;
        for(int j = localCol; j < localCol+filterWidth; j++){
            sum += localImage[offset+j] *
                filter[filterIdx++];
        }
    }
    /*
```

```
// Inner loop unrolled
for(int i = localRow; i < localRow+filterWidth; i++) {
   int offset = i*localWidth+localCol;

      sum += localImage[offset++] * filter[filterIdx++];
      sum += localImage[offset++] * filter[filterIdx++];
      sum += localImage[offset++] * filter[filterIdx++];
      sum += localImage[offset++] * filter[filterIdx++];
      sum += localImage[offset++] * filter[filterIdx++];
      sum += localImage[offset++] * filter[filterIdx++];
      sum += localImage[offset++] * filter[filterIdx++];
}
*/

/*
// Completely unrolled
int offset = localRow*localWidth+localCol;

sum += localImage[offset+0] * filter[filterIdx++];
sum += localImage[offset+1] * filter[filterIdx++];
sum += localImage[offset+2] * filter[filterIdx++];
sum += localImage[offset+3] * filter[filterIdx++];
sum += localImage[offset+4] * filter[filterIdx++];
sum += localImage[offset+5] * filter[filterIdx++];
sum += localImage[offset+6] * filter[filterIdx++];

offset += localWidth;

sum += localImage[offset+0] * filter[filterIdx++];
sum += localImage[offset+1] * filter[filterIdx++];
sum += localImage[offset+2] * filter[filterIdx++];
sum += localImage[offset+3] * filter[filterIdx++];
sum += localImage[offset+4] * filter[filterIdx++];
sum += localImage[offset+5] * filter[filterIdx++];
sum += localImage[offset+6] * filter[filterIdx++];

offset += localWidth;

sum += localImage[offset+0] * filter[filterIdx++];
sum += localImage[offset+1] * filter[filterIdx++];
sum += localImage[offset+2] * filter[filterIdx++];
sum += localImage[offset+3] * filter[filterIdx++];
sum += localImage[offset+4] * filter[filterIdx++];
sum += localImage[offset+5] * filter[filterIdx++];
sum += localImage[offset+6] * filter[filterIdx++];

offset += localWidth;

sum += localImage[offset+0] * filter[filterIdx++];
sum += localImage[offset+1] * filter[filterIdx++];
sum += localImage[offset+2] * filter[filterIdx++];
sum += localImage[offset+3] * filter[filterIdx++];
```

```
    sum += localImage[offset+4] * filter[filterIdx++];
    sum += localImage[offset+5] * filter[filterIdx++];
    sum += localImage[offset+6] * filter[filterIdx++];

    offset += localWidth;

    sum += localImage[offset+0] * filter[filterIdx++];
    sum += localImage[offset+1] * filter[filterIdx++];
    sum += localImage[offset+2] * filter[filterIdx++];
    sum += localImage[offset+3] * filter[filterIdx++];
    sum += localImage[offset+4] * filter[filterIdx++];
    sum += localImage[offset+5] * filter[filterIdx++];
    sum += localImage[offset+6] * filter[filterIdx++];

    offset += localWidth;

    sum += localImage[offset+0] * filter[filterIdx++];
    sum += localImage[offset+1] * filter[filterIdx++];
    sum += localImage[offset+2] * filter[filterIdx++];
    sum += localImage[offset+3] * filter[filterIdx++];
    sum += localImage[offset+4] * filter[filterIdx++];
    sum += localImage[offset+5] * filter[filterIdx++];
    sum += localImage[offset+6] * filter[filterIdx++];

    offset += localWidth;

    sum += localImage[offset+0] * filter[filterIdx++];
    sum += localImage[offset+1] * filter[filterIdx++];
    sum += localImage[offset+2] * filter[filterIdx++];
    sum += localImage[offset+3] * filter[filterIdx++];
    sum += localImage[offset+4] * filter[filterIdx++];
    sum += localImage[offset+5] * filter[filterIdx++];
    sum += localImage[offset+6] * filter[filterIdx++];
    */

    // Write the data out
    imageOut[(globalRow+filterRadius)*cols +
        (globalCol+filterRadius)] = sum;
    }
    return;
}
```

Reference

NVIDIA Corporation. (2009). *NVIDIA OpenCL Programming Guide for the CUDA Architecture.* Santa Clara, CA: NVIDIA Corporation.

OpenCL Case Study: Histogram

INTRODUCTION

This chapter discusses specific optimizations for a memory-bound kernel. The kernel we choose for this chapter is an image histogram operation. The source data for this operation is an 8-bit-per-pixel image with a target of counting into each of 256 32-bit histogram bins.

The principle of the histogram algorithm is to perform the following operation over each element of the image:

```
for( many input values ) {
    histogram[ value ]++;
}
```

This algorithm performs many scattered read-modify-write accesses into a small histogram data structure. On a CPU, this application will use the cache, although with a high rate of reuse of elements. On a GPU, these accesses will be resolved in global memory, which will produce a worst-case scenario in terms of performance.

To address the high degree of contention of access in global memory, the algorithm chosen parallelizes the histogram over a number of workgroups, each of which summarizes its block of source data into a number of sub-histograms stored in on-chip local memory. These local histograms are finally reduced into a single global histogram, storing the result for the overall image. The overview of the algorithm is shown in Figure 9.1.

CHOOSING THE NUMBER OF WORKGROUPS

When we begin to map an OpenCL kernel to target hardware, we may encounter some constraints on the number of work-items and workgroups that follow from the design of the algorithm, the target architecture, and the size of the various memory regions distributed throughout the target machine. Local memory is shared within a workgroup, and a given group summarizes data into a sub-histogram stored in a region within local memory. This allows many work-items to contribute to the same local memory area, collaborating to reduce memory overhead. Given that the final stage of the histogram computation is a global reduction with a separate local region

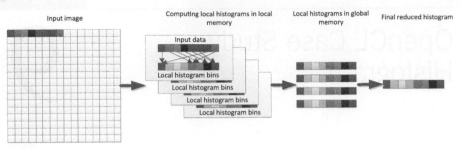

FIGURE 9.1

Computing the histogram involves first producing local histograms from the input image and then exporting those to global memory and performing a global reduction operation to produce the final histogram.

per workgroup, creating too many workgroups would transfer more local data into global memory, increasing memory usage and require a larger reduction operation.

To most efficiently use local memory and to reduce the overhead of global memory transactions, the number of workgroups should be as close as possible to the number of compute units, or SIMD cores, in the device. The local memory resources exist physically on a per-SIMD core basis in AMD and NVIDIA GPUs and are intended in the OpenCL specification to support access at least as efficient as global memory. It is important to make maximal use of the high bandwidth to such dedicated memory regions and that we use as many local memory spaces as possible to maximise parallel memory access. As just noted, we should avoid creating many more workgroups than the actual number of SIMD cores because this wastes global memory bandwidth.

Through the OpenCL API, we can query the number of compute units on the device at runtime:

```
clGetDeviceInfo(..., CL_DEVICE_MAX_COMPUTE_UNITS,...);
```

Note that in this case, using the naive single work-item per input pixel is highly inefficient. This is due largely to the low number of pixels mapping to a single histogram bin and hence generates a higher cost during the reduction phase. This inefficiency is also caused by per-work-item and per-group execution costs becoming significant due to high work-item counts.

CHOOSING THE OPTIMAL WORKGROUP SIZE

The optimal workgroup size for a given algorithm can be difficult to identify. At a minimum, workgroup sizes should be selected to be an even multiple of the width of the hardware scheduling units. Because targeted architectures are often vector based, it is inefficient to use half vectors for scheduling OpenCL work-items. On AMD GPUs, the hardware scheduling unit is a wavefront—a logical vector of 32 or 64 work-items that runs on a hardware SIMD unit. OpenCL workgroups execute as sets of wavefronts.

A single wavefront per compute unit is inadequate to fully utilize the machine. The hardware schedules two wavefronts at a time interleaved through the ALUs of the SIMD unit, and it schedules additional wavefronts to perform memory transactions. An absolute minimum to satisfy the hardware and fill instruction slots on an AMD GPU is then three wavefronts per compute unit, or 196 work-items on high-end APU GPUs. However, to enable the GPU to perform efficient hiding of global memory latency in fetch-bound kernels, at least seven wavefronts are required per SIMD.

We cannot exceed the maximum number of work-items that the device supports in a workgroup, which is 256 on current AMD GPUs. At a minimum, we need 64 work-items per group and at least three groups per compute unit. At a maximum, we have 256 work-items per group, and the number of groups that fit on the compute unit will be resource limited. There is little benefit to launching a very large number of work-items. Once enough work-items to fill the machine and cover memory latency have been dispatched, nothing is gained from scheduling additional work-items, and there may be additional overhead incurred. Within this range, it is necessary to fine-tune the implementation to find the optimal performance point.

OPTIMIZING GLOBAL MEMORY DATA ACCESS PATTERNS

A histogram is a highly memory-bound operation: Very few arithmetic operations are needed per pixel of the input image. We cannot rely on the often extensive floating point capabilities of OpenCL devices to attain high performance. Instead, we must make as efficient use of the memory system as possible, optimizing memory accesses when moving from one type of device to another.

For the histogram operation, the order of reads from global memory is order independent. This means that we can freely optimize the access pattern without concerns about correctly ordering reads with respect to each other.

The memory subsystems of both AMD GPUs and CPUs are optimized to perform 128-bit read operations, matching the common four-component pixel size of four 32-bit floats. On the GPU, single reads are inefficient because of the availability of vector hardware that can hold up to 64 work-items, so multiples of this 128-bit read allow the memory system to take full advantage of wide and high-speed data paths to memory. The ideal read pattern is for all simultaneously executing work-items to read adjacent 128-bit quantities, forming a 256-byte read burst across the 16 work-items executing in parallel on a given core and directly mapping to a GPU memory channel.

The result is that we transform memory accesses as follows. Each work-item reads unsigned integer quantities, packed into four-wide vectors (unit4), starting at the global work-item index and continuing with a stride that is equal to the total number of work-items to be read.

An efficient access pattern for reading input data is shown in the following code and in Figure 9.2:

```
uint gid    = get_global_id(0);
uint Stride = get_global_size(0);

for( i=0, idx = gid; i < n4VectorsPerWorkItem; i++, idx += Stride ) {
    uint4 temp = Image[idx];
    ...
```

Although the similar code shown in Figure 9.3 is a less efficient implementation when run on the GPU (in which each work-item reads serially), this implementation is perfect for a CPU, in which the total number of work-items in the system should not significantly exceed the number of cores.

```
uint gid= get_global_id(0);

for( i=0, idx = gid * n4VectorsPerWorkItem;
     I < n4VectorsPerWorkItem;
     i++, idx++) {

  uint4 temp = Image[idx];
  ...
```

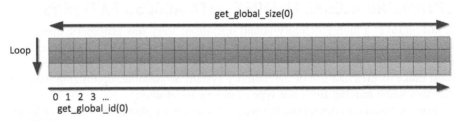

FIGURE 9.2

An efficient read pattern for the GPU in which work-items read consecutive addresses and stride through memory to find the next data item to read.

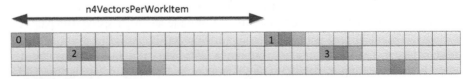

FIGURE 9.3

Serial reads in which each work item reads a series of locations in a contiguous section of memory and the next work item starts some distance through memory are more efficient for the CPU, in which temporal locality in a single work-item is more of a benefit than coalesced reading between serially executed work-items.

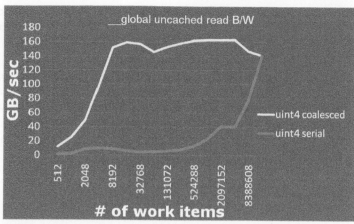

FIGURE 9.4

Serial coalesced trade-off: A graph of memory system throughput scalar and vector serial and coalesced reads against the number of work-items on the AMD Radeon HD™6970 GPU. Note that when the number of work-items becomes very large as the data set size is fixed, the two read styles converge to be the same coalesced read; hence, they have identical performance. The graph assumes a data set size of 256 MB.

We can see how the difference between these trades off as a function of the number of work-items in Figure 9.4. A clear performance benefit initially, but as we increase the number of work-items performing coalesced reads, performance declines because too many work-items are active in the system. Serial performance is very poor when strides are long, but as strides reduce, cache line reuse and coalescing benefits in the memory system improve performance until the two types of reads converge when they become identical with one data element read per work-item.

USING ATOMICS TO PERFORM LOCAL HISTOGRAM

When we execute this application on a CPU, we execute a workgroup with a single thread and hence have no read-after-write hazards. When targeting an AMD Radeon™ GPU, we can use a wide SIMD vector and provide for fine-grained threading. The combination of these features means that many work-items execute in parallel (16 work-items on high-end GPUs), and we can potentially interleave instruction execution from multiple executing wavefronts. As a result, we cannot guarantee the ordering of read-after-write dependencies on our local histogram bins.

To address this issue, we could reproduce the histogram bins multiple times, but this would require a copy of each bin for each work-item in the group (we do not know what order they will execute in). The resulting memory pressure would be too great.

The alternative solution is to use hardware atomics. The hardware atomics on the AMD Radeon HD6970 architecture are associated with each lane of the local data storage and can improve performance significantly. We can rely on these atomics with little concern about the overhead for our algorithm.

Performing the histogram operation in a local memory buffer becomes as simple as the following code. Note that because we have performed a 128-bit read of 16 pixels simultaneously (where each pixel is really a single 8-bit channel), we repeat this code in the core loop for each channel and use masks and shifts to extract this data. Performing the mask and shift operations explicitly on a uint4 vector maps efficiently to the underlying hardware architecture.

```
for( int i=0, idx=gid; i<n4VectorsPerWorkItem; i++, idx += Stride ) {
    uint4 temp = Image[idx];
    uint4 temp2 = (temp & mask);

    (void) atomic_inc( subhists + temp2.x );
    (void) atomic_inc( subhists + temp2.y );
    (void) atomic_inc( subhists + temp2.z );
    (void) atomic_inc( subhists + temp2.w );

    temp = temp >> 8;
    temp2 = (temp & mask);
    ...
```

OPTIMIZING LOCAL MEMORY ACCESS

Directly targeting histogram bins in global memory is a recipe for a nonscalable algorithm (i.e., the performance will not scale when we introduce additional hardware resources to the execution). There is a severe bottleneck when performing binning operations, whether using atomic functions or multiple bins per group, through the DRAM interface that will limit performance due to a significant increase in the total amount of memory traffic.

To avoid this issue, we choose to use separate small histograms for each workgroup using local memory buffers. These local memories are very high bandwidth, whether we are running on a CPU or a GPU. Using small histograms guarantees cache independence on a CPU and effective use of the dedicated high-bandwidth scratchpad memories on many GPUs. Although we are able to map to the scratchpad memory on a GPU, given that we are using wide SIMD vectors to access this memory, care must be taken to access this local data efficiently. Taking the local memory structure on the AMD Radeon 6970 GPU as an example (i.e., local data shares (LDS)), we have an SRAM array with 32 banks addressed using bits 2–7 of the address. Bank conflicts occur if we have multiple work-items from a 16-wide parallel SIMD issue attempt to read or write the same LDS bank.

Because we are limiting ourselves to a small number of workgroups relative to the amount of input data, we know that each work-item will process a significant number of input pixels. We already know that this reduces the size of the final reduction and concentrates work into local memory, localizing memory traffic and hence improving performance. It also gives us a further advantage in that we can afford to expand our local memory buffer slightly, such that instead of a single histogram for the entire workgroup, we use a subset of histograms and perform a reduction at the end. Given the large number of pixels per work-item, the overhead of the reduction stage should be negligible.

The benefit of using multiple histogram bins is apparent if we are careful with our layout. Figure 9.5 shows how we can reproduce the histogram multiple times to reduce bank conflicts. The AMD hardware has 32 memory banks in LDS and a single set of histogram bins. To attempt to increment the same histogram bin (guaranteed in a single color image) or sets of histogram bins that map to the same bank, sets of 16 work-items are dispatched in a single SIMD instruction. Any collisions will cause the application to stall.

To avoid these stalls, we can reproduce the entire set of histogram bins such that each work-item is guaranteed, whichever histogram bin it aims to use, to access the same bank. In this way, we can guarantee that a single bank will be used per work-item, and no two work-items will use the same bank. The cost is an increase in local memory use per workgroup and the addition of a local reduction stage to the computation.

Figure 9.6 shows the impact of this trade-off when accessing a random data set, where conflicts were few, so the overhead of the reduction is more noticeable. A uniform data set created a significant number of bank conflicts when using a single set of histogram bins and so benefits immediately when increasing the number of copies.

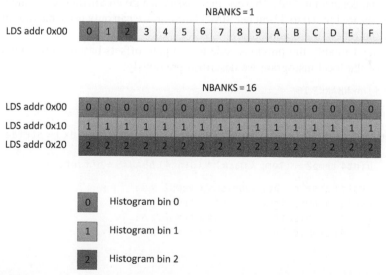

FIGURE 9.5

With a single set of histogram bins and 16 hardware banks, every 16th bin will map to the same hardware bank, causing conflicts if for any two work-items in a single SIMD vector address two histogram bins a and b, where $a\%16 = b\%16$. By reproducing the histogram for each work item, we alleviate these collisions.

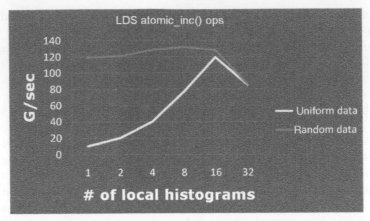

FIGURE 9.6

Trading off the number of banks. As we increase the number of copies of the local histogram in a given workgroup, we reduce the number of conflicts at the cost of introducing a local reduction operation and, eventually, reducing concurrent execution in the system due to resource constraints.

Realistic data sets would lie between these two extremes. Note that the peak is found at 16 banks, even though this evaluation is performed on the Radeon HD6970 device with 32 banks in total. Only 16 work-items issue in a given SIMD vector, and atomic operations are limited to 32-bit per SIMD lanes, so we can only use a maximum of 16 banks; the other 16 are unused.

We next modify the previous code to compute offsets based on the number of copies of the local histogram we described previously:

```
#define NBANKS 16

uint offset = (uint) lid % (uint) (NBANKS);

for( int i=0, idx=gid; i<n4VectorsPerWorkItem; i++, idx += Stride ) {
    uint4 temp = Image[idx];
    uint4 temp2 = (temp & mask) * (uint4) NBANKS + offset;

    (void) atomic_inc( subhists + temp2.x );
    (void) atomic_inc( subhists + temp2.y );
    (void) atomic_inc( subhists + temp2.z );
    (void) atomic_inc( subhists + temp2.w );
    ...
```

LOCAL HISTOGRAM REDUCTION

Before we conclude the local histogram kernel discussion, we must reduce the data across the copies we created and output this to global memory. We can mask out work-items in the group higher numbered than the number of bins. We can alternatively iterate through bins (if there are more bins than work-items) and then, for each bin histogram, copy the bins and output this to global memory.

```
barrier( CLK_LOCAL_MEM_FENCE );
for( int binIndex = lid;
     binIndex < NBINS;
     binIndex += get_local_size(0) ) {

    uint bin = 0;

    for( int i=0; i<NBANKS; i++ ) {
        bin += subhists[
            (lid * NBANKS) + ((i + lid) % NBANKS) ];
    }

    globalHistogram[
        (get_group_id(0) * NBINS) + binIndex ] = bin;
}
```

Note that in the previous code, we modify the code to avoid bank conflicts within the summation loop, as we otherwise guarantee NBANKS-way conflicts.

THE GLOBAL REDUCTION

The final step necessary in our histogram algorithm is to reduce the local bins. Because we have carefully limited the number of workgroups, the work to perform the global reduction is minor. Accordingly, we can avoid performing complicated tree-based reductions and multipass algorithms. Instead, we enqueue a single summation kernel similar to the reduction used for the local histograms:

```
__kernel void reduceKernel(
    __global uint * globalHistogram,
    uint nSubHists ) {

    uint gid = get_global_id(0);
    uint bin = 0;

    for( int i=0; i < nSubHists; i++ )
        bin += globalHistogram [ (i * NBINS) + gid ];
    globalHistogram [ gid ] = bin;
}
```

FULL KERNEL CODE

```
__kernel __attribute__((reqd_work_group_size(NBINS,1,1)))
void histogramKernel(__global uint4 *Image,
                     __global uint  *globalHistogram,
                         uint  n4VectorsPerWorkItem){
```

```
__local uint subhists[NBANKS * NBINS];

uint gid     = get_global_id(0);
uint lid     = get_local_id(0);
uint Stride  = get_global_size(0);
uint4 temp, temp2;
const uint shift = (uint) NBITS;
const uint mask = (uint) (NBINS-1);
uint offset = (uint) lid % (uint) (NBANKS);

uint localItems = NBANKS * NBINS;
uint localItemsPerWorkItem;
uint localMaxWorkItems;

// parallel LDS clear

// first, calculate work-items per data item,
// at least 1:
localMaxWorkItems = min( 1, get_local_size(0) / localItems );
// but no more than we have items:
localMaxWorkItems = max( 1, localMaxWorkItems / localItems );
// calculate threads total:
localMaxWorkItems = localItems / localMaxWorkItems;
// but no more than LDS banks:
localMaxWorkItems = min( get_local_size(0), localMaxWorkItems );

localItemsPerWorkItem = localItems / localMaxWorkItems;

// now, clear LDS
__local uint *p = (__local uint *) subhists;

if( lid < localMaxWorkItems ) {
   for(i=0, idx=lid;
       i<localItemsPerWorkItem;
       i++, idx+=localMaxWorkItems)
   {
      p[idx] = 0;
   }
}

barrier( CLK_LOCAL_MEM_FENCE );

// read & scatter phase

for( int i=0, idx=gid;
     i<n4VectorsPerWorkItem;
     i++, idx += Stride ) {

   temp = Image[idx];
   temp2 = (temp & mask) * (uint4) NBANKS + offset;

   (void) atomic_inc( subhists + temp2.x );
   (void) atomic_inc( subhists + temp2.y );
   (void) atomic_inc( subhists + temp2.z );
```

```
        (void) atomic_inc( subhists + temp2.w );

        temp = temp >> shift;
        temp2 = (temp & mask) * (uint4) NBANKS + offset;

        (void) atomic_inc( subhists + temp2.x );
        (void) atomic_inc( subhists + temp2.y );
        (void) atomic_inc( subhists + temp2.z );
        (void) atomic_inc( subhists + temp2.w );

        temp = temp >> shift;
        temp2 = (temp & mask) * (uint4) NBANKS + offset;

        (void) atomic_inc( subhists + temp2.x );
        (void) atomic_inc( subhists + temp2.y );
        (void) atomic_inc( subhists + temp2.z );
        (void) atomic_inc( subhists + temp2.w );

        temp = temp >> shift;
        temp2 = (temp & mask) * (uint4) NBANKS + offset;

        (void) atomic_inc( subhists + temp2.x );
        (void) atomic_inc( subhists + temp2.y );
        (void) atomic_inc( subhists + temp2.z );
        (void) atomic_inc( subhists + temp2.w );
    }

    barrier( CLK_LOCAL_MEM_FENCE );

    // reduce __local banks to single histogram per work-group

    for( int binIndex = lid;
         binIndex < NBINS;
         binIndex += get_local_size(0) ) {

        uint bin = 0;

        for( int i=0; i<NBANKS; i++ ) {
          bin += subhists[
              (lid * NBANKS) + ((i + lid) % NBANKS) ];
        }

        globalHistogram[
            (get_group_id(0) * NBINS) + binIndex ] = bin;
    }
}

__kernel void reduceKernel(
    __global uint *globalHistogram,
    uint nSubHists ) {

    uint gid = get_global_id(0);
    uint bin = 0;
```

```
        // Reduce work-group histograms into single histogram,
        // one work-item for each bin.

        for( int i=0; i < nSubHists; i++ )
            bin += globalHistogram[ (i * NBINS) + gid ];

        globalHistogram[ gid ] = bin;
}
```

PERFORMANCE AND SUMMARY

Combining these activities, we can process a significant amount of input data with very high performance. As measured on the AMD Radeon HD6970 architecture with 256 histogram bins, we can achieve the following:

1. 158 GB/s of input data performing only reads from global memory into registers
2. 140 GB/s of input data adding scattering into local histograms to 1
3. 139 GB/s adding the local reduction operation to 1 and 2
4. 128 GB/s adding the final global reduction, requiring enqueuing a second kernel, to 1–3

In this chapter, we focused on the steps needed to optimize a memory-bound algorithm. We discussed how to restructure reads and to use local memory to reduce access overhead. We showed that we can improve application throughput when performing a full histogram compared with reading data only. We also showed that compared with reading data only, performing a full histogram need only marginally reduce application throughput if implemented efficiently. Techniques to reduce local memory bank conflicts and to improve global memory performance have wide application in other algorithms.

OpenCL Case Study: Mixed Particle Simulation

INTRODUCTION

This case study examines leveraging both the CPU and the GPU to implement a mixed-sized particle simulation. Without a loss of generality, this example is restricted to two dimensions to keep the kernels easily understandable. In addition, this case study leverages OpenCL's ability to share data between the CPU and the GPU, which is beneficial on highly integrated devices such as AMD's APUs.

Implementing a simple simulation with uniform particle sizes on data-parallel devices such as GPUs is relatively straightforward in OpenCL. Unfortunately, the efficiency of the simulation decreases if the assumption breaks and the particle size varies. The inefficiency results from the non-uniform granularity of the computation, especially for the collision detection, which is the most expensive part in a particle simulation. If there is a single large particle and many small particles, the number of collisions detected on the large particle can be significantly more than the number detected on the small particles. This difference can cause inefficiency because most GPUs execute in SIMD manner over wide vectors. If a GPU SIMD engine executes small particles for most SIMD lanes and in a single lane computes the result for a large particle, the "large" lane runs for longer than the "small" lanes. This means that the lanes computing collisions for small particles have to wait for the large lane to finish. The work imbalance results in load imbalance and poor utilization of the hardware as the vector width increases. However, the CPU has no problem dealing with this variation in the granularity of computation. Accordingly, the approach we present here is to use the CPU for the collision of large particles, whereas the GPU is used only for the collision of the uniformly sized small particles. This chapter discusses how to realize the collaboration of the GPU and the CPU for a mixed-sized particle simulation using OpenCL.

OVERVIEW OF THE COMPUTATION

Figure 10.1 is a screen shot from the simulation. You can see a large number of small particles rendered in blue interacting with varying-sized particles rendered in green and red. The green and the red colors represent dynamic and static particles, respectively. The collisions between the particles are classified into three types: small–small, large–small, and large–large. The granularity of the small–small collision is uniform, so the work is dispatched to the GPU. However, as discussed previously, the granularity of large–small and large–large is varying, so the CPU is better suited for performing these computations. If there are no large–small interactions, the two simulations are completely disjoint, so the GPU simulates the small particles and the CPU simulates the large particles. The mixed-sized particle simulation is implemented as an extension of the two disjoint computations. The challenge is to efficiently realize the interaction between the simulations because the physical properties of small particles live in GPU memory, whereas those of large particles live in CPU memory. If the memories are allocated without care, the data on the GPU has to be read back to the host every time it calculates the interaction. By using OpenCL buffers that are shared between and accessed by both the CPU and the GPU, the read back is no longer necessary.

Figure 10.2 shows an overview of the algorithm and the interaction between the GPU manager thread and the CPU work thread, both of which run on the host CPU. There are three major phases of computation per iteration: (1) data structure construction (2) computation of forces resulting from (3) collisions and force integration.

FIGURE 10.1

A screen shot from the mixed particle simulation. (Please see front cover of the book)

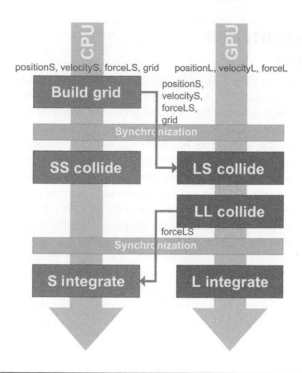

FIGURE 10.2

Overview of the computation for a single iteration.

First, the GPU kernel data structure is built. Then the GPU and CPU are synchronized to guarantee that the computation of the new data structure is complete and we can share the updated data and physical properties of the small particles with the CPU thread. After the first synchronization, threads start processing collisions. The GPU performs the small–small collisions, and the CPU performs the large–small and large–large collisions. To accelerate the collision detection of small particles against large particles, the data structure built on the GPU is also used on the CPU. The output from the collisions is a set of forces on particles. Two force buffers are prepared for the small particles: One is filled with small–small forces, resulting from the small–small collisions, and the other is shared with the CPU, which fills the buffer with the forces resulting from the large–small collisions. After the collisions are completed, the GPU and CPU threads are synchronized again so that the CPU is known to have finished writing to the force buffer, which is going to be used in the integration stage. Then, the GPU integrates forces on small particles, and the CPU integrates forces on large particles. Note that there are no write conflicts between the CPU and the GPU for the shared buffer. The CPU only writes to the shared buffer during the large–small collision phase. The buffer is only accessed by the GPU during the integration phase, after the GPU and CPU synchronize.

GPU IMPLEMENTATION
Buffer Creation

First, the buffers have to be created so that the runtime has the option of sharing data between the GPU and the CPU. A shared buffer can be created with the CL_MEM_ALLOC_HOST_PTR flag, which indicates the CPU will access the buffer. If the buffer is created with this flag, the runtime must return a location in host memory where data can be accessed between map and unmap function calls. We have the option of maintaining the data in host memory permanently (although this is not a requirement).[1] If this data is located permanently in host memory, the map and unmap operations applied to the buffer will introduce little execution overhead, requiring only synchronization overhead. However, this benefit does not come for free on a discrete GPU. Because the memory is stored in the CPU memory, whenever the GPU accesses the buffer the request must utilize the PCI Express bus. This transfer can result in larger latency compared with memory allocated on the GPU. On AMD's Fusion APU architecture and similar heterogeneous multiprocessors-on-a-chip where the GPU and the CPU share memory, we avoid the overhead of using the PCI Express bus. Removing this bottleneck leads to better performance. The following code shows an allocation of a shared buffer. Note that we are passing the CL_MEM_ALLOC_HOST_PTR flag as an argument:

```
buffer = clCreateBuffer(
    context,
    CL_MEM_READ_WRITE | CL_MEM_ALLOC_HOST_PTR,
    bufferSize,
    0,
    &status );
```

Although this buffer is created to be shared between the CPU and the GPU, we cannot access the data from the buffer pointer because the memory space is not unified in OpenCL. To access the data from the CPU, the buffer has to be mapped into the host's address space:

```
ptr = clEnqueueMapBuffer(
    commandQueue,
    buffer,
    false,
    CL_MAP_READ | CL_MAP_WRITE,
    0,
    bufferSize,
    0,
    0,
    0,
    &status );
```

---

[1]Note that CL_MEM_ALLOC_HOST_PTR guarantees that when map is called on the buffer, the passed pointer becomes the host pointer returned by map. Data is still only valid at the host pointer between calls to map and unmap.

The `clEnqueueMapBuffer` call returns a pointer to the buffer data. If a buffer is created without the flag being mapped, the data will be copied over from the device to the host, and the map operation is expensive. However, the map is almost free when a buffer is created using the flag and combined with appropriate runtime and hardware support, the buffer then lives in the host memory.

Building the Acceleration Structure

For accelerating the collision detection of particles, we use a uniform grid (a grid with a spatially invariant cell size) with a fixed capacity for each cell. Fast build and query are properties of a uniform grid that make it well suited for collision detection in a particle simulation, if the simulation does not have to extend to infinite space. The uniform grid has two buffers: a counter buffer storing cell counters and an index buffer storing particle indices or cell data. A work-item assigned to a particle fetches the particle position from global memory to a register and converts the world space position to a grid space coordinate. The work-item reads from the counter buffer the number of particles stored in the cell and adds the particle index to the index buffer. Care must be taken when accessing the counter because there can be several particles that fall into the same cell. In that case, several work-items try to read and write to the same counter. To guarantee the success of the memory access, we use an atomic operation as shown here:

```
for( all particles ) {
    idx = convertToGridIdx( particle[i] );
    count = atomic_inc( grid_count[idx] );
    grid[ calcAddr( idx, count ) ] = I;
}
```

The code listed under Kernels for Simulation has some additional logic to handle the boundary conditions and to prevent too many particles from being stored in a single cell.

Computing Collisions

This step calculates the force on each particle from the colliding particles. The uniform grid is used to efficiently locate the colliding particles associated with each particle. The particle position is converted to a grid coordinate system, which is used to calculate the address in memory of the grid cell. Because the size of each cell is defined to be equal to the diameter of the particles, potential colliding particles are only in the 3^2 grid cells (in three dimensions, 3^3) around the cell to which the particle belongs. Note that the granularity of the computation is uniform because the particles we are calculating have a uniform diameter, so all work-items check nine cells without any exceptions. A work-item iterates over the nine cells and reads the number of particles and particle indices stored in each cell to calculate the force on the particle. This force is a function of the colliding particle positions and velocities. After interparticle collision, each work-item checks for particle collisions with the boundary. These forces are accumulated and then written out to a force buffer.

```
for( all particles ) {
    force = 0;

    // compute particle interaction
    for( neighborhood ) {
        for( particles in grid cell[n] ) {
            j = getStoredParticleIdx();
            force += calcForce( particle[i], particle[j] );
        }
    }
    // compute boundary interaction
    force += calcForce( particle[i], top );
    force += calcForce( particle[i], bottom );
    force += calcForce( particle[i], left );
    force += calcForce( particle[i], right );
    forceOut[i] = force;
}
```

Integration

After the forces are computed on the CPU and GPU, a kernel is used to update the particles' positions and velocities via a process called integration. The velocity is computed as the sum of the forces resulting from the small–small particle interactions and the forces resulting from the large–small particle interactions. The particle position is updated based on the resulting particle velocity multiplied by the time step, dt. Finally, the buffer used to share force data with the CPU is zeroed for the next iteration. This kernel pseudo-code is fairly simple:

```
for( all particles ) {
    vel[i] += forceSmallSmall[i] + forceLargeSmall[i];
    pos[i] += vel[i]*dt;

    // zero forces for the CPU side
    forceBigParticles[i] = 0;
}
```

CPU IMPLEMENTATION

The CPU implementation does not differ much from the GPU version, but it runs in scalar rather than vector fashion. The collisions of particles are serialized so that we do not have to worry about the granularity. The collision of a large particle with small particles is performed using the uniform grid that was built on the GPU and shared with the CPU. It first calculates the extent of the large particle in the grid space and looks up all the cells in the extent. Figure 10.3 illustrates overlapping cells for a large particle. As the reader can see from this figure, the large particle overlaps many cells,

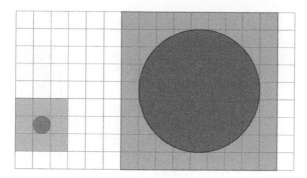

FIGURE 10.3

Small and large particles as mapped to the uniform grid.

whereas a small particle does not. If this code were to be executed on the GPU, it would waste many cycles as SIMD lanes were masked out.

LOAD BALANCING

Although we have shown the flow of the simulation using two threads in Figure 10.2, our implementation suffers from pool imbalance in terms of computation between the workloads. This imbalance results in low utilization of CPU threads. Of course, the degree of imbalance depends on the numbers of small and large particles present. Looking at the CPU work thread, it is easy to see that the large–small and large–large collisions are more expensive than the integration. Thus, the time between the first and the second synchronization is the largest amount of time. On the other hand, the most expensive part of the GPU execution is the small–small collision computation, followed by the construction of the uniform grid. Although the GPU is a powerful processor, the cost of building the uniform grid is not negligible. If the simulation is executed as shown in Figure 10.2, a thread has to wait before the first synchronization and the other has to wait before the second synchronization, which we can see more clearly in Figure 10.4A.

The computations can be reordered to improve load imbalance. Figure 10.2 shows the flow of a single iteration, but it is not necessary for grid creation to be the first step if we assume that particles do not move between the end of the previous iteration and the start of the current iteration. This is generally true unless a particle is directly moved, likely through user interaction, which is relatively rare. From this observation, grid creation can be moved to the end of the previous iteration. This modification makes two big blocks for the GPU thread, but the CPU's thread workload only involves the integration of particles (which is inexpensive). If we can move some computation to the CPU thread from the first half to the second half, then this should also ease load imbalance. Careful observation of the data flow of the pipeline shows that the second synchronization is necessary only for the buffer containing

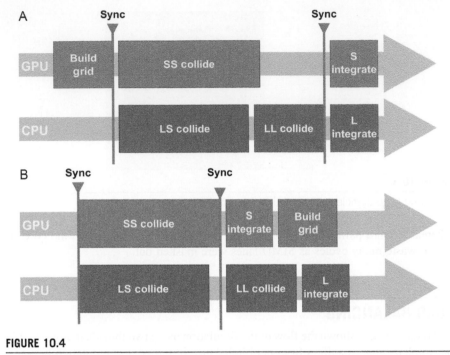

FIGURE 10.4

Load balancing.

forces for the small particles that were filled by the CPU. As a result, the large–large collision does not have to be performed during the first half given the removal of any data dependencies with the next GPU computation. This means that the large–large collision can be moved to the second half of the computation (as shown in Figure 10.4B). In this way, we improve the load balance on the CPU threads, which results in a reduction in total simulation time.

PERFORMANCE AND SUMMARY

Figure 10.1 is a screen shot from the mixed particle simulation with approximately 8200 small particles and 150 large particles running on an AMD A-series Fusion APU, on which the CPU and GPU are integrated on-chip. The bar at the right of the figure shows the computation times on two threads (one column per thread). The full height of the column is equal to 1/60 of a second. The blue and green blocks correspond to the time spent on the GPU and the CPU, respectively. Because there are four iterations per time step, one iteration takes approximately 4 ms in this simulation. The first four blocks are for the first iterations. As can be seen, the threads synchronize after the first GPU computation. The CPU work thread is waiting for the GPU thread to finish, producing the gap between the first green block and the synchronization.

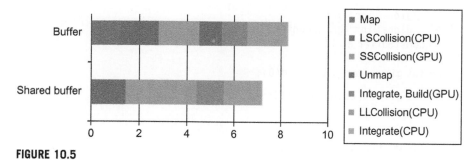

FIGURE 10.5

Breakdown of the simulation times.

If a buffer is created without the `CL_MEM_ALLOC_HOST_PTR` flag, the data has to be copied when the buffer is mapped and unmapped. The effect of the map operation is quantitatively compared between a simulation with a normal buffer and a simulation with a shared buffer. Figure 10.5 is the breakdown of the times. Although the simulation itself is the same, one can see a clear difference between the two versions with and without data sharing. The comparison shows a clear advantage of using a shared buffer. However, notice the extra execution time for the GPU-side small–small collision phase when using data sharing: This is due to the extra latency of accesses over the shared memory interface.

In this chapter, we discussed an implementation of a particle simulation that handles variably sized particles by leveraging the best features of both the CPU and the GPU. In addition, by sharing memory between the CPU and the GPU on tightly integrated devices such as AMD's Fusion APU architecture, the efficiency of the computation improved by eliminating wasteful memory copies. Although this example is designed to be simple to understand, the same technique can be applicable to more complicated applications.

KERNEL FOR UNIFORM GRID CREATION

```
typedef struct
{
    float4 m_max;
    float4 m_min;
    int4 m_nCells;
    float m_gridScale;
    u32 m_maxParticles;
}ConstBuffer;


__kernel
void GridConstructionKernel(
    __global float4* gPosIn,
```

```
        __global int* gridG,
        __global int* gridCounterG,
      ConstBuffer cb )
{
      int gIdx = get_global_id(0);

      if( gIdx >= cb.m_maxParticles ) {
         return;
      }

      float4 iPos = gPosIn[gIdx];

      int4 gridCrd = ugConvertToGridCrd(
         iPos-cb.m_min, cb.m_gridScale );

      if( gridCrd.x < 0 || gridCrd.x >= cb.m_nCells.x
         || gridCrd.y < 0 || gridCrd.y >= cb.m_nCells.y ) {
         return;
      }

      int gridIdx = ugGridCrdToGridIdx(
         gridCrd,
         cb.m_nCells.x,
         cb.m_nCells.y,
         cb.m_nCells.z );

      int count = atom_add(&gridCounterG[gridIdx], 1);

      if( count < MAX_IDX_PER_GRID ) {
         gridG[ gridIdx*MAX_IDX_PER_GRID + count ] = gIdx;
      }
}
```

KERNELS FOR SIMULATION

```
typedef struct
{
   float4 m_g;
   int m_numParticles;
   float m_dt;
   float m_scale;
   float m_e;

   int4 m_nCells;
   float4 m_spaceMin;
   float m_gridScale;
}ConstBuffer;

__kernel
void CollideGridKernel(
   __global float4* posIn,
```

```
        __global float4* velIn,
        __global int* grid,
        __global int* gridCounter,
        __global float4* forceOut,
    ConstBuffer cb)
{
    int gIdx = get_global_id(0);

    if(gIdx >= cb.m_numParticles ) {
        return;
    }

    int4 nCells = cb.m_nCells;
    float4 spaceMin = cb.m_spaceMin;
    float gridScale = cb.m_gridScale;
    float dt = cb.m_dt;
    float e = cb.m_e;

    float4 f = make_float4(0,0,0,0);

    float4 x_i = posIn[ gIdx ];
    float4 v_i = velIn[ gIdx ];

    float sCoeff, dCoeff;
    calcCoeffs(v_i.w, v_j.w, sCoeff, dCoeff);

    int4 iGridCrd = ugConvertToGridCrd( x_i-spaceMin, gridScale );

    //1. collide particles
    for(int i=-1;i<=1;i++) for(int j=-1;j<=1;j++) {
        int4 gridCrd = make_int4(
            iGridCrd.x+i,
            iGridCrd.y+j,
            iGridCrd.z+k,
            0);

        if( gridCrd.x < 0 || gridCrd.x >= nCells.x
            || gridCrd.y < 0 || gridCrd.y >= nCells.y ) {
            continue;
        }

        int gridIdx = ugGridCrdToGridIdx(
            gridCrd,
            nCells.x,
                nCells.y,
                nCells.z );

            int numElem = gridCounter[ gridIdx ];
            numElem = min(numElem, MAX_IDX_PER_GRID);

            for(int ie=0; ie<numElem; ie++) {
                int jIdx = grid[ MAX_IDX_PER_GRID*gridIdx + ie ];
```

```
                    if( jIdx == gIdx ) {
                        continue;
                    }
                    float4 x_j = posIn[jIdx];
                    float4 v_j = velIn[jIdx];
                    f += calcForce(
                        x_i,
                        x_j,
                        v_i,
                        v_j,
                        x_i.w,
                        x_j.w,
                        v_i.w,
                        v_j.w,
                        dt,
                        sCoeff,
                        dCoeff );
                }
            }

            //2. collide with boundary
            {
                float sCoeff, dCoeff;
                calcCoeffs(v_i.w, sCoeff, dCoeff);

                float4 planes[4];
                planes[0] = make_float4(0,1,0,cb.m_scale);
                planes[1] = make_float4(-1,0,0,cb.m_scale);
                planes[2] = make_float4(1,0,0,cb.m_scale);
                planes[3] = make_float4(0,-1,0,cb.m_scale);

                for(int j=0; j<4; j++) {
                    float4 eqn = planes[j];
                    float dist = dot3w1( x_i, eqn );
                    f += calcForceB(
                        x_i,
                        v_i,
                        x_i.w,
                        dist,
                        eqn,
                        dt,
                        sCoeff,
                        dCoeff );
                }
            }
            forceOut[ gIdx ] = f;
        }
```

```
__kernel
void IntegrateKernel(
    __global float4* pos,
    __global float4* vel,
    __global float4* forceSS,
    __global float4* forceLS,
    ConstBuffer cb)
{
    int gIdx = get_global_id(0);
    if( gIdx >= cb.m_numParticles ) {
        return;
    }

    float4 x = pos[gIdx];
    float4 v = vel[gIdx];

    v += (forceSS[gIdx]+ forceLS[gIdx])*cb.m_dt/v.w+cb.m_g;
    x += v*cb.m_dt;

    pos[gIdx] = make_float4(x.x, x.y, x.z, pos[gIdx].w);
    vel[gIdx] = make_float4(v.x, v.y, v.z, vel[gIdx].w);

    forceLS[gIdx] = make_float4(0,0,0,0);
}
```

OpenCL Extensions

11

INTRODUCTION

Similar to most programming languages and frameworks, the OpenCL specification provides support for optional extensions. They represent a small but important set of extended OpenCL capabilities. In this chapter, we discuss a number of these extensions that can provide programmers an extended set of tools to implement OpenCL applications.

OVERVIEW OF EXTENSION MECHANISM

OpenCL defines three types of extensions:

- KHR extension: Formally ratified by the OpenCL working group and comes with a set of conformance tests that any application claiming to support the extension must have passed. All KHR extensions are included as part of the OpenCL specification. In general, the goal is to keep the set of KHR extensions small to avoid differences between implementations. Unfortunately, in some cases, a feature must be an extension because it is not possible to support on all platforms. DirectX interoperability is a good example because it is only relevant to OpenCL implementations that support Microsoft Windows. A KHR extension is assigned a unique string name of the form cl_khr_<name>, where name is the name given to the particular extension.
- EXT extension: Developed by one or more of the OpenCL working group members, but it has not been formally approved. There is no requirement for an EXT feature to pass conformance tests. An EXT extension is often used to provide early access to features being worked on by a subgroup of the OpenCL working group, many of which will appear in the specification core or as a KHR at a later date. An EXT extension is assigned a unique string name of the form cl_ext_<name>, where name is the name given to the particular extension.
- Vendor extension: Developed by a single vendor, most likely to expose some feature that is only accessible on the vendor's hardware or platform (and thus would

not be of general application). An example is AMD's Device Attribute Query, which allows the developer to query additional information specific to AMD devices. A Vendor extension is assigned a unique string name of the form `cl_<vendor>_<name>`, where `vendor` is a given vendor-defined string (e.g., `amd` is used by AMD), and `name` is the name given to the particular extension.

Extensions can be associated with a given OpenCL platform and in those cases are likely to be always enabled. For example, AMD's Event Callback extension (`cl_amd_event_callback`) is always enabled. Other extensions can be specific to a particular set of devices (e.g., double precision support (`cl_khr_fp64`)).

In general, the application must query either the platform or a particular device to determine what extensions are supported. Using the C++ Wrapper API, the following code demonstrates how to query both the platform and a device for the extension information:

```
std::vector<cl::Platform> platforms;

cl::Platform::get(&platforms);
std::string  platformExts  =  platforms[0].getInfo<CL_PLATFORM_
EXTENSIONS>();

cl_context_properties cprops[] = {
    CL_CONTEXT_PLATFORM,(cl_context_properties)platforms[1](),0 };

cl::Context context(devType, cprops);
std::vector<cl::Device>  devices  =  context.getInfo<CL_CONTEXT_
DEVICES>();

// Check that double is supported
std::string deviceExts = devices[0].getInfo<CL_DEVICE_EXTENSIONS>
();
```

Of course, because we now have a value of type `std::string` for platform and device extensions, we can simply use the method `find()`. For example, to check that a device supports 64-bit Atomics (defined with the name `cl_khr_int64_base_atomics`), you could use the following code:

```
bool has64Atomics = deviceExts.find("cl_khr_int64");
```

Because extensions are optional, there is no requirement for an implementation to provide any externally defined symbols that the host application can call. Accordingly, a host program cannot be statically linked against any extension APIs. Instead, we can query the particular function's address equipped with the following API:

```
void * clGetExtensionFunctionAdddress(const char *funcname);
```

This returns the address of the extension function named by `funcname`. The pointer returned can be cast to a function pointer of the expected type. `Typedefs` for each function pointer are declared for all extensions that add API entry points. For example, the EXT extension Atomic Counters, exposed in the OpenCL extension header `cl_ext.h`, provides low-latency atomic append/consume counters and defines the following:

```
typedef CL_API_ENTRY cl_counter_ext (
CL_API_CALL * clCreateCounterEXT_fn)(
    cl_context          /* context */,
    cl_counter_flags_amd /* flags */,
    cl_uint             /* value */,
    cl_int *            /* error_ret */) CL_API_SUFFIX__VERSION_1_0;
```

Then, assuming that a particular OpenCL device supports the extension `cl_ext_atomic_counters`, the following call will set `clCreateCounterEXT_pfn` to a non-NULL value:

```
clCreateCounterEXT_fn clCreateCounterEXT_pfn =
    clGetExtensionFunctionAdddress("clCreateCounterEXT");
```

In practice, it is often useful to use the following macro to enable quick allocation of these functions:

```
#define __INIT_CL_EXT_FCN_PTR(name) \
    if(!##name_fn) { \
    ##name_pfn = (##name_fn) \
        clGetExtensionFunctionAddress(#name); \
    if(!##name_pfn) { \
    } \
    }
```

To get the same behavior as the function pointer definition previously, we can write the following:

```
__INIT_CL_EXT_FCN_PTR(clCreateContextEXT)
```

The examples presented later in this chapter go a step further and use the OpenCL C++ Wrapper API, which, if a particular extension is enabled, directly exposes a class interface and implicitly takes care of allocating and querying function pointers (as required).

Once an application has verified that a particular extension is supported by a device and has allocated any required API function addresses, it can then use any corresponding OpenCL C source extensions. However, these extension must also be enabled, this time in the OpenCL C source itself. These features are controlled using a pragma directive. The pragma is of the form

```
#pragma OPENCL EXTENSION extension_name : behavior
```

where `extension_name` is the corresponding name of the extension being enabled or disabled, such as `cl_khr_int64`, and `behavior` can be either `enable` or `disable`. The impact of enabling or disabling an extension follows from the position in the source code of the last seen pragma for a given extension. For example, to enable 64-bit atomics in an OpenCL C source program, the following code would do the job:

```
#pragma OPENCL EXTENSION cl_khr_int64 : enable
```

Images are the one exception to the rules described previously. To check if a device supports this feature (which is optional), a separate device query is required:

```
bool hasImages = devices[0].getInfo<CL_DEVICE_IMAGE_SUPPORT>;
```

If the result of this call is true, then images are supported by the device in question and the OpenCL C source is not required to explicitly enable this feature.

There are many KHR, EXT, and vendor extensions—too many to discuss in detail in this chapter. The remainder of this chapter discusses two important extensions in wide use today:

- Device fission—the ability for some devices to be divided into smaller subdevices
- Double precision—the ability for some devices to support double as well as float data types

DEVICE FISSION

The EXT extension Device Fission (Bellows *et al.*, 2010) provides an interface for subdividing an OpenCL device into multiple subdevices. As an example, consider an AMD six-core Istanbul x86 CPU shown symbolically in Figure 11.1A. We view all six cores as a single OpenCL device by default, as shown in Figure 11.1B. Using Device Fission, the six cores can be subdivided into six OpenCL devices as shown in Figure 11.1C, each capable of supporting one or more command queues. Because these command queues are asynchronous and run in their own threads, it is possible to use Device Fission to build a portable and powerful threading application based on task parallelism. To date, Device Fission is supported only on CPU-like devices, but in the future this functionality will spread across all devices in the platform, including GPUs. Next, we motivate and describe the basic use of Device Fission through an example.

An interesting application of Device Fission is to use it to build and study concurrent runtimes, similar to Microsoft's Concurrent Runtime (ConcRT) (Microsoft, 2010) and Intel's Threading Building Blocks (TBB) (Intel, 2011). We present a case study of building a simple C++ class that supports a parallel *for* construct that distributes work across a set of devices created using Device Fission. Although this example has little in common with the kind of production functionality provided by runtimes such as ConcRT and TBB, it provides enough to show that with only a small amount of effort we can build portable, scalable, parallel applications that go beyond basic data-parallel computations. For this example, the goal is to implement a simple class `Parallel` that provides a `parallelFor` method to distribute work across x86 cores, each having a corresponding OpenCL device generated by Device Fission. The class `Parallel` has the following public interface:

```
class Parallel
{
public:
    Parallel();
    static unsigned int atomicAdd(
        unsigned int inc,
        volatile unsigned int *dest);
    bool parallelFor(int range, std::function<void (int i)> f);
};
```

We demonstrate its use with a simple application that counts the number of prime numbers in an input array of randomly generated integers. The implementation uses the OpenCL C++ Wrapper API (Gaster, 2010). To enable Device Fission, we simply need to define `USE_CL_DEVICE_FISSION` and include `cl.hpp`:[1]

```
#define USE_CL_DEVICE_FISSION 1
#include <CL/cl.hpp>
```

As described previously, we encapsulate the parallel features of our simple runtime in the class `Parallel`. All OpenCL state for the program is held in the private part of this class definition. The default constructor initializes OpenCL and divides the CPU device into single core subdevices. As is standard with all OpenCL initialization, we need to first query a platform, then create a context (in this case, using `CL_DEVICE_TYPE_CPU`), and finally inspect the list of devices (as shown in Figure 11.1B, this will always be presented as a single element):

```
std::vector<cl::Platform> platforms;
cl::Platform::get(&platforms);

cl_context_properties properties[] =
{
    CL_CONTEXT_PLATFORM,
    (cl_context_properties)(platforms[1])(),
    0
};
context_ = cl::Context(CL_DEVICE_TYPE_CPU, properties);

std::vector<cl::Device> devices =
    context_.getInfo<CL_CONTEXT_DEVICES>();
```

Before we can use the Device Fission extension, the program must check that it is an exported extension for the device:

---

[1]We also enable C++ exceptions for OpenCL as shown in the full program source, given in Listing 11.1.

```
if (devices[0].getInfo<CL_DEVICE_EXTENSIONS>().find(
    "cl_ext_device_fission") == std::string::npos) {

  std::cout << "Required that device support "
          << "cl_ext_device_extension"
          << std::endl;
  exit(-1);
}
```

Given an OpenCL `cl::Device`, in this case `devices[0]`, the method `createSubDevices` creates subdevices,

```
cl_int createSubDevices(
    const cl_device_partition_property_ext * properties,
    VECTOR_CLASS<Device>* devices)
```

which, given a list of partition properties (as defined in Table 11.1), creates a set of subdevices, returned in the parameter devices.

The following code then creates the subdevices, using the partition `CL_DEVICE_PARTITION_EQUALLY_EXT` to equally subdivide (in this case), producing a one-to-one mapping between subdevice and core:

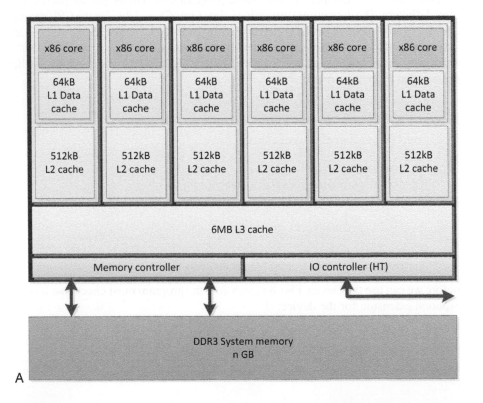

A

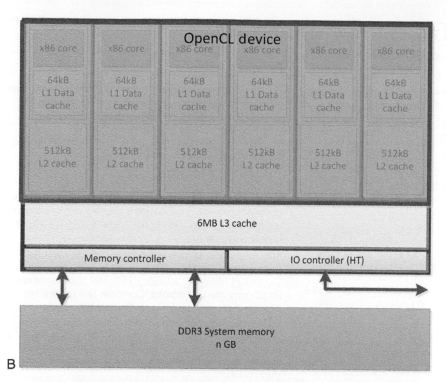

B

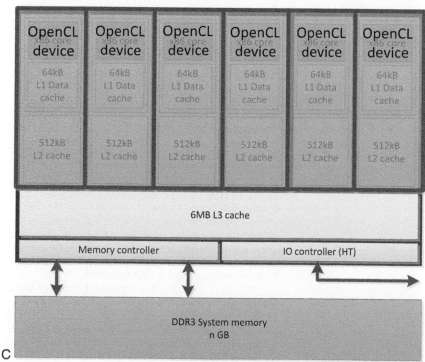

C

FIGURE 11.1

CPU as seen by OpenCL with and without device fission. (A) Phenom II 6 core. (B) Phenom II 6 core represented as a single OpenCL device for all cores. (C) Phenom II 6 core represented as an OpenCL device for each core.

Table 11.1 Subdevice Partition Properties

cl_device_partition _property_ext	Description
CL_DEVICE_PARTITION_ EQUALLY_EXT	Split the aggregate device into as many smaller devices as can be created, each containing N compute units. The value N is passed as the value accompanying this property. If N does not divide evenly into CL_DEVICE_MAX_COMPUTE_UNITS, then the remaining compute units are not used.
CL_DEVICE_PARTITION_ BY_COUNTS_EXT	This property is followed by a CL_PARTITION_BY_COUNTS_LIST_END_EXT terminated list of compute unit counts. For each non-zero count M in the list, a subdevice is created with M compute units in it. CL_PARTITION_BY_COUNTS_LIST_END_EXT is defined to be 0.
CL_DEVICE_PARTITION_ BY_NAMES_EXT	This property is followed by a list of compute unit names. Each list starts with a CL_PARTITION_BY_NAMES_LIST_END_EXT terminated list of compute unit names. Compute unit names are integers that count up from zero to the number of compute units less 1. CL_PARTITION_BY_NAMES_LIST_END_EXT is defined to be −1. Only one subdevice may be created at a time with this selector. An individual compute unit name may not appear more than once in the subdevice description.
CL_DEVICE_PARTITION_ BY_AFFINITY_ DOMAIN_EXT	Split the device into smaller aggregate devices containing one or more compute units that all share part of a cache hierarchy. The value accompanying this property may be drawn from the following CL_AFFINITY_DOMAIN list: CL_AFFINITY_DOMAIN_NUMA_EXT—Split the device into subdevices composed of compute units that share a NUMA band. CL_AFFINITY_DOMAIN_L4_CACHE_EXT—Split the device into subdevices composed of compute units that share a level 4 data cache. CL_AFFINITY_DOMAIN_L3_CACHE_EXT—Split the device into subdevices composed of compute units that share a level 3 data cache. CL_AFFINITY_DOMAIN_L2_CACHE_EXT—Split the device into subdevices composed of compute units that share a level 2 data cache. CL_AFFINITY_DOMAIN_L1_CACHE_EXT—Split the device into subdevices composed of compute units that share a level 1 data cache. CL_AFFINITY_DOMAIN_NEXT_FISSIONABLE_EXT— Split the device along the next fissionable CL_AFFINITY_DOMAIN. The implementation shall find the first level along which the device or subdevice may be further subdivided in the order NUMA, L4, L3, L2, L1, and fission the device into subdevices composed of compute units that share memory subsystems at this level. The user may determine what happened by calling clGetDeviceInfo (CL_DEVICE_PARTITION_STYLE_EXT) on the subdevices.

```
cl_device_partition_property_ext subDeviceProperties[] =
{
  CL_DEVICE_PARTITION_EQUALLY_EXT,
  1,
  CL_PROPERTIES_LIST_END_EXT,
  0
};

devices[0].createSubDevices(subDeviceProperties, &subDevices_);
if (subDevices_.size() <= 0) {
    std::cout << "Failed to allocate sub-devices" << std::endl;
    exit(-1);
}
```

The following code concludes the default constructor definition by iterating through the list of subdevices, creating a command queue for each one:

```
for (auto i = subDevices_.begin(); i != subDevices_.end(); i++) {
    queues_.push_back(cl::CommandQueue(context_, *i));
}
```

Figure 11.2 shows each CPU core paired with its corresponding command queue. It is important to note that commands submitted via each queue run asynchronously and concurrently with each other.

The implementation for atomicAdd is straightforward and is provided later. Here, we focus on the definition of parallelFor, which takes two arguments. The first argument represents the bounds of the iteration space, and the second argument is a function object that will be applied to each index across this space. This second argument is a native C++ function object,[2] but OpenCL clEnqueueNDRangeKernel operations are valid only for OpenCL C kernels, and so we need another approach to support native C++ functions. Fortunately, OpenCL has just such a function, clEnqueueNativeKernel, which can enqueue a C function. With some careful marshaling, this can also be made to work for a C++ function. Native kernels were described in Chapter 5.

Using clEnqeueNativeKernel, the definition of parallelFor is straightforward:[3]

```
bool parallelFor(int range, std::function<void (int i)> f)
{
    std::vector<cl::Event> events;

    size_t args[2];

    args[0] = reinterpret_cast<size_t>(&f);
```

---

[2]The term native is used to imply that the function in question has been compiled by the host compiler and not the OpenCL C compiler.

[3]Note that we use the OpenCL C++ Wrapper API (rather than the clEnqueueNativeKernel from the C API), as described previously.

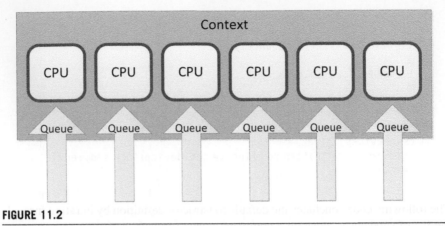

FIGURE 11.2

OpenCL subdevices with associated command queues.

```
int index = 0;
for (int x = 0; x < range; x++) {

    int numQueues =
        range - x > queues_.size() ? queues_.size() : range - x;

    cl::Event event;
    while(numQueues > 0) {

        args[1] = static_cast<size_t>(index++);

        queues_[numQueues-1].enqueueNativeKernel(
            funcWrapper,
            std::make_pair(
                static_cast<void *>(args),
                sizeof(size_t)*2),
            NULL,
            NULL,
            NULL,
            &event);

        events.push_back(event);

        numQueues-;
        x++;
    }
    cl::Event::waitForEvents(events);
}
return true;
}
```

The first part of the function sets up the argument, which in this case is the actual function we want to run. This is required because it is a C++ function object (often called a functor), and OpenCL is expecting a C function. Thus, we provide a wrapper function called funcWrapper that takes as an argument a pointer to the functor. The wrapper function "unboxes" it and calls the function object when executed. The main body of the function is the loop executing the functor for the 0 . . . range, with the inner loop mapping some subset of this to the number of actual subdevices. Note that these are all submitted asynchronously, and each call returns an event that we wait on at the end of each set of submissions. A more optimized version might wait until a large number of submissions have happened and control a finer grain of control using queue.flush() and so on. We leave this as an exercise for the reader.

Finally, we put this all together in Listing 11.1, which shows the complete implementation of our primes checking example, including the main function. One interesting and important aspect of this example is that no OpenCL C device code is used, and it is simply using the OpenCL runtime as a portable threading library.

Listing 11.1

```cpp
// Enable OpenCL C++ exceptions
#define __CL_ENABLE_EXCEPTIONS

// Enable Device Fission
#define USE_CL_DEVICE_FISSION 1

#include <CL/cl.hpp>

#include <cstring>
#include <cstdlib>
#include <cassert>
#include <cmath>
#include <iostream>
#include <fstream>
#include <vector>

#include <functional>
#include <memory>

class Parallel
{
private:
    cl::Context context_;
    std::vector<cl::Device> subDevices_;
    cl::CommandQueue queue_;
    std::vector<cl::CommandQueue> queues_;

    static void CL_CALLBACK funcWrapper(void * a)
    {
        size_t * args = static_cast<size_t *>(a);

        std::function<void (int i)> * f =
            reinterpret_cast<std::function<void (int i)>*>(args[0]);
```

```
        (*f)(static_cast<int>(args[1]));
    }
public:
    Parallel()
    {
        std::vector<cl::Platform> platforms;
        cl::Platform::get(&platforms);

        cl_context_properties properties[] =
        {
            CL_CONTEXT_PLATFORM,
            (cl_context_properties)(platforms[1])(),
            0
        };

        context_ = cl::Context(CL_DEVICE_TYPE_CPU, properties);

        std::vector<cl::Device> devices =
            context_.getInfo<CL_CONTEXT_DEVICES>();

        // Check that device fission is supported
        if (devices[0].getInfo<CL_DEVICE_EXTENSIONS>().find(
            "cl_ext_device_fission") == std::string::npos) {
            std::cout << "Required that device support "
                    << "cl_ext_device_extension"
                    << std::endl;
            exit(-1);
        }

    cl_device_partition_property_ext subDeviceProperties[] =
    {
        CL_DEVICE_PARTITION_EQUALLY_EXT,
        1,
        CL_PROPERTIES_LIST_END_EXT,
        0
    };
    devices[0].createSubDevices(subDeviceProperties, &subDevices_);
    if (subDevices_.size() <= 0) {
        std::cout << "Failed to allocate sub-devices" << std::endl;
        exit(-1);
    }

    for (auto i = subDevices_.begin(); i != subDevices_.end(); i++) {
    queues_.push_back(cl::CommandQueue(context_, *i));
    }

    std::cout << "Number of sub-devices "
            << subDevices_.size()
            << std::endl;
    }

    static unsigned int atomicAdd(
        unsigned int inc,
        volatile unsigned int *dest)
    {
```

```
#if defined(_MSC_VER)
        return (unsigned int)_InterlockedExchangeAdd(
            (volatile long*)dest,
            (long)inc);
#else
        return __sync_fetch_and_add(dest, inc);
#endif
    }

    bool parallelFor(int range, std::function<void (int i)> f)
    {
        std::vector<cl::Event> events;

        size_t args[2];

        args[0] = reinterpret_cast<size_t>(&f);

        int index = 0;
        for (int x = 0; x < range; x++) {

            int numQueues =
                range - x > queues_.size() ? queues_.size() : range - x;

            cl::Event event;
            while(numQueues > 0) {

                args[1] = static_cast<size_t>(index++);

                queues_[numQueues-1].enqueueNativeKernel(
                    funcWrapper,
                    std::make_pair(
                        static_cast<void *>(args),
                        sizeof(size_t)*2),
                    NULL,
                    NULL,
                    NULL,
                    &event);

                events.push_back(event);

                numQueues-;
                x++;
            }

            cl::Event::waitForEvents(events);

        }

        return true;
    }

};

const unsigned int numNumbers = 1024;
```

```cpp
int
main(int argc, char** argv)
{
    volatile unsigned int numPrimes = 0;
    int * numbers = new int[numNumbers];
    ::srand(2009);

    // Random initialize
    for (size_t i = 0; i < numNumbers; ++i) {
        numbers[i] = ::rand();
    }

    try {
        Parallel parallel;

        parallel.parallelFor(numNumbers, [numbers, &numPrimes]
        (int x) {

            auto isPrime = [] (unsigned int n) -> bool {
                if (n == 1 || n == 2) {
                    return true;
                }
                if (n % 2 == 0) {
                    return false;
                }

                for (unsigned int odd = 3;
                    odd <= static_cast<unsigned int>(
                        sqrtf(static_cast<float>(n)));
                    odd +=2) {

                    if (n % odd == 0) {
                        return false;
                    }
                }
                return true;
            };

            if (isPrime(numbers[x])) {
                Parallel::atomicAdd(1, &numPrimes);
            }
        });
        std::cout << "Number of primes found = " << numPrimes <<
        std::endl;
    }
    catch (cl::Error err) {
        std::cerr
            << "ERROR: "
            << err.what()
            << "("
            << err.err()
            << ")"
```

```
            << std::endl;
      return EXIT_FAILURE;
   }
   delete[] numbers;
   return EXIT_SUCCESS;
}
```

DOUBLE PRECISION

Floating point formats were created to allow programmers to work with very large and very small non-integral data values. For many applications, single precision floating point does not provide enough range for the targeted application. Many applications (particularly in science and engineering) require part or all of a particular computation to use double precision. OpenCL does not require that a particular compute device support double precision. For critical applications in which double precision is required, OpenCL provides the optional `cl_khr_fp64` extension. This is enabled by including the following directive before any double precision use in an OpenCL C program:

```
#pragma cl_khr_fp64 : enable
```

Once enabled, the double precision support provides access to the following data types:

Type	Description
Double	Double precision floating point number
double2	2-component double vector
double3	3-component double vector
double4	4-component double vector
double8	8-component double vector
double16	16-component double vector

The double type conforms to the IEEE 754 double precision storage format.

There is a one-to-one mapping with the corresponding single precision float types. On an AMD CPU, when the OpenCL device is `CL_DEVICE_TYPE_CPU`, vector types are mapped directly to SSE and AVX packed registers. In the case in which a vector type is larger than the underlying hardware vector, the resulting implementation is expanded into multiples of the hardware width. All of the conversion rules defined by the OpenCL specification for float types are also defined for doubles. The built-in math functions provided for float have been extended to include appropriate versions that work on double, double2, double3, double4, double8, and double16 as arguments and return values.

As a simple example, Listing 11.2 shows OpenCL C code to implement a block matrix multiple using double precision. Note that the first line of the OpenCL source file enables the extension.

Listing 11.2

```
#pragma OPENCL EXTENSION cl_khr_fp64 : enable

#include "matrixmul.h"

#define AS(i, j) As[(j) * BLOCK_SIZE + (i)]
#define BS(i, j) Bs[(j) * BLOCK_SIZE + (i)]

__kernel void
matrixMul(
    __global double* C,
    __global double* A,
    __global double* B,
    int wA,
    int wB,
    __local double* As,
    __local double* Bs)
{
    // Block index
    int bx = get_group_id(0);
    int by = get_group_id(1);

    int tx = get_local_id(0);
    int ty = get_local_id(1);

    // Index of the first sub-matrix of A processed by the block
    int aBegin = wA * BLOCK_SIZE * by;

    // Index of the last sub-matrix of A processed by the block
    int aEnd = aBegin + wA - 1;

    // Step size used to iterate through the sub-matrices of A
    int aStep = BLOCK_SIZE;

    // Index of the first sub-matrix of B processed by the block
    int bBegin = BLOCK_SIZE * bx;

    // Step size used to iterate through the sub-matrices of B
    int bStep = BLOCK_SIZE * wB;

    // Csub is used to store the element of the block sub-matrix
    // that is computed by the thread
    double Csub = 0;

    // Loop over all the sub-matrices of A and B
    // required to compute the block sub-matrix
    for (int a = aBegin, b = bBegin;
            a <= aEnd;
```

```
                    a += aStep, b += bStep) {

            // Load the matrices from device memory
            // to local memory; each work-item loads
            // one element of each matrix
            AS(ty, tx) = A[a + wA * ty + tx];
            BS(ty, tx) = B[b + wB * ty + tx];

            // Synchronize to make sure the matrices are loaded
            barrier(CLK_LOCAL_MEM_FENCE);

            // Multiply the two matrices together;
            // each work-item computes one element
            // of the block sub-matrix
            for (int k = 0; k < BLOCK_SIZE; ++k)
                Csub += AS(ty, k) * BS(k, tx);

            // Synchronize to make sure that the preceding
            // computation is done before loading two new
            // sub-matrices of A and B in the next iteration
            barrier(CLK_LOCAL_MEM_FENCE);
        }
        // Write the block sub-matrix to device memory;
        // each work-item writes one element
        int c = wB * BLOCK_SIZE * by + BLOCK_SIZE * bx;
        C[c + wB * ty + tx] = Csub;
    }
```

The host OpenCL program, written using the OpenCL C++ Wrapper API, is given in Listing 11.3, with the shared header, matrixmul.h, given in Listing 11.4. The example is straightforward, but two points are worth discussing further. First, to avoid unexpected runtime errors, the application must check that the device supports the extension cl_khr_fp64, and this is achieved with the following code:

```
if (devices[0].getInfo<CL_DEVICE_EXTENSIONS>().find("cl_khr_fp64")
    ==
    std::string::npos) {

    std::cout << "Required that device support cl_khr_fp64" << std::
    endl;
    exit(-1);
}
```

In this case, if the device does not support the extension, then the application simply exits. A more robust solution might drop back to the host to perform the computation if necessary. Second, this example uses the profiling API for command queues to collect information on the time taken to execute the matrix multiply.

Listing 11.3

```cpp
#include <CL/cl.hpp> // C++ Wrapper API (no need to include cl.h)

#include <cstring>
#include <cstdlib>
#include <cassert>
#include <cmath>
#include <iostream>
#include <fstream>
#include <vector>
#include <matrixmul.h>

template <size_t X, size_t Y>
class Matrix
{
private:
    cl_double data_[X * Y];

public:
    template <typename Functor>
    Matrix(Functor init) { init(data_, X, Y); }
    Matrix() { ::memset(data, '\0', X * Y * sizeof(cl_double)); }

    Matrix<X,Y> operator -= (const Matrix<X,Y>& rhs)
    {
        for (size_t i = 0; i < (X * Y); ++i) {
            data_[i] -= rhs.data_[i];
        }
        return *this;
    }

    Matrix<X,Y> operator - (const Matrix<X,Y>& rhs)
    {
        Matrix<X,Y> result = *this;
        return result -= rhs;
    }

    bool operator == (const Matrix<X,Y>& rhs)
    {
        for (size_t i = 0; i < (X * Y); ++i) {
            if (data_[i] != rhs.data_[i]) {
                return false;
            }
        }
        return true;
    }

    bool operator != (const Matrix<X,Y>& rhs)
    {
        return !(*this == rhs);
    }
```

```
bool  compareL2fe(const  Matrix<X,Y>&  reference,  cl_double
epsilon)
{
    cl_double error = 0.0f;
    cl_double ref = 0.0f;

    for (size_t i = 0; i < (X * Y); ++i) {
        cl_double diff = reference.data_[i] - data_[i];
        error += diff * diff;
        ref += reference.data_[i] * reference.data_[i];
    }

    cl_double normRef =::sqrt((double) ref);
    if (::fabs((double) ref) < 1e-7f) {
        return false;
    }
    cl_double normError = ::sqrtf((double) error);
    error = normError / normRef;

    return error < epsilon;
}

void printOn(std::ostream& out)
{
    for (size_t y = 0; y < Y; ++y) {
        for (size_t x = 0; x < X; ++x) {
            out << data_[y * X + x] << " ";
        }
        out << "\n";
    }
}

cl_double* data() { return data_; }
size_t size() const { return X * Y * sizeof(cl_double); }
};
static void
randomInit(cl_double* data, size_t width, size_t height)
{

    for (size_t i = 0; i < width*height; ++i) {
        data[i] = ::rand() / (double) RAND_MAX;
    }
}

static void
nop(cl_double*, size_t, size_t)
{
}

static void
computeGold(
    cl_double* C, const cl_double* A, const cl_double* B,
    cl_uint hA, cl_uint wA, cl_uint wB)
{
    for (cl_uint i = 0; i < hA; ++i) {
```

```
        for (cl_uint j = 0; j < wB; ++j) {
            cl_double sum = 0;
            for (cl_uint k = 0; k < wA; ++k) {
                cl_double a = A[i * wA + k];
                cl_double b = B[k * wB + j];
                sum += a * b;
            }
            C[i * wB + j] = (cl_double)sum;
        }
    }
}

int
main(int argc, char** argv)
{
    cl_device_type devType = CL_DEVICE_TYPE_CPU;
    cl_int err, err1, err2, err3;
    ::srand(2009);

    Matrix<WA,HA> A(&randomInit);
    Matrix<WB,HB> B(&randomInit);

    // Initialize the OpenCL runtime.
    std::vector<cl::Platform> platforms;
    cl::Platform::get(&platforms);

    cl_context_properties cprops[] = {
        CL_CONTEXT_PLATFORM,   (cl_context_properties)platforms[1]
        (), 0 };

    cl::Context context(devType, cprops);
    std::vector<cl::Device> devices = context.getInfo<
        CL_CONTEXT_DEVICES>();
    if (devices.size() == 0) {
        std::cerr << "Device not available\n";
        return EXIT_FAILURE;
    }

    // Check that double is supported
    if (devices[0].getInfo<CL_DEVICE_EXTENSIONS>().find(
        "cl_khr_ fp64") ==
            std::string::npos) {

            std::cout << "Required that device support cl_khr_fp64"
                << std::endl;
            exit(-1);
    }

    std::ifstream file("matrixmul_kernels.cl");
    if (!file.is_open()) {
        std::cerr << "We couldn't load CL source code\n";
        return EXIT_FAILURE;
    }

    std::string prog(
```

```
            std::istreambuf_iterator<char>(file),
            (std::istreambuf_iterator<char>()));

    cl::Program::Sources source(
        1,
        std::make_pair(prog.c_str(),prog.length()+1));

    cl::Program program(context, source);

    err = program.build(devices, "-I.");
    if (err != CL_SUCCESS) {
        std::string str;
        str = program.getBuildInfo<CL_PROGRAM_BUILD_LOG>(devices
        [0]);
        std::cout << "Program Info: " << str;
        exit(1);
    }

    cl::Kernel matrixMul(program, "matrixMul", &err);
    if (err != CL_SUCCESS) {
        std::cerr << "Could not create kernel \"matmult\"\n";
        return EXIT_FAILURE;
    }

    cl::Buffer in0(context, CL_MEM_USE_HOST_PTR, A.size(),
        A.data(), &err1);
    cl::Buffer in1(context, CL_MEM_USE_HOST_PTR, B.size(),
        B.data(), &err2);
    cl::Buffer out(context, CL_MEM_ALLOC_HOST_PTR,
        WC * HC * sizeof(cl_double), NULL, &err3);
    if (err1 != CL_SUCCESS || err2 != CL_SUCCESS || err3 != CL_SUCCESS) {
        std::cerr << "Could not create memory objects\n";
        return EXIT_FAILURE;
    }

    err = matrixMul.setArg(0, out);
    err |= matrixMul.setArg(1, in0);
    err |= matrixMul.setArg(2, in1);
    err |= matrixMul.setArg(3, WA);
    err |= matrixMul.setArg(4, WB);
    const size_t localSize = sizeof(double[BLOCK_SIZE][BLOCK_SIZE]);
    err |= matrixMul.setArg(5, cl::__local(localSize));
    err |= matrixMul.setArg(6, cl::__local(localSize));
    if (err != CL_SUCCESS) {
        std::cerr << "Could not set matrixMul's args\n";
        return EXIT_FAILURE;
    }

    cl_command_queue_properties properties =
        CL_QUEUE_PROFILING_ ENABLE;
    cl::CommandQueue queue(context, devices[0], properties, &err);
    if (err != CL_SUCCESS) {
        std::cerr << "Could not create the command queue\n";
        return EXIT_FAILURE;
```

```cpp
    }
    cl::Event event;
    err1 = queue.enqueueNDRangeKernel(
        matrixMul, cl::NullRange,
        cl::NDRange(WC, HC),
        cl::NDRange(BLOCK_SIZE, BLOCK_SIZE),
        NULL,
        &event);

    Matrix<WC,HC> C(&nop);
    err2 = queue.enqueueReadBuffer(out, CL_TRUE, 0, C.size(),
        C.data());
    if (err1 != CL_SUCCESS || err2 != CL_SUCCESS) {
        std::cerr << "matrixMul execution failed\n";
        return EXIT_FAILURE;
    }

    Matrix<WC, HC> reference(&nop);
    computeGold(reference.data(), A.data(), B.data(), HA, WA, WB);

    if (!C.compareL2fe(reference, 1e-6f)) {
        Matrix<WC, HC> difference = reference - C;
        difference.printOn(std::cout);
        std::cout << "FAILED\n";
        return EXIT_FAILURE;
    }
    if ((properties & CL_QUEUE_PROFILING_ENABLE) != 0) {
        cl_long start = event.getProfilingInfo<
            CL_PROFILING_COMMAND_START>();
        cl_long end = event.getProfilingInfo<
            CL_PROFILING_COMMAND_END>();
        std::cout << "Elapsed time: "
                << (double)(end - start) / 1e6
                << "ms\n";
    }

    std::cout << "PASS!\n";
    return EXIT_SUCCESS;
}
```

Listing 11.4

```cpp
// Thread block size
#define BLOCK_SIZE 16

// Matrix dimensions
// (chosen as multiples of the thread block size for simplicity)
#define WA (3 * BLOCK_SIZE) // Matrix A width
#define HA (5 * BLOCK_SIZE) // Matrix A height
#define WB (8 * BLOCK_SIZE) // Matrix B width
```

```
#define HB WA // Matrix B height
#define WC WB // Matrix C width
#define HC HA // Matrix C height
```

References

Bellows, G., Gaster, B. R., Munshi, A., Ollmann, I., Rosenberg, O., & Watt, B. (2010). *Device Fission*. Khronos OpenCL Working Group.

Gaster, B. R. (2010). *The OpenCL C++ Wrapper API, Version 1.1*. Khronos OpenCL Working Group.

Intel. (2011). *Threading Building Blocks 3.0 for Open Source*. http://threadingbuildingblocks.org.

Microsoft. (2010). *Concurrency Runtime: Visual Studio 2010*. http://msdn.microsoft.com/en-us/library/dd504870.aspx.

Foreign Lands: Plugging OpenCL In

12

INTRODUCTION

Up to this point, we have considered OpenCL in the context of the system programming languages C and C++; however, there is a lot more to OpenCL. In this chapter, we look at how OpenCL can be accessed from a selection of different programming language frameworks, including Java, Python, and the functional programming language Haskell.

BEYOND C AND C++

For many developers, C and C++ are the programming language of choice. For many others, this is not the case: for example, a large amount of the world's software is developed in Java or Python. These high-level languages are designed with productivity in mind, often providing features such as automatic memory management, and performance has not necessarily been at the forefront of minds of the systems' designers. An advantage of these languages is that they are often highly portable, think of Java's motto "write once, run everywhere," and reduce the burden on the developer to be concerned with low-level system issues. However, it is often the case that it is not easy, sometimes even impossible, to get anything close to peak performance for applications written in these languages.

To address both the performance gap and also to allow access to a wide set of libraries not written in a given high-level language, a foreign function interface (FFI) is provided to allow applications to call into native libraries written in C, C++, or other low-level programming languages. For example, Java provides the Java Native Interface, while Python has its own mechanism. Both Java (e.g., JOCL (Java bindings for OpenCL (JOCL), 2012)) and Python (e.g., PyOpenCL (Klöckner, 2012)) have OpenCL wrapper APIs that allow the developer to directly access the compute capabilities offered by OpenCL. These models are fairly low level and provide the plumbing between the managed runtimes and the native, unmanaged, aspects of OpenCL. To give a flavor of what is on offer, Listing 12.1, is a PyOpenCL implementation of vector addition.

Listing 12.1

```python
import pyopencl as cl
import numpy
import numpy.linalg as la

a = numpy.random.rand(50000).astype(numpy.float32)
b = numpy.random.rand(50000).astype(numpy.float32)

ctx   = cl.create_some_context()
queue = cl.CommandQueue(ctx)

mf       = cl.mem_flags
a_buf    = cl.Buffer(ctx, mf.READ_ONLY | mf.COPY_HOST_PTR, hostbuf=a)
b_buf    = cl.Buffer(ctx, mf.READ_ONLY | mf.COPY_HOST_PTR, hostbuf=b)
dest_buf = cl.Buffer(ctx, mf.WRITE_ONLY, b.nbytes)

prg = cl.Program(ctx, """
    __kernel void vecadd(__global const float *a,
    __global const float *b, __global float *c)
    {
int gid = get_global_id(0);
c[gid] = a[gid] + b[gid];
    }
    """).build()

prg.vecadd(queue, a.shape, None, a_buf, b_buf, dest_buf)

a_plus_b = numpy.empty_like(a)
cl.enqueue_copy(queue, a_plus_b, dest_buf)

print la.norm(a_plus_b - (a+b))
```

An example of moving beyond simple wrapper APIs is Aparapi (2012). Originally developed by AMD but now a popular open source project, Aparapi allows Java developers to take advantage of the compute power of GPU and other OpenCL devices by executing data-parallel code fragments on the GPU rather than confining them to the local CPU. The Aparapi runtime system achieves this by converting Java bytecode to OpenCL at runtime and executing on the GPU. If for any reason Aparapi cannot execute on the GPU, it will execute in a Java thread pool. An important goal of Aparapi is to stay within the Java language both from a syntax point of view and from one of sprit. This design requirement can be seen from the source code to perform a vector addition, given in Listing 12.2, where there is no OpenCL C code or OpenCL API calls.

Listing 12.2

```
package com.amd.aparapi.sample.add;
import com.amd.aparapi.Kernel;
import com.amd.aparapi.Range;
public class Main{
  public static void main(String[] _args) {
    final int size = 512;
    final float[] a = new float[size];
    final float[] b = new float[size];
    for (int i = 0; i < size; i++) {
        a[i] = (float)(Math.random()*100);
        b[i] = (float)(Math.random()*100);
    }
    final float[] sum = new float[size];
    Kernel kernel = new Kernel(){
      @Override public void run() {
          int gid = getGlobalId();
          sum[gid] = a[gid] + b[gid];
      }
    };
    kernel.execute(Range.create(512));
    for (int i = 0; i < size; i++) {
        System.out.printf("%6.2f + %6.2f = %8.2f\n", a[i], b[i], sum[i]);
    }
    kernel.dispose();
  }
}
```

Instead, the Aparapi developer expresses OpenCL computations by generating instances of Aparapi classes, overriding methods that describe the functionality of a kernel that will be dynamically compiled to OpenCL at runtime from the generated Java bytecode.

Aparapi is an example of a more general concept of embedding a Domain-Specific Language (DSL) within a hosting programming language: in this case, Java. DSLs focus on providing an interface for a domain expert and commonly a DSL will take the form of a specific set of features for a given science domain, for example, medical imaging. In this case, the domain is that of data-parallel computations and in particular that of GPGPU computing.

HASKELL OPENCL

Haskell is a pure functional language and along with Standard ML (SML), and its variants is one of the most popular modern functional languages. Unlike many of the other managed languages, Haskell (and SML) programming consists of describing functions, in terms of expressions, and evaluating them by application to argument expressions. In general, the model differs from imperative programming by not defining sequencing of statements and not allowing side effects. There is usually no assignment outside of declarations. This is often seen as both a major advantage and a major disadvantage of Haskell. Combining side-effect free programming with Haskell's large and often complex type system can often be an off-putting experience for the newcomer used to the imperative models of C, C++, or Java. However, side-effect free can be liberating in the presence of parallel programming, as in this case evaluating an expression will produce a single isolated result, which is thread-safe by definition. For this reason, Haskell has recently gained a lot of interest in the parallel programming research community. For the interested reader new to Haskell, they would do well to read Hutton's excellent book on programming in Haskell (Hutton, 2007) and Meijer's companion video series on Microsoft's Channel 9 (Meijer, 2009).

Due to certain aspects of Haskell's type system, it has proven to be an excellent platform for the design of Embedded Domain-Specific Languages (EDSLs), which in turn provide abstractions that automatically compile to GPUs. See, for example, Accelerate (Chakravarty *et al.*, 2011) or Obsidian (Svensson *et al.*, 2011) for two excellent examples of this approach. However, this is a book about low-level programming with OpenCL and so here we stay focused, instead considering how the Haskell programmer can get direct access to the GPU via OpenCL. The benefits of accessing OpenCL via Haskell are manyfold but in particular:

1. OpenCL brings a level of performance to Haskell not achievable by existing CPU threading libraries.
2. The high-level nature of Haskell significantly reduces the complexity of OpenCL's host API and leads to a powerful and highly productive development environment.

There has been more than one effort to develop wrapper APIs for OpenCL in Haskell; however, we want more than a simple FFI binding for OpenCL. In particular, we want something that makes accessing OpenCL simpler, while still providing full access to the power of OpenCL. For this, we recommend HOpenCL (Gaster and Morris, 2012), which is an open source library providing both a low-level wrapper to OpenCL and a higher level interface that enables Haskell programmers to access the OpenCL APIs in an idiomatic fashion, eliminating much of the complexity of interacting with the OpenCL platform and providing stronger static guarantees than other Haskell OpenCL wrappers. For the remainder of this chapter, we focus on the latter higher level API; however, the interested reader can learn more about the low-level API in HOpenCL's documentation.

As a simple illustration we again consider the vector addition of Chapter 1. The kernel code is unchanged and again embedded as a string, but the rest is all Haskell.

Module Structure

HOpenCL is implemented as a small set of modules all contained under the structure `Langauge.OpenCL`.

— `Language.OpenCL.Host.Constants` — defines base types for the OpenCL Core
API
— `Langauge.OpenCL.Host.Core` — defines low-level OpenCL Core API
— `Language.OpenCL.GLInterop` — defines the OpenGL interoperability API
— `Language.OpenCL.Host` — defines the high-level OpenCL API

For the most part, the following sections introduce aspects of the high-level API, and in the cases where reference to the core is necessary, it will be duly noted. For details of the low-level API, the interested reader should reference the HOpenCL documentation (Gaster and Garrett Morris, 2012).

Environments

As described in early chapters, many OpenCL functions require either a context, which defines a particular OpenCL execution environment, or a command queue, which sequences operations for execution on a particular device. In much OpenCL code, these parameters function as "line noise," that is, which technically necessary, they do not change over large portions of the code. To capture this notion, HOpenCL provides two type classes, `Contextual` and `Queued`, to qualify operations that require contexts and command queues, respectively.

In general, an application using HOpenCL will want to embed computations that are qualified into other qualified computations, for example, embedding Queued computations within Contextual computations and thus tying the knot between them. The `with` function is provided for this purpose.

```
with :: Wraps t m n => t -> m u -> n u
```

Reference Counting

For OpenCL objects whose life is not defined by a single C scope, the C API provides operations for manual reference counting (e.g., `clRetainContext`/`clReleaseContext`). HOpenCL generalizes this notion with a type class `LifeSpan` which supports operations `retain` and `release`.

```
retain  :: (LifeSpan t, MonadIO m) => t -> m ()
release :: (LifeSpan t, MonadIO m) => t -> m ()
```

The using function handles constructing and releasing new reference-counted objects. It introduces the ability to automatically manage OpenCL object lifetimes.

```
using :: (Lifespan t m, CatchIO m) => m t -> (t -> m u) -> m u
```

To simplify the use of OpenCL contexts (Context) and command queues (CommandQueue), which are automatically reference-counted in HOpenCL, the operation withNew combines the behavior of the with function and the using function.

```
withNew :: (Wraps t m n, Lifespan t, CatchIO n) => n t -> m u -> n u
```

Platform and Devices

The API function platforms is used to discover the set of available platforms for a given system.

```
platforms :: MonadIO m => m [Platform]
```

Unlike the C API, there is no need to call platforms twice, first to determine the number of platforms and second to get the actual list of platforms; HOpenCL manages all of the plumbing automatically. The only complicated aspect of the definition of platforms is that the result is returned within a monad m, which is constrained to be an instance of the type class MonadIO. This constraint enforces that the particular OpenCL operation happens within a monad that can perform IO. This is true for all OpenCL actions exposed by HOpenCL and is required to capture the fact that the underlying API may perform unsafe operations and thus needs sequencing.

After platforms have been discovered they can be queried, using the overloaded (?) operator, to determine which implementation (vendor) the platform was defined by. For example, the following code selects the first platform and displays the vendor.

```
(p:_) <- platforms
putStrLn . ("Platform is by: " ++) =<< p ? PlatformVendor
```

In general, any OpenCL value that can be queried by a function of the form clGetXXXInfo, where **XXX** is the particular OpenCL type, can be queried by an instance of the function:

```
(?) :: MonadIO m => t -> qt u -> m u
```

For platform queries the type of the operator (?) is

```
(?) :: MonadIO m => Platform -> PlatformInfo u -> m u
```

Similar to the OpenCL C++ Wrapper API's implementation of clGetXXXInfo, the type of the value returned by the operator (?), is dependent on the value being queried, providing an extra layer of static typing. For example, in the case of PlatformVendor, the result is the Haskell type String.

The devices function returns the set of devices associate with a platform.

It takes arguments of a platform and a device type. The device type argument can be used to limit the devices to GPUs only (GPU), CPUs only (CPU), all devices (ALL), as well as other options. As with platforms the operator (?) is called to retrieve information such as name and type.

```
devicesOfType :: MonadIO m => Platform -> [DeviceType] -> m [Device]
```

The Execution Environment

As described earlier, a host can request that a kernel be executed on a device. To achieve this, a context must be configured on the host that enables it to pass commands and data to the device.

Contexts

The function `context` creates a context from a platform and a list of devices.

```
context :: MonadIO m => Platform -> [Device] -> m Context
```

In the case that it is necessary to restrict the scope of the context, e.g., to enable graphics interoperability, then properties may be passed using the `contextFromProperties` function.

```
contextFromProperties :: MonadIO m =>
ContextProperties -> [Device] -> m Context
```

Context properties are built with the operations `noProperties`, which defines an empty set of properties and `pushContextProperty` that adds a context property to an existing set. `noProperties` and `pushContextProperty` are defined as part of the core API in `Language.OpenCL.Host.Core`.

```
noProperties :: ContextProperties
pushContextProperty :: ContextProperty t u =>
t u -> u -> ContextProperties -> ContextProperties
```

Command Queues

Communication with a device occurs by submitting commands to a **command queue**. The function `queue` creates a command queue within the current `Contextual` computation.

```
queue :: Contextual m => Device -> m CommandQueue
```

As `CommandQueue` is reference-counted and defined within a particular `Contextual` computation, a call to `queue` will often be combined with `withNew`, embedding the command queue into the current context.

```
withNew (queue gpu) $
  --computation dependent on newly created command queue
```

Buffers

The function `buffer` allocates an OpenCL buffer, assuming the default set of flags. The function `bufferWithFlags` allocates a buffer with the associated set of user-supplied memory flags. (`MemFlag` is defined in `Language.OpenCL.Host.Constants`.)

```
buffer :: (Storable t, Contextual m) => Int -> m (Buffer t)
bufferWithFlags :: (Storable t, Contextual m) =>
                                Int -> [MemFlag] -> m (Buffer t)
```

As buffers are associated with a Contextual computation (a Context), the `using` function can be used to make this association.

Data contained in host memory is transferred to and from an OpenCL buffer using the commands `writeTo` and `readFrom`, respectively.

```
readFrom :: (Readable cl hs, Storable t, Queued m) =>
                                    cl t -> Int -> Int -> m (hs t)
writeTo   :: (Writable cl hs, Storable t, Queued m) =>
                                    cl t -> Int -> hs t -> m Event
```

Creating an OpenCL Program Object

OpenCL programs are compiled at runtime through two functions, `programFrom-Source` and `buildProgram`, that create a program object from source string and build a program object, respectively.

```
programFromSource :: Contextual m => String -> m Program
buildProgram :: MonadIO m => Program -> [Device] -> String -> m ()
```

The OpenCL Kernel

Kernels are created with the function `kernel`.

```
kernel :: MonadIO m => Program -> String -> m Kernel
```

Arguments can be individually set with the function `fixArgument`. However, often the arguments can be set at the point when the kernel is invoked and HOpenCL provides the function `invoke` for this use case.

```
fixArgument :: (KernelArgument a, MonadIO m) => Kernel -> Int -> a -> m ()
invoke :: KernelInvocation r => Kernel -> r
```

Additionally, it is possible to create a kernel invocation, which one can think of as a kernel closure, from a kernel and a set of arguments using the function `setArgs`. This can be useful in a multi-threaded context.

```
setArgs :: Kernel -> [Co.Kernel -> Int -> IO ()] -> Invocation
```

A call to `invoke` by itself is not enough to actually enqueue a kernel; for this, an application of `invoke` is combined with the function `overRange`, which describes the execution domain and results in an event representing the enqueue, within the current computation.

```
overRange :: Queued m => Invocation -> ([Int], [Int], [Int]) -> m Event
```

Full Source Code Example for Vector Addition

The following example source code implements the vector addition OpenCL application, originally given in Chapter 2, and is reimplemented here using HOpenCL.

```
module VecAdd where

import Language.OpenCL.Host
import Language.OpenCL.Host.FFI

import Control.Monad.Trans (liftIO)
```

```
source =
  "__kernel void vecadd(                                        \n" ++
  "    __global int *C, __global int* A, __global int *B) {     \n" ++
  "    int tid = get_global_id(0);                              \n" ++
  "    C[tid] = A[tid] + B[tid];                                \n" ++
  "}                                                              "

elements = 2048 :: Int;

main = do (p:_) <- platforms
          [gpu] <- devicesOfType p [GPU]
          withNew (context p [gpu]) $
             using (programFromSource source) $ \ p ->
             using (buffer elements) $ \ inBufA ->
             using (buffer elements) $ \ inBufB ->
             using (buffer elements) $ \ outBuf ->
                  do { buildProgram p [gpu] ""
                     ; using (kernel p "vecadd") $ \ vecadd ->
                       withNew (queue gpu) $
                         do writeTo inBufA 0 [0.. elements - 1 ]
                            writeTo inBufB 0 [0.. elements - 1 ]
                            invoke vecadd outBuf inBufA inBufB
                               `overRange` ([0], [elements], [1])
                            (x::[Int]) <- readFrom outBuf 0 elements
                            liftIO (if and $ zipWith (\a b -> a == b+b)
                                              x [0.. elements - 1 ]
                              then print "Output is correct"
                              else print "Output is incorrect") }
```

This is the complete program! Compare these 33 lines of Haskell code to the 208 lines (not counting comments) for the same example given at the end of Chapter 2.

SUMMARY

In this chapter, we have shown that accessing OpenCL's compute capabilities need not be limited to the C or C++ programmer. We highlighted that there are production level bindings for OpenCL for many languages, including Java and Python, and focused on a high-level abstraction for programming OpenCL from the functional language Haskell.

References

Aparapi, (2012). http://Aparapi.googlecode.com.

Chakravarty, M. M., Keller, G., Lee, S., McDonell, T. L., & Grover, V. (2011). Accelerating Haskell array codes with multicore GPUs. In: *Proceedings of the Sixth Workshop on Declarative Aspects of Multicore Programming* (pp. 3–14), New York, NY, USA: ACM DAMP'11.

Gaster, B. R., & Garrett Morris, J. (2012). *HOpenCL. https://github.com/bgaster/hopencl.git.*

Gaster, Benedict, R., & Morris, Garrett (2012). *HOpenCL.*

Hutton, G. (2007). *Programming in Haskell.* Cambridge University Press.

Java bindings for OpenCL (JOCL), (2012). http://www.jocl.org/.

Klöckner, Andreas (2012). *PyOpenCL. http://mathema.tician.de/software/pyopencl.*

Meijer, Erik (2009). *Functional Programming Fundamentals. Channel 9 Lectures.* http://channel9.msdn.com/Series/C9-Lectures-Erik-Meijer-Functional-Programming-Fundamentals/Lecture-Series-Erik-Meijer-Functional-Programming-Fundamentals-Chapter-1.

Svensson, J., Sheeran, M., & Claessen, K. (2011). Obsidian: A domain specific embedded language for parallel programming of graphics processors. In: S.-B. Scholz & O. Chitil (Eds.), *Implementation and Application of Functional Languages, Volume 5836 of Lecture Notes in Computer Science* (pp. 156–173). Heidelberg: Springer Berlin.

OpenCL Profiling and Debugging

INTRODUCTION

Our motivation for writing programs in OpenCL is not limited to writing isolated high-performance kernels but to speed up parallel applications. Previous chapters discussed how we can optimize kernels running on OpenCL devices by targeting features of the architecture. In this chapter, we discuss how we can study the interaction between the computational kernels on the device and the host. We need to measure the performance and study an application as a whole to understand bottlenecks.

An OpenCL application can include kernels and a large amount of input/output (IO) between the host and device. Profiling such an application can help us to improve performance by answering some of the following questions regarding an application:

- Which kernel should be optimized when multiple kernels exist in an application?
- How much time is spent by the kernels waiting in command queues versus actually executing?
- What is the ratio between execution time and the time spent initializing the OpenCL runtime and compiling kernels for an application?
- What is the ratio of time spent in host device IO to computation time for an application?

The first two sections of this chapter examine how the OpenCL API provides some basic features for application profiling and how operating system APIs can be used for timing sections of code, respectively. The following two sections discuss two tools from AMD that can help with profiling an application for performance:

- AMD Accelerated Parallel Processing (APP) Profiler is a performance analysis tool that gathers data from the OpenCL runtime and AMD Radeon GPUs during the execution of an OpenCL application.
- AMD Accelerated Parallel Processing (APP) KernelAnalyzer is a static analysis tool to compile, analyze, and disassemble an OpenCL kernel for AMD Radeon GPUs.

Each of the profiling approaches discussed above can help a developer quickly determine why an application is not performing as expected and, in combination with the debugging features described later in this chapter, can greatly improve the development process.

We conclude this chapter by discussing debugging OpenCL code. Debugging of parallel programs is traditionally more complicated than conventional serial code due to subtle bugs such as race conditions, which are difficult to detect and reproduce. We give a brief overview of gDEBugger. AMD gDEBugger is an OpenCL™ and OpenGL debugger and memory analyzer, that provides the ability to debug OpenCL™ & OpenGL API calls and OpenCL™ kernels and step through the source code to find bugs, optimize performance and reduce memory consumption. We also briefly explain the `printf` extension provided by AMD, which allows us to view kernel data.

PROFILING WITH EVENTS

OpenCL supports 64-bit timing of commands submitted to command queues using `clEnqueueXX()`commands, such as `clEnqueueNDRangeKernel()`. Generally, commands are enqueued into a queue asynchronously, and as described in previous chapters, the developer uses events to keep track of a command's status as well as to enforce dependencies. Events provide a gateway to a command's history: They contain information detailing when the corresponding command was placed in the queue, when it was submitted to the device, and when it started and ended execution. Access to an event's profiling information is through the following API `clGetEventProfilingInfo`, which provides an interface for queuing timing information:

Enabling Profiling

Profiling of OpenCL programs using events has to be enabled explicitly on a per command queue basis. Profiling is enabled when creating a command queue by setting the `CL_QUEUE_PROFILING_ENABLE` flag.

Once a command queue has been created, it is not possible to turn event profiling on and off.

```
cl_int clGetEventProfilingInfo (
    cl_event event,
    cl_profiling_info param_name,
    size_t param_value_size,
    void *param_value,
    size_t *param_value_size_ret)
```

The first argument, `event`, is the event being queried, and the second argument is an enumeration value describing the query. Valid values for the enumeration are given in the following table:

CL_PROFILING	Return Type	Information Returned in param_value
CL_PROFILING_COMMAND_QUEUED	cl_ulong	A 64-bit value that describes the current device time counter in nanoseconds when the command identified by *event* is enqueued in a command queue by the host.
CL_PROFILING_COMMAND_SUBMIT	cl_ulong	A 64-bit value that describes the current device time counter in nanoseconds when the command identified by the event that has been enqueued is submitted by the host to the device associated with the command queue.
CL_PROFILING_COMMAND_START	cl_ulong	A 64-bit value that describes the current device time counter in nanoseconds when the command identified by *event* starts execution on the device.
CL_PROFILING_COMMAND_END	cl_ulong	A 64-bit value that describes the current device time counter in nanoseconds when the command identified by *event* has finished execution on the device.

As discussed previously, OpenCL command queues work asynchronously—that is, the functions return as soon as the command is enqueued. For this reason, querying an OpenCL event for timestamps after a kernel enqueue necessitates a `clFinish` call or other event synchronization before the call to `clGetEventProfilingInfo` to ensure that the task associated with the event has completed execution.

Event profiling information is not enabled by default and instead is enabled on a per command queue basis. To explicitly enable a command queue for event profiling, the following bit-field value is passed at creation:

```
CL_QUEUE_PROFILING_ENABLE
```

Once a command queue has been created, it is not possible to turn event profiling on and off.

The following is a simple example of the use of events to profile a kernel execution:

```
// Sample Code that can be used for timing kernel execution duration
// Using different parameters for cl_profiling_info allows us to
// measure the wait time
cl_event timing_event;
cl_int err_code;
```

```
//! We are timing the clEnqueueNDRangeKernel call and timing
//information will be stored in timing_event
err_code = clEnqueueNDRangeKernel (
   command_queue, kernel,
   work_dim,
   global_work_offset,
   global_work_size,
   local_work_size,
   0,
   NULL,
   &timing_event);
clFinish(command_queue);

cl_ulong starttime;
cl_ulong endtime;
err_code = clGetEventProfilingInfo(
   timing_event,
   CL_PROFILING_COMMAND_START,
   sizeof(cl_ulong),
   &starttime, NULL);

kerneltimer = clGetEventProfilingInfo(
   timing_event,
   CL_PROFILING_COMMAND_END,
   sizeof(cl_ulong),
   &endtime,
   NULL);

unsigned long elapsed = (unsigned long)(endtime - starttime);

printf("Kernel Execution\t%ld ns\n",elapsed);
```

AMD ACCELERATED PARALLEL PROCESSING PROFILER

The AMD Accelerated Parallel Processing (APP) Profiler is a performance analysis tool that gathers data from the OpenCL runtime and AMD Radeon GPUs during the execution of an OpenCL application. We can then use this information to discover bottlenecks in an application and find ways to optimize the application's performance for AMD platforms. Hereafter, we refer to the AMD APP Profiler as the profiler.

The profiler can be installed as part of the AMD APP SDK installation or individually using its own installer package. You can download the profiler from the AMD developer website at http://developer.amd.com.

In this section, we describe the major features in Version 2.5 of the profiler with the described version is included with Version 2.7 of the AMD APP SDK. Because the profiler is still being rapidly developed, please consult the profiler documentation for the latest features of the tool.

The profiler supports two usage models:

1. As a Microsoft Visual Studio 2008 or 2010 plug-in
2. As a command line utility tool for both Windows and Linux platforms

Using the profiler as a Visual Studio plug-in is the recommended usage model because one can visualize and analyze the results in multiple ways. To start the profiler in the Visual Studio plug-in, simply load a solution into Visual Studio. Select a C/C++ project as the startup project, and click on the Collect Application Trace or Collect GPU Performance Counters button on the APP Profiler Session Explorer panel. By default, the APP Profiler Session Explorer panel will be docked in the same window panel as the Visual Studio Solution Explorer panel. No code or project modifications are required to profile the application. The profiler will query Visual Studio for all the project settings required to run the application. When the application completes, the profiler will generate and display the profile information.

The command line utility tool is a popular way to collect data for applications for which the source code is not available. The output text files generated by the profiler can be analyzed directly. They can also be loaded by the Visual Studio plug-in to be visualized.

Two modes of operation are supported by the profiler: collecting OpenCL application traces and collecting OpenCL kernel GPU performance counters.

Collecting OpenCL Application Trace

The OpenCL application trace lists all the OpenCL API calls made by the application. For each API call, the profiler records the input parameters and output results. In addition, the profiler also records the CPU timestamps for the host code and device timestamps retrieved from the OpenCL runtime. The output data is recorded in a text-based AMD custom file format called an Application Trace Profile file. Consult the tool documentation for the specification. This mode is especially useful in helping to understand the high-level structure of a complex application.

From the OpenCL application trace data, we can do the following:

- Discover the high-level structure of the application with the Timeline View. From this view, we can determine the number of OpenCL contexts and command queues created and the relationships between these items in the application. The application code, kernel execution, and data transfer operations are shown in a timeline.
- Determine if the application is bound by kernel execution or data transfer operations, find the top 10 most expensive kernel and data transfer operations, and find the API hot spots (most frequently called or most expensive API call) in the application with the Summary Pages View.
- View and debug the input parameters and output results for all API calls made by the application with the API Trace View.

The Timeline View (Figure 13.1) provides a visual representation of the execution of the application. Along the top of the timeline is the time grid, which shows the

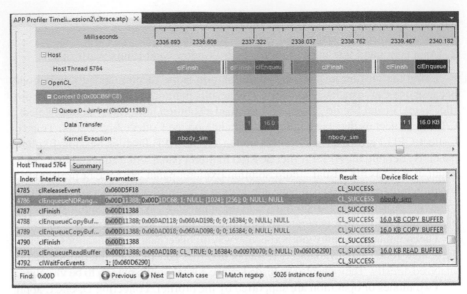

FIGURE 13.1

The Timeline and API Trace View of AMD APP Profiler in Microsoft Visual Studio 2010.

total elapsed time of the application when fully zoomed out, in milliseconds. Timing begins when the first OpenCL call is made by the application and ends when the final OpenCL call is made. Directly below the time grid, each host (OS) thread that made at least one OpenCL call is listed. For each host thread, the OpenCL API calls are plotted along the time grid, showing the start time and duration of each call. Below the host threads, the OpenCL tree shows all contexts and queues created by the application, along with data transfer operations and kernel execution operations for each queue. We can navigate in the Timeline View by zooming, panning, collapsing/expanding, or selecting a region of interest. From the Timeline View, we can also navigate to the corresponding API call in the API Trace View and vice versa.

The Timeline View can be useful for debugging your OpenCL application. The following are examples:

- You can easily confirm that the high-level structure of your application is correct. By examining the timeline, you can verify that the number of queues and contexts created match your expectations for the application.
- You can gain confidence that synchronization has been performed properly in the application. For example, if kernel A execution is dependent on a buffer operation and outputs from kernel B execution, then kernel A execution should appear after the completion of the buffer execution and kernel B execution in the time grid. It can be difficult to find this type of synchronization error using traditional debugging techniques.

- Finally, you can see that the application has been utilizing the hardware efficiently. For example, the timeline should show that nondependent kernel executions and data transfer operations occur simultaneously.

Summary Pages View

The Summary Pages View shows various statistics for your OpenCL application. It can provide a general idea of the location of the application's bottlenecks. It also provides useful information such as the number of buffers and images created on each context, the most expensive kernel call, etc.

The Summary Pages View provides access to the following individual pages:

- API Summary page: This page shows statistics for all OpenCL API calls made in the application for API hot spot identification.
- Context Summary page: This page shows the statistics for all the kernel dispatch and data transfer operations for each context. It also shows the number of buffers and images created for each context. This is shown in Figure 13.2.
- Kernel Summary page: This page shows statistics for all the kernels that are created in the application.
- Top 10 Data Transfer Summary page: This page shows a sorted list of the 10 most expensive individual data transfer operations.
- Top 10 Kernel Summary page: This page shows a sorted list of the 10 most expensive individual kernel execution operations.
- Warning(s)/Error(s) Page: The Warning(s)/Error(s) Page shows potential problems in your OpenCL application. It can detect unreleased OpenCL resources, OpenCL API failures and provide suggestions to achieve better performance. Clicking on a hyperlink takes you to the corresponding OpenCL API that generates the message.

From these summary pages, it is possible to determine whether the application is bound by kernel execution or data transfer (Context Summary page). If the application is bound by kernel execution, we can determine which device is the bottleneck.

Context ID	# of Buffers	# of Images	# of Kernel Dispatch CPU_Device	Total Kernel Time(ms) CPU_Device	# of Kernel Dispatch Juniper	Total Kernel Time (ms) - Juniper	# of Memory Transfer	Total Memory Time (ms)	# of Read	Total Read Time (ms)	Size of Read	# of Write	Total Write Time (ms)	Size of Write	# of Map	Total Map Time (ms)	Size of Map	# of Copy	Total Copy Time (ms)	Size of Copy
0	2	0	1	67.43930	1	15.86929	2	1.21196	0	0	0 Byte	2	1.21196	512.00 KB	0	0	0 Byte	0	0	0 Byte
1	2	0	1	36.10200	NA	NA	1	0.13787	0	0	0 Byte	1	0.13787	256.00 KB	0	0	0 Byte	0	0	0 Byte
2	2	0	NA	NA	1	1.38887	1	1.71825	0	0	0 Byte	1	1.71825	256.00 KB	0	0	0 Byte	0	0	0 Byte
3	2	0	1	36.32298	NA	NA	1	0.13444	0	0	0 Byte	1	0.13444	256.00 KB	0	0	0 Byte	0	0	0 Byte
4	2	0	NA	NA	1	1.38915	1	1.66952	0	0	0 Byte	1	1.66952	256.00 KB	0	0	0 Byte	0	0	0 Byte
Total	10	0	3	139.86428	3	18.64731	6	4.87205	0	0	0 Byte	6	4.87205	1.50 MB	0	0	0 Byte	0	0	0 Byte

FIGURE 13.2

The Context Summary Page View of AMD APP Profiler in Microsoft Visual Studio 2010.

From the Kernel Summary page, we can find the name of the kernel with the highest total execution time. Or, from the Top 10 Kernel Summary page, we can find the individual kernel instance with the highest execution time. If the kernel execution on a GPU device is the bottleneck, the GPU performance counters can then be used to investigate the bottleneck inside the kernel. We describe the GPU performance counters view later in this chapter.

If the application is bound by the data transfers, it is possible to determine the most expensive data transfer type (read, write, copy, or map) in the application from the Context Summary page. We can investigate whether we can minimize this type of data transfer by modifying the algorithm if necessary. With help from the Timeline View, we can investigate whether data transfers have been executed in the most efficient way—that is, concurrently with a kernel execution.

API Trace View

The API Trace View (Figure 13.1) lists all the OpenCL API calls made by the application.

Each host thread that makes at least one OpenCL call is listed in a separate tab. Each tab contains a list of all the API calls made by that particular thread. For each call, the list displays the index of the call (representing execution order), the name of the API function, a semicolon delimited list of parameters passed to the function, and the value returned by the function. When displaying parameters, the profiler will attempt to dereference pointers and decode enumeration values to give as much information as possible about the data being passed in or returned from the function. Double-clicking an item in the API Trace View will display and zoom into that API call in the Host Thread row in the Timeline View.

The view allows us to analyze and debug the input parameters and output results for each API call. For example, we can easily check that all the API calls are returning CL_SUCCESS or that all the buffers are created with the correct flags. We can also identify redundant API calls using this view.

Collecting OpenCL GPU Kernel Performance Counters

The GPU kernel performance counters can be used to find possible bottlenecks in the kernel execution. You can find the list of performance counters supported by AMD Radeon GPUs in the tool documentation.

Once we have used the trace data to discover which kernel is most in need of optimization, we can collect the GPU performance counters to drill down into the kernel execution on a GPU device. Using the performance counters, we can do the following:

- Find the number of resources (General Purpose Registers, Local Memory size, and Flow Control Stack size) allocated for the kernel. These resources affect the possible number of in-flight wavefronts in the GPU. A higher number of wavefronts better hides data latency.
- Determine the number of ALU, global, and local memory instructions executed by the GPU.

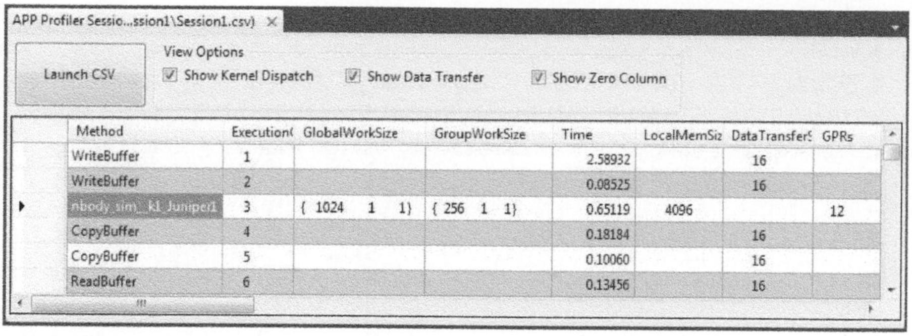

FIGURE 13.3

The Session View of AMD APP Profiler in Microsoft Visual Studio 2010.

- Determine the number of bytes fetched from and written to the global memory.
- Determine the utilization of the SIMD engines and memory units in the system.
- View the efficiency of the Shader Compiler in packing ALU instructions into the VLIW instructions used by AMD GPUs.
- View any local memory (Local Data Share (LDS)) bank conflicts where multiple lanes within a SIMD unit attempt to read or write the same LDS bank and have to be serialized, causing access latency.

The Session View (Figure 13.3) shows the performance counters for a profile session. The output data is recorded in a comma-separated-variable (csv) format. You can also click on the kernel name entry in the "Method" column to view the OpenCL kernel source, AMD Intermediate Language, GPU ISA, or CPU assembly code for that kernel.

AMD ACCELERATED PARALLEL PROCESSING KERNELANALYZER

The AMD APP KernelAnalyzer is a static analysis tool to compile, analyze, and disassemble an OpenCL kernel for AMD Radeon GPUs. It can be used as a graphical user interface tool for interactive tuning of an OpenCL kernel or in command line mode to generate detailed reports. Hereafter, we refer to this tool as the KernelAnalyzer.

The KernelAnalyzer can be installed as part of the AMD APP SDK installation or individually using its own installer package. You can download the KernelAnalyzer package from the AMD developer website at http://developer.amd.com.

To use the KernelAnalyzer, the AMD OpenCL runtime is required to be installed on the system. However, no GPU is required in the system.

To compile an OpenCL kernel in the KernelAnalyzer, simply drop the source containing the OpenCL kernel anywhere within the KernelAnalyzer's main window (Figure 13.4). We do not require the entire OpenCL application to compile or analyze the OpenCL kernel.

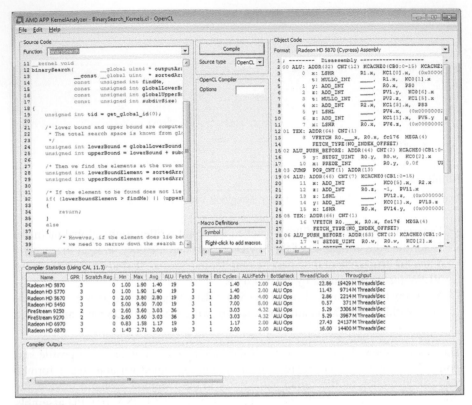

FIGURE 13.4

AMD APP KernelAnalyzer.

With the KernelAnalyzer, we can do the following:

- Compile, analyze, and disassemble the OpenCL kernel for multiple Catalyst driver versions and GPU device targets.
- View any kernel compilation errors and warnings generated by the OpenCL runtime.
- View the AMD Intermediate Language code generated by the OpenCL runtime.
- View the ISA code generated by the AMD Shader Compiler. Typically, device-specific kernel optimizations are performed by analyzing the ISA code.
- View various statistics generated by analyzing the ISA code.
- View General Purpose Registers and spill registers allocated for the kernel.

Because the KernelAnalyzer can quickly compile a kernel for multiple GPU device targets, it is very useful for rapid prototyping of OpenCL kernels.

WALKING THROUGH THE AMD APP PROFILER

In this section, we walk through the usage of AMD APP Profiler to profile the MatrixMultiplication application from the AMD APP SDK Version 2.4 samples.

We show you a step-by-step process that includes running the AMD APP Profiler, using the generated data to find a bottleneck in the application, and improving the performance of the application.

Starting the AMD APP Profiler

1. Load the AMD APP SDK samples solution file (`OpenCLSamplesVS10.sln`) in Microsoft Visual Studio.
2. Set the MatrixMultiplication project as the start-up project.
3. Confirm that the project can compile and run normally.
4. Confirm that the APP Profiler has been installed properly.
   a. From the Visual Studio main menu bar, select the `Help -> About Microsoft Visual Studio` menu item. Under the `Installed products`, you should see an AMD APP Profiler entry. If you do not see this entry, please re-install the profiler.
   b. Check that the APP Profiler Session Explorer is docked in the same window panel as the Visual Studio Solution Explorer. If you do not see the APP Profiler Session Explorer panel, enable it by selecting `View -> Other Windows -> APP Profiler Session Explorer` from the Visual Studio main menu bar.

Using the Application Trace to Find the Application Bottleneck

1. On the APP Profiler Session Explorer, click on the `Collect Application Trace` button to start collecting a trace for the application.
2. After the trace has been completed, the APP Profiler Timeline (Figure 13.5) will be shown and docked in the same window panel as the Visual Studio editor window.
   a. From the API Trace View in Figure 13.5, we can confirm that the application runs successfully without generating any errors from the OpenCL runtime by verifying that all return error codes of the API calls are `CL_SUCCESS`. From this view, we can also inspect the input arguments and output results of each API call. For example, the first two buffers are created with a `CL_MEM_READ_ONLY` flag, and the third buffer is created with a `CL_MEM_WRITE_ONLY` flag. These buffers are of size 16 MB.
   b. From the Timeline View in Figure 13.5, we can learn the following facts about the application:
      • The application contains one OpenCL context and one command queue.
      • The command queue is created for a GPU device called Juniper, which is the internal name for the AMD Radeon HD5770 GPU.

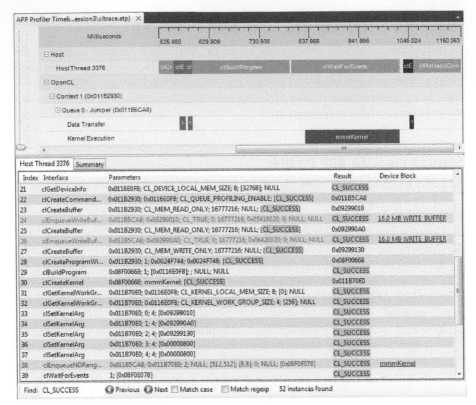

FIGURE 13.5

The APP Profiler Timeline and API Trace View of the MatrixMultiplication application.

- The application contains three data transfer operations: Two input buffers are sent to the device, and one output buffer is read from the device.
- There is one kernel execution on the GPU device.
- The application likely has correct dependency for the data transfers and kernel operations. Two input buffers are sent to the device prior to the start of the kernel execution operation, and the output buffer is read from the device after the completion of the kernel execution. Short of exhaustive testing or model checking, this is good support for correct implementation of the intent.

3. Click on the Summary tab (Figure 13.5) to view the Summary Pages View.
   a. Navigate to the Context Summary page (Figure 13.6; the default view after you click on the Summary tab) by selecting the Context Summary from the drop-down combo box on the Summary Pages View.
      - From this page, we find that the kernel operation on the GPU device is the bottleneck. The total kernel execution on the GPU device takes 195 ms compared to the total data transfer operations, which take 32 ms.

b. Navigate to the Top10 Kernel Summary page (Figure 13.7) by selecting the `Top10 Kernel Summary` from the drop-down menu.
   • Using this page, we can find the kernel instance (`mmmKernel`) that is in most need of optimization. In this example, however, there is only one kernel instance.

Using the GPU Performance Counters to Find the Bottleneck in the Kernel

Once we have discovered the kernel instance that is in most need of optimization, we can collect the GPU performance counters (click the `Collect GPU Performance Counters` button on the APP Profiler Session Explorer panel) to guide us in finding the possible bottlenecks in the kernel.

Figure 13.8 shows the resulting GPU performance counters of multiplying two matrices of size 2048 × 2048 together using three different methods:

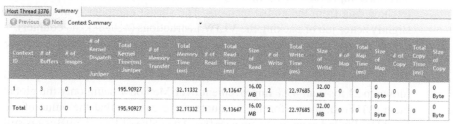

Context ID	# of Buffers	# of Images	# of Kernel Dispatch Juniper	Total Kernel Time(ms) Juniper	# of Memory Transfer	Total Memory Time (ms)	# of Read	Total Read Time (ms)	Size of Read	# of Write	Total Write Time (ms)	Size of Write	# of Map	Total Map Time (ms)	Size of Map	# of Copy	Total Copy Time (ms)	Size of Copy
1	3	0	1	195.90927	3	32.11332	1	9.13647	16.00 MB	2	22.97685	32.00 MB	0	0	0 Byte	0	0	0 Byte
Total	3	0	1	195.90927	3	32.11332	1	9.13647	16.00 MB	2	22.97685	32.00 MB	0	0	0 Byte	0	0	0 Byte

FIGURE 13.6

The Context Summary page of the MatrixMultiplication application.

Kernel Name	Context ID	Command Queue ID	Device Name	Duration (ms)	Global Work Size	Group Work Size	Thread ID	Call Index
mmmKernel	1	0	Juniper	195.90927	{512,512}	{8,8}	3376	38

FIGURE 13.7

The Top10 Kernel Summary page of the MatrixMultiplication application.

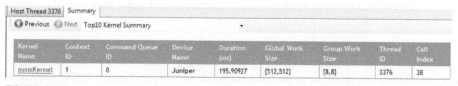

Method	Time	GPRs	Wavefronts	ALUInsts	FetchInsts	WriteInsts	LDSFetchInsts	LDSWriteInsts	ALUBusy	ALUPacking	CacheHit	FetchUnitBusy	FetchUnitStalled	LDSBankConflict
mmmKernel	195.90927	17	4096	15383	4096	4	0	0	13.32	77.31	0	98.10	42.28	0
mmmKernel_local	114.16687	20	4096	20577	2304	4	4096	512	30.87	82.45	0	97.67	43.69	20.14
mmmKernel_image	21.40209	31	2048	21008	6144	8	0	0	83.78	84.83	69.31	98.09	0.09	0

FIGURE 13.8

The resulting GPU performance counters for three different methods of multiplying two matrices of size 2048 × 2048. The first row employs a method of using only the global memory, whereas the second row adds the usage of local memory. The third method uses OpenCL image objects.

1. Row 1 is the result from the MatrixMultiplication sample: This method uses the global memory to store the matrices.
   a. The result shows that the kernel uses 17 general-purpose registers (GPRs). This is good because it is less likely that the number of wavefronts in-flight will be limited by the GPR usage. There are 4096 wavefronts generated. With a maximum of 24 SIMD cores on current devices, this is at least 170 wavefronts per core—far more than the device resources can run concurrently and easily enough to keep the device busy.
   b. From the low value of `ALUBusy` and high value of `FetchUnitBusy` and `Fetch-UnitStalled` counters, we can conclude that the kernel is bottlenecked by fetching data from the global memory.
2. Row 2 is the result from the MatrixMultiplication sample with a `mmmKernel_local` kernel: This method uses the global memory to store the matrices but also utilizes the local memory to cache the results.
   a. The result shows that we have improved the kernel running time from 195 to 114 ms (a 42% improvement) by utilizing the local memory to reduce the pressure of fetching data from the global memory. The shader compiler is also doing a slightly better job of packing the VLIW instructions (`ALUPacking` counter).
3. Row 3 is the result from the MatrixMulImage sample: This method uses the OpenCL image objects to store the matrices.
   a. The result shows that the kernel running time has been significantly improved (down to 21 ms—an 89% improvement over Method 1 using only the global memory). From the performance counters, we can see that the value of the FetchUnitStalled counter is now near 0%. The value of FetchUnitBusy is still very high; this shows that this kernel is still bottlenecked over the data fetching from the global memory. However, using the image objects helps due to the support for data caching of image objects (69% cache hit for the `CacheHit` counter). The value of the `ALUBusy` counter is now quite high, signifying that the SIMDs are now utilized properly.

From these three methods, we have seen that the MatrixMultiplication kernel is bottlenecked by fetching data from the global memory. The second and third methods try to address this problem by utilizing the local memory and image buffer objects to cache the results from the global memory.

DEBUGGING OPENCL APPLICATIONS

From the previous sections, we have seen how we can optimize performance of our OpenCL code. However, the paramount requirement is correctness. In this section, we discuss debugging in a heterogeneous environment and give an overview of the tools provided.

Debugging of parallel programs is traditionally more complicated than conventional serial code due to subtle bugs such as race conditions, which are difficult to detect and reproduce. The difficulties of debugging parallel applications running on heterogeneous devices are exacerbated by the complexity and "black box" nature of the accelerated parallel platform.

The developer works on top of an API that hides the parallel platform's implementation. Debuggers and profilers transform the developer's view into a "white box" model, letting the developer peer into OpenCL to see how individual commands affect the parallel computing system. This allows developers to find bugs caused by incorrect OpenCL usage and optimize their applications for the system on which it runs. In the remainder of this chapter, we give a brief overview of gDEBugger, which is an advanced debugger and profiler for OpenCL, and we explain (briefly) the `printf` extension provided by AMD, a simpler but sometimes effective alternative to a full debugger.

OVERVIEW OF GDEBUGGER

gDEBugger is an OpenCL and OpenGL debugger, profiler, and memory analyzer. It helps developers find bugs and optimize OpenCL performance and memory consumption.

gDEBugger consists of the following components:

- gDEBugger Visual Studio plug-in—a plug-in that adds advanced OpenCL and OpenGL debugging capabilities into Microsoft's Visual Studio
- gDEBugger (stand-alone)—a stand-alone product that offers advanced OpenCL and OpenGL debugging and profiling capabilities over multiple platforms (Windows, Linux, and Mac)

Figure 13.9 shows a simplified high-level overview of how gDEBugger interacts with OpenCL devices. It shows some of the important modules/components. When gDEBugger is used, it intercepts the API calls between the Application and the OpenCL Installable Client Driver. This enables gDEBugger to log all API calls, identify all used OpenCL objects, and gather data on these objects. In addition, gDEBugger can actively modify some of the API calls, add calls to query additional information, and can eliminate some calls to help the developer analyze the performance bottlenecks.

In the following sections, we briefly describe the debugging capabilities of gDEBugger to advocate its usage in development environments.

Debugging Parallel OpenCL Applications with gDEBugger

As previously discussed, there are two distinct regions of code in heterogeneous applications:

1. API-level code (`clEnqueue` calls, `clCreateBuffer`, etc.), which runs on the host
2. Compute kernel (run on devices) code

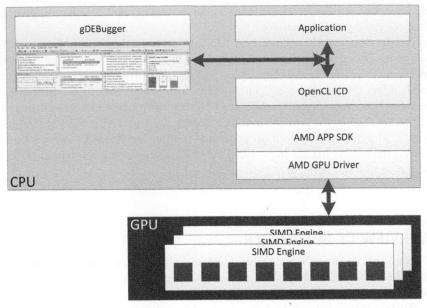

FIGURE 13.9

A high-level overview of where gDEBugger links to the application and OpenCL.

We give brief details about the debugging capabilities of gDEBugger for both the API-level code and compute kernels.

API-Level Debugging

API-level debugging is provided by gDEBugger to view the parameters that a runtime function is called with. The following are features provided by API-level debugging:

- API function breakpoints: gDEBugger will break the debugged application before the function is executed. This allows viewing the call stack that led to the function call, as well as the function's parameters.
- Record the OpenCL API call history: When the debugged process is suspended, gDEBugger shows us the last OpenCL function call (and its parameters) made in the currently selected context. Figure 13.10 shows how gDEBugger provides a back-trace of the OpenCL commands invoked by the program.
- Program and kernel information: OpenCL contexts contain multiple program and kernel objects within them. gDEBugger allows us to verify which programs are associated with each context. If the program was created using `clCreateProgramWithSource`, we can also view the source code passed to this function.
- Image and buffers' data: An OpenCL context will contain buffers and images. gDEBugger allows us to view the object's data. For Image types, gDEBugger allows us to see the image data visualized in the "Image view."

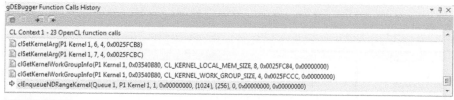

FIGURE 13.10

gDEBugger function call history.

- Memory checking: gDEBugger allows us to view the memory consumption for a specific context's buffers. The memory checking functionality provided by gDE-Bugger can be used to trace memory leaks and unneeded objects that were created or were not released in time, consuming device memory and making debugging more difficult.
- API usage statistics: gDEBugger shows statistical information about the currently selected context's API usage. By viewing a breakdown of the OpenCL API calls made in this context by various categories, we can see the number of times a function is called. This allows us to understand the performance of different runtime functions for different implementations and devices.

Kernel Debugging

gDEBugger also enables debugging within the compute kernel that is executing on the device. There are two ways to start debugging an OpenCL kernel with gDEBugger:

1. Setting a breakpoint in the kernel code
2. Stepping into the kernel execution from its corresponding `clEnqueuNDRangeKernel` **call**

A common concern when debugging an OpenCL application is keeping track of state in the presence of a large number of work items. A kernel on a GPU device will commonly be launched with many thousands of work items. gDEBugger assists the developer by allowing us to focus on a particular active work item by displaying the work item's variable's values and enforcing possible breakpoints for the work item. Figure 13.11 shows the appearance of OpenCL kernel code while debugging with gDEBugger.

AMD `PRINTF` EXTENSION

The AMD `printf` extension is another useful debugging tool. The `printf` extension is enabled by adding the line `#pragma OPENCL EXTENSION cl_amd_printf : enable` to the kernel source code. OpenCL extensions were described in detail in Chapter 11.

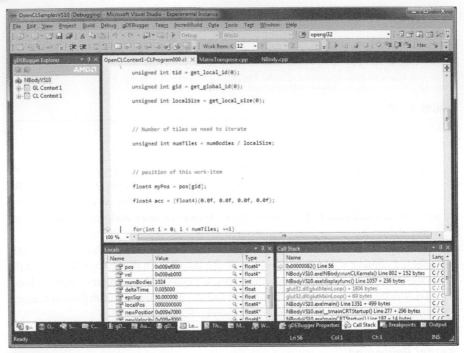

FIGURE 13.11

Kernel source view seen in gDEBugger for an application kernel.

The pragma lets the OpenCL compiler know about the possible usage of the `printf` function within a kernel body.

As seen in the following vector addition code, the usage of `printf` for OpenCL kernels is similar to its usage in C/C++ programming. Note that `printf` outputs the results of the format string for every work item of the NDRange on which it will be executed.

```
#pragma OPENCL EXTENSION cl_amd_printf : enable

//! Simple example showing usage of printf in a vector add kernel.
__kernel void vec_add(__global float * d_ip1, __global float * d_ip2,
__global float d_op, int N)
{
    int tid = get_global_id(0)
    if (tid < N)
```

```
    {
        float value_0 = d_ip0[tid];
        float value_1 = d_ip0[tid];
        //This line will print out the format string below 'N' times.
        printf("Values read in %f\t %f\n", value_0, value_1);
        d_op[tid] = value_0 + value_1;
    }

}
```

CONCLUSION

In this chapter, we examined different OpenCL profiling and debugging tools. OpenCL tools such as the APP Profiler and the KernelAnalyzer help us to understand the location of performance bottlenecks in our code. gDEBugger helps us to debug our programs.

Performance Optimization of an Image Analysis Application

14

INTRODUCTION

Chapter 13 discussed step by step how to use AMD CodeAnalyst, Profiler, gDEBugger, and KernelAnalyzer to profile and debug an OpenCL application. While Chapter 13 gave a very basic introduction to the tools, in this chapter, we use a real-world application as an example to walk through the steps from migrating a single-threaded application to one that utilizes the GPU and APU power using OpenCL. We will see how some of the profiling techniques that these, and other, tools provide can be used to investigate bottlenecks and improve peak performance of an application. After all, high performance is generally the reason to put time into porting code to use OpenCL.

This chapter dives into detailed profiling techniques provided by the software development tools described in Chapter 13, and applies them to a real application. We port a medical image analysis pipeline from a traditional CPU multithreaded execution and optimized for execution in OpenCL on a GPU. In this chapter, we see both static analysis and profiling and the trade-offs involved in optimizing a real application for data-parallel execution on a GPU.

In this chapter, we use AMD tools as an example. More thorough descriptions of all the tools are available in their documentation, and tools from other vendors provide similar capabilities. You should use whatever tools are appropriate for the architecture you are targeting.

We present a vasculature image enhancement module, which is the first and most important step for a vessel analysis application. The automatic and real-time enhancement of the vessels potentially facilitates diagnosis and later treatment of vascular diseases. The performance and power consumption of the proposed algorithms are evaluated on single-core CPU, multicore CPU, discrete GPU, and finally an accelerated processing unit (APU).

In this chapter, we first discuss the algorithm to give a background to the problem being solved. We then show how the CPU implementation may be ported to OpenCL and run on a GPU. In this section, we show how different tools may be used to inform the developer about what parts of the application should move to OpenCL and how to optimize them once they are there. We examine some trade-offs in kernel code and how they affect performance. Finally, we see how these changes may affect energy use by the application and show that the GPU can give an energy consumption benefit.

DESCRIPTION OF THE ALGORITHM

The algorithm chosen is a coarse segmentation of the coronary arteries in CT images based on a multiscale Hessian-based vessel enhancement filter (Frangi, 2001). The filter utilizes the second-order derivatives of the image intensity after smoothing (using a Gaussian kernel) at multiple scales to identify bright tubular-like structures. The six second-order derivatives of the Hessian matrix at each voxel can be either computed by convolving the image with second-order Gaussian derivatives at preselected scale value or approximated using a finite difference approach.

Various vessel enhancement techniques have been proposed in the past decade. Three of the most popular techniques for curvilinear structure filtering have been proposed by Frangi (2001), Lorenz et al (1997), and Sato et al (1998). All these approaches are based on extracting information from the second-order intensity derivatives at multiple scales to identify local structures in the images. Based on that information, it is possible to classify the local intensity structure as tubular-like, plane-like, or block-like.

In this chapter, we use a multiscale Hessian-based vessel enhancement filter by Frangi (2001) because of its superior performance compared with other tubular filters (Olabarriaga et al. 2003). The filter utilizes the second-order derivatives of the image intensity after smoothing using a Gaussian kernel at multiple scales to identify bright tubular-like structures with various diameters. The six second-order derivatives of the Hessian matrix at each voxel are computed by convolving the image with the second-order Gaussian derivatives at preselected scales.

Assuming a continuous image function $\mathbf{I}(\mathbf{x}), \mathbf{x} = (x, y, z)$, the Hessian matrix $\mathbf{H}$ for the 3D image at any voxel $\mathbf{x}$ is defined as

$$\mathbf{H}(\mathbf{x}) = \begin{pmatrix} \dfrac{\partial^2 \mathbf{I}(\mathbf{x})}{\partial x \partial x} & \dfrac{\partial^2 \mathbf{I}(\mathbf{x})}{\partial x \partial y} & \dfrac{\partial^2 \mathbf{I}(\mathbf{x})}{\partial x \partial y} \\[3mm] \dfrac{\partial^2 \mathbf{I}(\mathbf{x})}{\partial y \partial x} & \dfrac{\partial^2 \mathbf{I}(\mathbf{x})}{\partial y \partial y} & \dfrac{\partial^2 \mathbf{I}(\mathbf{x})}{\partial y \partial z} \\[3mm] \dfrac{\partial^2 \mathbf{I}(\mathbf{x})}{\partial z \partial x} & \dfrac{\partial^2 \mathbf{I}(\mathbf{x})}{\partial z \partial y} & \dfrac{\partial^2 \mathbf{I}(\mathbf{x})}{\partial z \partial z} \end{pmatrix}$$

At a predefined scale σ, Hessian $\mathbf{H}$ can be computed by convolving the image $\mathbf{I}(\mathbf{x})$ with the second-order Gaussian derivatives shown in Figure 14.1(a).

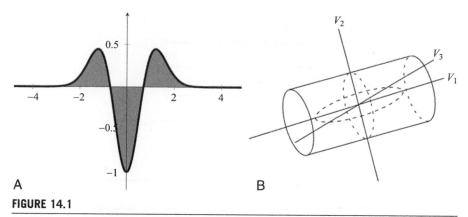

A   **B**

FIGURE 14.1

Illustrations of second-order Gaussian derivative and ellipsoid. (a) The second-order derivative of a Gaussian kernel at scale $\sigma = 1$. (b) The ellipsoid that locally describes the second-order structure of the image with illustration of the principal directions of curvature.

A vesselness term $v_\sigma(\mathbf{x})$ is defined as in Frangi (2001) and is based on the eigenvalues and eigenvectors of $\mathbf{H}\sigma(\mathbf{x})$. Let $|\lambda_1| \leq |\lambda_2| \leq |\lambda_3|$ denote the eigenvalues of the Hessian $\mathbf{H}\sigma(\mathbf{x})$, and $\mathbf{v}_1, \mathbf{v}_2, \mathbf{v}_3$ are the corresponding eigenvectors. The principal curvature directions are then given by $\mathbf{v}_2$ and $\mathbf{v}_3$, as shown in Figure 14.1(b).

Since arteries have higher intensity values in computerized tomographic angiography (CTA) images than surrounding soft tissues, the vessel center points are the ones with maximal local intensities after smoothing. Thus, the corresponding eigenvalues λ_2 and λ_3 should be negative for voxels on the arteries in CTA image; otherwise, the vesselness response should be zero. As in Frangi (2001), the vesselness response $v_\sigma(\mathbf{x})$ at voxel $\mathbf{x}$ with scale σ is formulated as

$$v_\sigma(\mathbf{x}) = \begin{cases} 0 & \text{if } \lambda_2 > 0 \text{ or } \lambda_3 > 0 \\ \left(1 - e^{-(A^2/2\alpha^2)}\right) e^{-(B^2/2\beta^2)} \left(1 - e^{-(S^2/2\gamma^2)}\right) & \text{otherwise} \end{cases}$$

where $A = \frac{|\lambda_2|}{|\lambda_3|}$, $\quad B = \frac{|\lambda_1|}{\sqrt{|\lambda_2\lambda_3|}}$, $\quad S = \sqrt{\lambda_1^2 + \lambda_2^2 + \lambda_3^2}$

Controlled by α, parameter A discriminates plate-like from line-like structures; B, dominated by β, accounts for deviation from blob-like structures, and S, controlled by γ, differentiates between high-contrast region, for example, one with bright vessel structures on a dark background, and low-contrast background regions. This approach achieves scale normalization by multiplying $\mathbf{H}$ by σ^2 before eigenvalue decomposition. The weighting factors α, β, and γ are to be specified in order to determine the influence of A, B, and S.

Because the size of the cross-sectional profile of the coronaries varies substantially from the root to the distal end, a single-scale vesselness response is not sufficient to capture the whole range of coronaries. The vesselness response of the filter

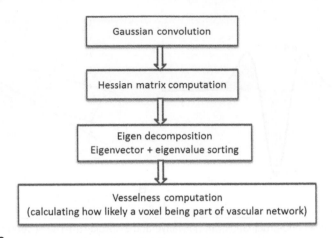

FIGURE 14.2

Flowchart of the vessel enhancement algorithm described in this chapter.

reaches a maximum at a scale that approximately matches the size of the vessel to detect. Thus, integrating the vesselness response at different scales is necessary to support varying vessel sizes. Here, the response is computed at a range of scales, exponentially distributed between σ_{min} and σ_{max}. The maximum vesselness response $V_\sigma(\mathbf{x})$ with the corresponding optimal scale $\sigma_{optimal}(\mathbf{x})$ is then obtained for each voxel of the image:

$$V(\mathbf{x}) = \max_{\sigma_{min} \leq \sigma \leq \sigma_{max}} v_\sigma(\mathbf{x})$$

The scale $\sigma_{optimal}(\mathbf{x})$ approximates the radius of the local vessel segment centered at $\mathbf{x}$. There are two groups of outputs of this vessel enhancement algorithm:

(1) The final vesselness image denoted as I_v is constructed using the maximum response $V_\sigma(\mathbf{x})$ of each voxel $\mathbf{x}$ as the intensity value;

(2) The optimal scale $\sigma_{optimal}(\mathbf{x})$ is selected for each voxel $\mathbf{x}$ (Figure 14.2).

In this chapter, we use a 3D cardiac CTA image with voxel dimensions 256 by 256 by 200, voxel resolution $0.6 \times 0.6 \times 0.5$ mm^3.

MIGRATING MULTITHREADED CPU IMPLEMENTATION TO OPENCL

At the time of writing, AMD offers the following development tools: APP Kernel-Analyzer, CodeAnalyst, APP Profiler, and gDEBugger. The first two are used in this section to port the multithreaded CPU-based image analysis application to GPU. The APP Profiler will be utilized in the next section for performance optimization.

KernelAnalyzer is a static analysis tool for viewing details about OpenCL kernel code (among other possible inputs). It compiles the code to both AMD's intermediate language and the particular hardware ISA of the target device and performs analyses on that data such that it can display various statistics about the kernel in a table. This can be useful for catching obvious issues with the compiled code before execution as well as for debugging compilation.

CodeAnalyst is traditionally a CPU profiling tool that supports timer-based and counter-based sampling of applications to build up an impression of the application's behavior. Recent editions of CodeAnalyst have added support for profiling the OpenCL API.

The APP Profiler supports counter-based profiling for the GPU. The approach it uses is not interrupt based in the way that CodeAnalyst is, rather it gives accumulated values during the execution of the kernel. This information is useful for working out where runtime bottlenecks are, in particular, those arising from computed memory addresses that are difficult or impossible to predict offline.

Finally, gDEBugger is a debugging tool that supports step-through debugging of OpenCL kernels.

Hotspot Analysis

Before implementing and optimizing for GPU and APU platforms, we first need to identify the hot spots in the multithreaded CPU-based implementation with the time-based profiling (TBP) facility in CodeAnalyst. These hot spots are the most time-consuming parts of a program that are the best candidates for optimization.

At the time of writing, CodeAnalyst 3.7 offers eight predefined profile configurations, including time-based profile, event-based profile (access performance, investigate L2 cache access, data access, instruction access, and branching), instruction-based sampling and thread profile. It also offers three other profile configurations that can be customized. The profile configuration controls which type of performance data to be collected. For example, if we are interested in finding detailed information about the mispredicted branches and subroutine returns, the "investigate branching" configuration is the ideal choice. Note that you can also profile a Java or OpenCL application in CodeAnalyst to help identify the bottlenecks of your applications.

Here we focus on getting an overall assessment of the performance of this application and identifying the hot spots for further investigation and optimization purpose. Hence, two configurations suit our requirement: *access performance* and *time-based profiling*.

In TBP, the application to be analyzed is run at full speed on the same machine that is running CodeAnalyst. Samples are collected at predetermined intervals to be used to identify possible bottlenecks, execution penalties, or optimization opportunities.

TBP uses statistical sampling to collect and build a program profile. CodeAnalyst configures a timer that periodically interrupts the program executing on a processor core using the standard operating system interrupt mechanisms. When a timer interrupt occurs, a sample is created and stored for postprocessing. Postprocessing builds up an event histogram, showing a summary of what the system and its software components were doing. The most time-consuming parts of a program will have the most samples, as there would be more timer interrupts generated and more samples taken in that region. It is also important to collect enough samples to draw a statistically meaningful conclusion of the program behavior and to reduce the chance of features being missed entirely.

The number of TBP samples collected during an experimental run depends upon the sampling frequency (or, inversely, on the timer interval) and the measurement period. The default timer interval is one millisecond. Using a one millisecond interval, a TBP sample is taken on a processor core approximately every millisecond of wall clock time. The timer interval can be changed by editing the current time-based profile configuration. By specifying a shorter interval time, CodeAnalyst can take samples more frequently within a fixed-length measurement window. However, the overhead of sampling will increase too, which leads to higher load on the test system. The process of taking samples and the incurred overhead have an intrusive effect that might perturb the test workload and bias the statistical results.

The measurement period refers to the length of time over which samples are taken. It depends upon the overall execution time of the workload and how CodeAnalyst data collection is configured. The measurement period can be configured to collect samples for all or part of the time that the workload executes. If the execution time of a program is very short (for example, less than 15 s), it helps to increase program runtime by using a larger data set or more loop iterations to obtain a statistically useful result. However, it depends on the characteristics of the workload being researched to decide how many samples should be taken at what interval that would provide sufficient information for the analysis and, in some circumstances, increasing the length of the workload's execution may change the behavior enough to confuse the results.

The system configuration for this work is an AMD Phenom II X6 1090T, Radeon HD 6970, with CodeAnalyst Performance Analyzer for Windows version 3.5.

The access performance configuration shows 95% average system CPU utilization and 44% average system memory utilization. Given that TBP provides a system-wide profiling, to use the information provided in TBP efficiently, we need to select the entries corresponding to the application itself and perform postanalysis. The table below provides the four most time-consuming segments of the application, accounting for 95% of the application runtime. It also illustrates the percentage of function execution over the execution time of the whole application. Given that all these routines are inherently parallel for an image analysis workload, we can start by porting the eigenanalysis function into an OpenCL kernel first, followed by the convolution, Hessian, and vesselness computations.

Function	Convolution	Hessian	Eigenanalysis	Vesselness
Ratio	30%	8%	55%	2%

Kernel Development and Static Analysis

In this chapter, we use the latest release of AMD APP KernelAnalyzer, version 1.12. KernelAnalyzer is a tool for analyzing the performance of OpenCL kernels for AMD Radeon Graphics cards. It compiles, analyzes, and disassembles the OpenCL kernel for multiple GPU targets and estimates the kernel performance without having to run the application on actual hardware or, indeed, having the target hardware in your machine. You can interactively tune the OpenCL kernel using its GUI. It is very helpful for prototyping OpenCL kernels in KernelAnalyzer and seeing in advance what compilation errors and warnings would be generated by the OpenCL runtime and subsequently for inspecting the statistics derived by analyzing the generated ISA code.

A full list of the compiler statistics can be found in the documentation of the KernelAnalyzer on AMD's Web site. Here we illustrate a subset of them that are important for providing hints for optimizing this application:

1. GPR shows the number of general purpose registers used or allocated. The impact of GPR usage on the kernel performance is discussed later in this chapter.
2. CF shows the number of control flow instructions in the kernel.
3. ALU:Fetch ratio shows whether there is likely to be extra ALU compute capacity available to spare. ALU:Fetch ratios of 1.2 or greater are highlighted in green and those of 0.9 or less are highlighted in red.
4. Bottleneck shows whether the likely bottleneck is ALU operations or global memory fetch operations.
5. Throughput is the estimated average peak throughput with no image filtering being performed.

Figure 14.3 shows the KernelAnalyzer user interface while analyzing the vesselness OpenCL kernel.

After developing all four major functions from this application in OpenCL and having it run on the GPU device, we inspect the performance of this newly migrated application in APP Profiler. Figure 14.4 shows the timeline view from APP Profiler. From the collected trace file, we can derive that the kernel execution takes 35.1% of the total runtime, the data transfer 32.7%, launch latency 9%, and other unaccounted activities that cover the setup time, and finalization time on the host-side account for the rest. We can see from the second to the last row of the trace that considerable time is spent copying data to and from the device. Given that all four functions are executed on device side and no host-side computation is left in between the kernels, we can safely eliminate the all interim data copies. This optimization reduces the total runtime by 23.4%. The next step is to inspect individual kernels and optimize them.

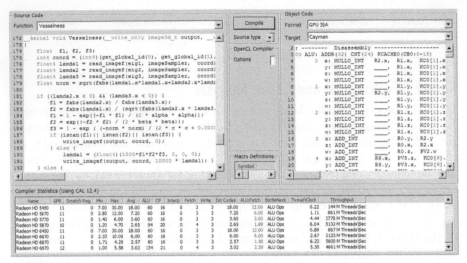

FIGURE 14.3

KernelAnalyzer user interface while analyzing the vesselness kernel and generating output for the Radeon HD6970 (Cayman) GPU.

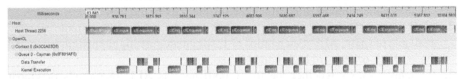

FIGURE 14.4

Execution trace of the application showing host code, data transfer, and kernel execution time using the timeline view of AMD APP Profiler.

PERFORMANCE OPTIMIZATION

APP Profiler has two main functionalities: collecting application trace and GPU performance counters. Counter selections include three categories: General (wavefronts, ALUInsts, FetchInsts, WriteInsts, ALUBusy, ALUFetchRatio, ALU-Packing), GlobalMemory (Fetchsize, CacheHit, fetchUnitBusy, fetchUnitStalled, WriteUnitStalled, FastPath, CompletePath, pathUtilisation), and LocalMemory (LDSFetchInsts, LDSWriteInsts, LDSBankConflict). For more detailed information about each of these counters, we refer to the APP Profiler documentation. In the rest of this section, we first discuss how to use kernel occupancy (a very important estimation provided in application trace) and a subset of GPU performance counters to guide the optimization.

Kernel Occupancy

This section provides an overview of the kernel occupancy calculation, including its definition and a discussion on the factors influencing its value and interpretation.

Kernel occupancy is a measure of the utilization of the resources of a compute unit on a GPU, the utilization being measured by the number of in-flight wavefronts, or threads as the hardware sees them, for a given kernel, relative to the number of wavefronts that could be launched, given the ideal kernel dispatch configuration depending on the workgroup size and resource utilization of the kernel.

The kernel occupancy value estimates the number of in-flight (active) wavefronts N_w^A on a compute unit as a percentage of the theoretical maximum number of wavefronts N_w^T that the compute unit can execute concurrently. Hence, the basic definition of the occupancy (O) is given by

$$O = \frac{N_w^A}{N_w^T}$$

The number of wavefronts that are scheduled when a kernel is dispatched is constrained by three significant factors: the number of GPRs required by each work item, the amount of shared memory (LDS for local data store) used by each workgroup, and the specified workgroup size.

Ideally, the number of wavefronts that can be scheduled corresponds to the maximum number of wavefronts supported by the compute unit because this offers the best chance of covering memory latency using thread switching. However, because the resources on a given compute unit are fixed and GPRs and LDS are hence shared among workgroups, resource limitations may lead to lower utilization. A workgroup consists of a collection of work items that make use of a common block of LDS that is shared among the members of the workgroup. Each workgroup consists of one or more wavefronts. Thus, the total number of wavefronts that can be launched on a compute unit is also constrained by the number of workgroups, as this must correspond to an integral number of workgroups, even if the compute unit has capacity for additional wavefronts. In the ideal situation, the number of wavefronts of a particular kernel that the compute unit is capable of hosting is an integral multiple of the number of wavefronts per workgroup in that kernel, which means that the maximum number of wavefronts can be achieved. However, in many situations this is not the case. In such a case, changing the number of work items in the workgroup changes the number of wavefronts in the workgroup and can lead to better utilization.

The factors that dominate kernel occupancy vary depending on the hardware features. In the following discussion, we focus on two major AMD GPU architectures: VLIW5/VLIW4 and Graphics Core Next.

Kernel Occupancy for AMD Radeon HD5000/6000 Series

The Radeon HD5000 and Radeon HD6000 series are based on a VLIW architecture such that operations are scheduled statically by the compiler across 4 or 5 SIMD ALUs. In this section, we discuss how this architecture affects some of the statistics.

1. LDS limits on the number of in-flight wavefronts

In the case that the LDS is the only constraint on the number of in-flight wavefronts, the compute unit can support the launch of a number of in-flight workgroups given by

$$WG_{max} = \frac{LDS_{CU}}{LDS_{WG}}$$

where WG_{max} is the maximum number of workgroups on a compute unit, LDS_{CU} is the shared memory available on the compute unit, and LDS_{WG} is the shared memory required by the workgroup based on the resources required by the kernel. The corresponding number of wavefronts is given as

$$WF_{max} = WG_{max} * WF_{WG}$$

where WF_{max} is the maximum number of wavefronts, WG_{max} is the maximum number of workgroups, and WF_{WG} is the number of wavefronts in a workgroup.

There is also another constraint whereby a compute unit can only support a fixed number of workgroups, a hard limit of $WG_{max} = 8$. This also limits the effectiveness of reducing the workgroup size excessively, as the number of wavefronts is also limited by the maximum workgroup size. Currently, the maximum workgroup size is 256 work items, which means that the maximum number of wavefronts is 4 when the wavefront size is 64 (and 8 when the wavefront size is 32).

Thus, when the only limit to the number of wavefronts on a compute unit is set by the LDS usage (for a given kernel), then the maximum number of wavefronts (LDS limited) is given by

$$WF_{LDS}^{max} = \min\{WG_{max}^{CU} * WF_{WG}, WG_{max} * WF_{WG}\}$$

2. GPR limits on the number of in-flight wavefronts

Another limit on the number of active wavefronts is the number of GPRs. Each compute unit has 16384 registers or 256 vector registers. These are divided among the work items in a wavefront. Thus, the number of registers per work item limits the number of wavefronts that can be launched. This can be expressed as

$$WF_{GPR} = \frac{N_{reg}^{max}}{N_{reg}^{used}}$$

where N_{reg} is the number of registers per work item; the superscripts "max" and "used" refer to the maximum number of registers and the actual number of registers used per wavefront.

As the number of in-flight wavefronts is constrained by the workgroup granularity, the number of GPR-limited wavefronts is given by

$$WF_{GPR}^{max} = floor\left(\frac{WF_{GPR}}{WF_{WG}}\right) * WF_{WG}$$

3. Other constraints

Another limit on the number of in-flight wavefronts is the flow control stack. However, this is generally an insignificant constraint, only becoming an issue in the presence of very deeply nested control flow, and so we do not consider it here.

The final factor in the occupancy is the workgroup size, as briefly discussed above. If there are no other constraints on the number of wavefronts on the compute unit, the maximum number of wavefronts is given by

$$\mathrm{WF}_{\mathrm{WG}}^{\max} = \min\left\{ \mathrm{floor}\left(\frac{\mathrm{WF}_{\max}^{\mathrm{CU}}}{\mathrm{WF}_{\mathrm{WG}}}\right), \mathrm{WF}_{\max}^{\mathrm{CU}} \right\} * \mathrm{WF}_{\mathrm{WG}}$$

where $\mathrm{WF}_{\max}^{\mathrm{CU}}$ is the maximum number of wavefronts on the compute unit and $\mathrm{WF}_{\mathrm{WG}}^{\max}$ is the maximum number of wavefronts on a compute unit when workgroup size is the only constraint.

This equation shows that having a workgroup size where the number of wavefronts divides the maximum number of wavefronts on the compute unit evenly generally yields the greatest number of active wavefronts, while indicating that making the workgroup size too small yields a reduced number of wavefronts. For example, setting a workgroup consisting of only 1 wavefront yields only 8 in-flight wavefronts, whereas (for example, given a maximum number of wavefronts on the compute unit of 32) a workgroup of 2 wavefronts will yield 16 wavefronts. Furthermore, having a single wavefront per workgroup doubles the LDS usage relative to having 2 wavefronts per workgroup as the LDS is shared only among the wavefronts in the same workgroup. Reuse of LDS may be a good thing for performance, too, reducing the number of times data is loaded from memory.

Given these constraints, the maximum number of in-flight wavefronts is given by

$$N_{\mathrm{W}}^{\mathrm{A}} = \min\left\{ \mathrm{WF}_{\mathrm{LDS}}^{\max}, \mathrm{WF}_{\mathrm{WG}}^{\max}, \mathrm{WF}_{\mathrm{GPR}}^{\max} \right\}$$

Thus, the occupancy, O, is given by:

$$O = \frac{\min\left\{ \mathrm{WF}_{\mathrm{LDS}}^{\max}, \mathrm{WF}_{\mathrm{WG}}^{\max}, \mathrm{WF}_{\mathrm{GPR}}^{\max} \right\}}{N_{\mathrm{W}}^{\mathrm{T}}}$$

The occupancy shown here is the estimated occupancy on a single compute unit. It is independent of the workloads on the other compute units on the GPU, as the occupancy is only really meaningful if there are sufficient work items to require all the resources of at least one compute unit. However, ideally, there should be a sufficient workload to ensure that more than one compute unit is needed to execute the work to explore the benefits of parallel execution. Higher occupancy allows for increased global memory latency hiding, as it allows wavefronts being swapped when there are global memory accesses. However, once there is a sufficient number of wavefronts on the compute unit to hide any global memory accesses, increasing occupancy may not increase performance.

Kernel Occupancy for AMD Radeon™ HD 7000

The Radeon HD7000 series is based on the Graphics Core Next architecture discussed in Chapter 6. This design separates the four VLIW-dispatched vector ALUs from the VLIW4-based designs and breaks it down into four separate SIMD units that are runtime scheduled. In addition, there is a separate scalar unit to manage control flow.

As a result of these architectural differences, the computation of occupancy on the HD7000 series GPUs differs in a number of significant ways from the previous occupancy calculation. While some features, such as the GPR, are still computed on the basis of individual SIMDs, these must be scaled to the whole compute unit. On the other hand, workgroup limits must be computed over the whole compute unit.

The first limit to the number of active wavefronts on the compute unit is the workgroup size. Each compute unit has up to 40 slots for wavefronts. If each workgroup is exactly one wavefront, then the maximum number of wavefronts WF_{max} is 40.

Otherwise, if there is more than one wavefront (WF) per workgroup (WG), there is an upper limit of 16 workgroups (WG) per compute unit (CU). Then, the maximum number of wavefronts on the compute unit is given by

$$WF_{WG}^{max} = \min\{16 * WF_{WG}, WF_{max}\}$$

where WF_{WG} is the number of wavefronts per workgroup.

The second limit on the number of active wavefronts is the number of VGPR (vector GPR) per SIMD.

$$WF_{VGPR}^{max} = \frac{VGPR_{max}}{VGPR_{used}}$$

where $VGPR_{max}$ is maximum number of registers per work item and $VGPR_{used}$ is the actual number of registers used per work item. However, for the total number of wavefronts per compute unit, we have to scale this value by the number of compute units:

$$WF_{VGPR}^{max} = WF_{VGPR}^{max} * SIMD_{Per_{CU}}$$

At the same time, the number of wavefronts cannot exceed WF_{max}, so

$$WF_{VGPR}^{max} = \min\{WF_{VGPR}^{max}, WF_{max}\}$$

However, the wavefronts are constrained by workgroup granularity, so the maximum number of wavefronts limited by the VGPR is given by

$$WF_{VGPR}^{max} = floor\left(\frac{WF_{VGPR}^{max}}{WF_{WG}}\right) * WF_{WG}$$

The third limit on the number of active wavefronts is the number of SGPR (Scalar GPR). SGPRs are allocated per wavefront but represent scalars rather than wavefront-wide vector registers. It is these registers that the scalar units discussed in Chapter 6 use. The SGPR limit is calculated by

$$WF_{SGPR}^{max} = floor \left(\frac{min\left\{ \frac{SGPR_{max}}{SGPR_{used}} * SIMD_{Per_{CU}}, WF_{max} \right\}}{WF_{WG}} \right) * WF_{WG}$$

The final limit on the number of active wavefronts is the LDS. The LDS limited number of wavefronts is given by

$$WG_{max} = \frac{LDS_{max}}{LDS_{used}}$$

where WG_{max} is the maximum number of workgroups determined by the LDS. Then, the maximum number of wavefronts is given by

$$WF_{LDS}^{max} = WG_{max} * WF_{WG}$$

Thus, the occupancy, O, is given by

$$O = \frac{min\left\{ WF_{LDS}^{max}, WF_{SGPR}^{max}, WF_{VGPR}^{max}, WF_{WG}^{max} \right\}}{WF_{max}}$$

Impact of Workgroup Size

The three graphs in Figure 14.5 provide a visual indication of how kernel resources affect the theoretical number of in-flight wavefronts on a compute unit. This figure is generated for the convolution kernel with workgroup size of 256 and 20 wavefronts on a Cayman GPU. The figure is generated directly by the profiler tool and its exact format depends on the device. There will be four subfigures if the kernel is dispatched to an AMD Radeon™ HD 7000 series GPU device (based on Graphics Core Next Architecture/Southern Islands) or newer. In this case, the extra subfigure is "Number of waves limited by SGPRs" that shows the impact of the number of scalar GPRs used by the dispatched kernel on the active wavefronts.

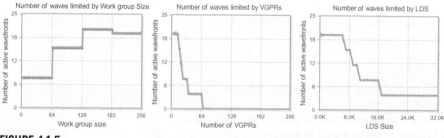

FIGURE 14.5

A visualization of the number of wavefronts on a compute unit as limited by (a) workgroup size, (b) vector GPRs, (c) LDS. This figure is generated by the AMD APP Profiler tool. The highlight on the title of (a) shows that the workgroup size is the limiting factor in this profile.

The title of the subfigure representing the limiting resource is highlighted. In this case, the highlight is placed on the first subfigure: "Number of waves limited by workgroup size." More than one subfigure's title is highlighted if there is more than one limiting resource. In each subfigure, the actual usage of the particular resource is highlighted with a small square.

The first subfigure, titled "Number of waves limited by workgroup size," shows how the number of active wavefronts is affected by the size of the workgroup for the dispatched kernel. Here the highest number of wavefronts is achieved when the workgroup size is in the range of 128–192. Similarly, the second and third subfigures show how the number of active wavefronts is influenced by the number of vector GPRs and LDS used by the dispatched kernel. In both case, as the amount of used resource increases, the number of active wavefronts decreases in steps.

In the same APP Profiler occupancy view, just below Figure 14.5, a table as shown below is generated with device, kernel information, and kernel occupancy. In the section "Kernel Occupancy," the limits imposed by each resource are shown, as well as which resource is currently limiting the number of waves for the kernel dispatch, with the occupancy ratio estimated in the last row.

Variable	Value	Device Limit
Device Info		
Device name	Cayman	
Number of compute units	48	
Max number of waves per compute unit	21	
Max number of workgroups per compute unit	8	
Wavefront size	64	
Kernel Info		
Kernel name	Convolution	
Vector GPR usage per work item	8	256
LDS usage per workgroup	0	32768
Flattened workgroup size	256	256
Flattened global work size	13107200	16777216
Number of waves per workgroup	4	4
Kernel Occupancy		
Number of waves limited by vector GPR and workgroup size	32	21
Number of waves limited by LDS and workgroup size	21	21
Number of waves limited by workgroup size	20	21
Limiting factor(s)	**Workgroup size**	
Estimated occupancy	95.24%	

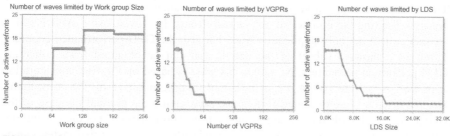

FIGURE 14.6

The same visualization as in Figure 14.5 but where the workgroup size is lowered to 128. All three factors now limit the occupancy.

Given this analysis provided by the kernel occupancy view, the limiting factors would be the optimization target. To keep it simple and for illustration purpose, we lower the workgroup size to 128 instead of 192 to check whether we can eliminate workgroup size as the limiting factor. A large workgroup size may not, after all, be necessary if enough wavefronts are present to cover memory latency. After this modification, we obtain a new set of kernel occupancy information as shown Figure 14.6, where the small square marks the current configuration with workgroup size 128 and wavefronts 16.

Variable	Value	Device Limit
Device Info		
Device name	Cayman	
Number of compute units	48	
Max number of waves per compute unit	21	
Max number of workgroups per compute unit	8	
Wavefront size	64	
Kernel Info		
Kernel name	Convolution	
Vector GPR usage per work item	8	256
LDS usage per workgroup	0	32768
Flattened workgroup size	128	256
Flattened global work size	13107200	16777216
Number of waves per workgroup	2	4
Kernel Occupancy		
Number of waves limited by vector GPR and workgroup size	16	21
Number of waves limited by LDS and workgroup size	16	21
Number of waves limited by workgroup size	16	21
Limiting factor(s)	**VGPR, LDS, workgroup size**	
Estimated occupancy	76.19%	

This change has a negative impact on the occupancy ratio, and all three factors are now limiting the number of active wavefronts. However, using APP Profiler, we can collect not only application trace but also the GPU performance counters. Table 14.1 shows a subset of the details that can be obtained from collecting GPU performance counters. Note that this table is based on the first configuration with workgroup size {64, 4, 1}, or a flattened workgroup size of 256 work items. Here four kernels are executed five times, each giving the gradual increase of the sigma value as described in the algorithm section. This trace does not include interim data transfers between kernels. As we discussed earlier, those interim transfers can be eliminated once all computations are performed on GPU device and so here we see only the first transfer from host to device and the end result being copied back after the data is processed.

In Table 14.1, we see more information than we have yet discussed. In summary,

> Global work size and workgroup size are the NDRange parameters used for the kernel dispatch.
> ALUBusy is the percentage of the execution during which the vector ALUs are being kept busy with work to do. If all the wavefronts on the SIMD unit are waiting for data to be returned from memory or blocking on colliding LDS writes the ALU will stall and its busy percentage will drop.
> ALUFetch is the ratio of ALU operations to memory operations. To a degree, the higher the better because the more ALU operations there are to execute on the compute unit, the more work there is to execute while waiting for data to return from memory.
> CacheHit is the hit rate of data in the cache hierarchy. In theory, higher is better, but that stands with the caveat that a kernel that performs only a single pass over the data does not need to reuse any data and hence is unlikely to hit frequently in the cache, for instance, the vesselness computation of a voxel only utilizing its own eigenvalues. In a kernel that frequently reuses data either temporally or between neighboring work items, the higher this value is, the more efficient that reuse is.
> The final two columns show when the memory fetch units are busy and stalled. A high busy value along with a high ALU busy value shows that the device is being effectively utilized. A high busy value with a low ALU busy value would imply that memory operations may be leading to underutilization of the compute capability of the device.

High kernel occupancy rate does not necessary indicate a more efficient execution. Take the convolution kernel as an example. The kernel occupancy rate increases from 76.19% to 95.24% while we increase the workgroup size from {64 2 1} to {64 4 1}. But the CacheHit and ALU utilization ratio reduced from 91.25% and 21.64% to 82.91% and 20.98%, respectively. As a result, the kernel execution time increases from 342 to 353 ms as shown in Table 14.2 created with numbers collected through the GPU performance counter in APP Profiler.

Table 14.1 A subset of the hardware performance counter values obtained from a profiling run.

Method	Call Index	GlobalWorkSize			Work Group Size			Time	Local Mem Size	VGPRs	FCStacks	ALUBusy	ALUFetch	CacheHit	FetchUnit	FetchUnit
Convolution_k1_Ca	50	{256	256	200}	{64	4	1}	352.1	0	8	5	20.98	3.72	82.91	45.09	0
Hessian_k2_Cayma	74	{256	256	200}	{64	4	1}	17.13	0	13	1	4.21	2	84.16	16.88	0.05
EigenAnalysis_k3_C	103	{256	256	200}	{64	2	1}	92.95	4608	15	5	44.88	356.6	75	1.01	0.01
Vesselness_k4_Cay	120	{256	256	200}	{64	4	1}	5.47	0	12	2	48.58	33.07	7.02	11.61	0.26
Convolution_k5_Ca	141	{256	256	200}	{64	4	1}	352.59	0	8	5	20.97	3.72	82.78	45.07	0
Hessian_k6_Cayma	165	{256	256	200}	{64	4	1}	16.75	0	13	1	4.23	2	83.84	16.95	0.05
EigenAnalysis_k7_C	194	{256	256	200}	{64	2	1}	93.47	4608	15	5	44.9	356.63	75	1.01	0.01
Vesselness_k8_Cay	211	{256	256	200}	{64	4	1}	5.38	0	12	2	48.7	33.08	7.21	11.64	0.25
Convolution_k9_Ca	232	{256	256	200}	{64	4	1}	352.58	0	8	5	20.97	3.72	82.74	17.05	0.05
Hessian_k10_Cayma	256	{256	256	200}	{64	4	1}	17.35	0	13	1	4.26	2	83.94	17.05	0.05
EigenAnalysis_k11_	285	{256	256	200}	{64	2	1}	92.57	4608	15	5	44.8	357.49	74.99	1.01	0.01
Vesselness_k12_Ca	302	{256	256	200}	{64	4	1}	5.35	0	12	2	48.63	33.06	7.12	11.62	0.25
Convolution_k13_C	323	{256	256	200}	{64	4	1}	352.76	0	8	5	20.97	3.72	82.63	45.07	0
Hessian_k14_Cayma	347	{256	256	200}	{64	4	1}	17.55	0	13	1	4.26	2	83.91	17.05	0.05
EigenAnalysis_k15_	376	{256	256	200}	{64	2	1}	92.44	4608	15	5	45	356.62	75	1.02	0.01
Vesselness_k16_Ca	393	{256	256	200}	{64	4	1}	5.37	0	12	2	48.55	33.07	7.08	1.02	0.01
Convolution_k17_C	414	{256	256	200}	{64	4	1}	352.53	0	8	5	20.96	3.72	82.82	45.06	0
Hessian_k18_Caym	438	{256	256	200}	{64	4	1}	17.11	0	13	1	4.87	2	83.73	19.55	0.09
EigenAnalysis_k19_	467	{256	256	200}	{64	2	1}	92.90	4608	15	5	44.82	357.75	75	1.01	0.01
Vesselness_k20_Ca	484	{256	256	200}	{64	4	1}	5.37	0	12	2	48.69	33.08	7.13	11.63	0.24

Table 14.2 Comparison of different workgroup sizes for the convolution kernel. Based on values obtained from APP Profiler.

Kernel	Platform	Global Work Size	Work Group Size	Time	LDS	VGPRS	SGPRs	Scratch Regs	FCStacks	ALUBusy	ALUFetch Ratio	CacheHit	Fetch Unit Busy	FetchUnit Stalled
Convolution	Cayman	{256 256 200}	{64 2 1}	342	0	8	NA		0	521.64	3.72	91.25	46.52	0
Convolution	Cayman	{256 256 200}	{64 4 1}	353	0	8	NA		0	520.98	3.72	82.91	45.09	0

Impact of VGPR and LDS

If a kernel is limited by register usage and not by LDS usage, then it is possible that moving some data into LDS will shift that limit. If a balance can be found between LDS use and registers such that register data is moved into LDS in such a way that the register count is lowered but LDS does not become a more severe limit on occupancy, then this could be a winning strategy. The same under some circumstances may be true of moving data into global memory.

However, care must be taken while making this change. Not only may LDS become the limiting factor on kernel occupancy, but accessing LDS is slower than accessing registers. Even if occupancy improves, performance may drop because the compute unit is executing more, or slower, instructions to compute the same result. This is even more true if global memory were to be used to reduce register count: this is exactly the situation we see with register spilling.

This section we show the impact of reducing kernel VGPR usage by moving some data storage to LDS to increase the kernel occupancy and improve the performance. Eigen decomposition of the Hessian matrix at each voxel of the image is used to illustrate this. The basic implementation of the eigenanalysis kernel is inserted below:

```
__kernel void eigenAnalysis(
     __read_only image3d_t h1, _
     _read_only image3d_t h2,
     __read_only image3d_t h3,
     __read_only image3d_t h4,
     __read_only image3d_t h5,
     __read_only image3d_t h6,
     __write_only image3d_t eig1,
     __write_only image3d_t eig2,
     __write_only image3d_t eig3)
{
     int4 coord=(int4)(get_global_id(0), get_global_id(1),
          get_global_id(2), 0);
     float matrix[9];
     float eigenvector[9];
     float eigenvalue[3];
     float4 value;
     value=read_imagef(h1, imageSampler,
          (int4)(coord.x, coord.y, coord.z, 0));
     matrix[0]=value.x;
     value=read_imagef(h2, imageSampler,
          (int4)(coord.x, coord.y, coord.z, 0));
     matrix[1]=matrix[3]=value.x;
     value=read_imagef(h3, imageSampler,
          (int4)(coord.x, coord.y, coord.z, 0));
     matrix[2]=matrix[6]=value.x;
     value=read_imagef(h4, imageSampler,
          (int4)(coord.x, coord.y, coord.z, 0));
```

```
    matrix[4]=value.x;
    value=read_imagef(h5, imageSampler,
        (int4)(coord.x, coord.y, coord.z, 0));
    matrix[5]=matrix[7]=value.x;
    value=read_imagef(h6, imageSampler,
        (int4)(coord.x, coord.y, coord.z, 0));
    matrix[8]=value.x;
    EigenDecomposition(eigenvalue, eigenvector, matrix, 3);
    write_imagef(eig1, coord,
        (float4)(eigenvalue[0], 0.0f, 0.0f, 0.0f));
    write_imagef(eig2, coord,
        (float4)(eigenvalue[1], 0.0f, 0.0f, 0.0f));
    write_imagef(eig3, coord,
        (float4)(eigenvalue[2], 0.0f, 0.0f, 0.0f));
}
```

In this implementation, each eigenanalysis kernel consumes 41 GPRs, with no LDS used. Profiling with APP Profiler, we can see that this high usage of the VGPR resource limits the number of wavefronts that can be deployed to 6. As a result, the estimated occupancy ratio is 29.57%. By allocating the storage for the array `matrix` in LDS as shown in the following code example, the vector GPR usage per work item is reduced to 15, with LDS usage reported at 4.5K, and the number of active wavefronts 14. Consequently, the estimated occupancy ratio increases substantially to 66.67%. The kernel runtime dropped from 180 to 93 ms on average on Cayman.

```
    __kernel __attribute__(
        (reqd_work_group_size(GROUP_SIZEx, GROUP_SIZEy, 1)))
    void EigenAnalysis(
        __read_only image3d_t h1,
        __read_only image3d_t h2,
        __read_only image3d_t h3,
        __read_only image3d_t h4,
        __read_only image3d_t h5,
        __read_only image3d_t h6,
        __write_only image3d_t eig1,
        __write_only image3d_t eig2,
        __write_only image3d_t eig3)
    {
        int4 coord=(int4)(get_global_id(0), get_global_id(1),
            get_global_id(2), 0);
        int localCoord=get_local_id(0);
        __local float matrix[GROUP_SIZEx*GROUP_SIZEy][9];
        float eigenvector[9];
        float eigenvalue[3];
        float4 value;
    ...
    }
```

The table below shows the profiler summary of the execution time of the final implementation with five different scales. These data are collected on a Radeon™ HD6970 GPU with five scales ranging from 0.5 to 4 mm and an image size of $256 \times 256 \times 200$.

Kernel Name	Device Name	# of Calls	Total Time (ms)	Avg Time (ms)	Max Time(ms)	Min Time (ms)
Convolution	Cayman	5	1711.34022	342.26804	343.05167	340.98611
Eigenanalysis	Cayman	5	463.57545	92.71509	93.19711	92.34878
Hessian	Cayman	5	86.11744	17.22349	20.16967	15.76600
Vesselness	Cayman	5	26.23067	5.24613	5.26400	5.23556

POWER AND PERFORMANCE ANALYSIS

We test the optimized application on a Trinity (A10-5800K) platform in three formats: a single-threaded CPU version, a multithreaded CPU version, and the GPU-based version. Using the AMD Graphics Manager software on the Trinity APU, we can collect the power consumption number at a fixed time interval on each device. In this case, two CPU modules (core pairs) listed as "CU" in the table and the GPU. In this test, power samples are collected at 100-ms time intervals and seven different scales for identifying vessel structure are used to increase the amount of samples collected for a more accurate analysis. Each row in the table below shows the average power consumption for each device and the total power consumption and execution time measured. Using this data, we calculate the total energy consumption. Note that despite the fact that all other applications are switched off, this approach still measures the whole system's power consumption, not just the running application. However, it is the easiest way to get an estimated analysis without extra hardware. Using the single-threaded CPU version as baseline, we can derive the performance and energy improvement for a multithreaded CPU version and GPU-based one. We perform a similar comparison with the multithreaded CPU as baseline in the third table. In total, we observe that, despite the GPU being powered down while not in use, the energy consumption of executing the application on GPU is significantly lower than the MT-CPU one.

	CU0	CU1	GPU	Power	Total Time (s)	Energy
ST-CPU	23.97	21.52	8.71	54.20	282.00	15285.45
MT-CPU	32.24	31.78	9.01	73.03	133.80	9772.01
GPU	16.01	15.21	24.48	55.70	19.35	1077.72

Baseline: ST-CPU		Performance Improvement	Energy Improvement
	ST-CPU	1	1
	MT-CPU	2.12	1.56
	GPU	14.57	14.18

Baseline: MT-CPU		Performance Improvement	Energy Improvement
	GPU	6.9	9

CONCLUSION

In this chapter, we showed how some of the profiling tools in the AMD APP SDK can be used to analyze and hence help optimize kernel performance. We applied runtime profiling and static analysis to a real-image analysis application to help optimize performance using OpenCL. Of course, in writing this chapter, we had to select a consistent set of tools, and in this case, to match the hardware example chapter and to make chapters link together, we choose the AMD tools. Similar data and optimizations are, of course, necessary on other architectures, and NVIDIA, Intel, and other vendors provide their own, often excellent, tools to achieve similar goals.

References

Frangi, A. F. (2001). Three-Dimensional Model-Based Analysis of Vascular and Cardiac Images. PhD thesis, University Medical Center Utrecht, The Netherlands.

Lorenz, C., Carlsen, I.-C., Buzug, T. M., Fassnacht, C., & Weese, J. (1997). Multi-scale line segmentation with automatic estimation of width, contrast and tangential direction in 2D and 3D medical images. In *Proceedings of the First Joint Conference on Computer Vision, Virtual Reality and Robotics in Medicine and Medial Robotics and Computer-Assisted Surgery* (pp. 233–242).

Olabarriaga, S. D., Breeuwer, M., & Niessen, W. (2003). Evaluation of Hessian-based filters to enhance the axis of coronary arteries in CT images. In *Computer Assisted Radiology and Surgery* (pp. 1191–1196). *International Congress Series* Vol. 1256, (pp. 1191–1196).

Sato, Y., Shiraga, N., Atsumi, H., Yoshida, S., Koller, T., Gerig, G., & Kikinis, R. (1998). Three-dimensional multi-scale line filter for segmentation and visualization of curvilinear structures in medical images. *Medical Image Analysis*, 2(2), 143–168.

Zhang, D. P. (2010). Coronary Artery Segmentation and Motion Modeling. PhD thesis, Imperial College London, UK.

Index

Note: Page numbers followed by *f* indicate figures and *t* indicate tables.

Printed and bound by CPI Group (UK) Ltd, Croydon, CR0 4YY

03/10/2024

01040327-0015